THE SLAVONIC & EAST EUROPEAN REVIEW

Volume 102, Number 1 — January 2024

POLITICAL MARTYRDOM IN LATE IMPERIAL RUSSIA

Guest editors: George Gilbert and Ben Phillips

Introduction: Political Martyrdom in Late Imperial Russia

GEORGE GILBERT and BEN PHILLIPS

WHAT is a martyr? The standard definition is that a martyr is someone who suffers persecution and death for advocating, renouncing or refusing to renounce or advocate a religious belief or other cause as demanded by an external party. Typically, the martyr is punished or executed by an oppressor for refusing to comply with a set of demands; this leads to a narrative being created in the left-behind community which focuses on the historical and socio-cultural role of the martyr. According to one reading, martyrdom myths and legends often (if by no means always) include the following six elements: a hero — a person of renown who is devoted to an admirable cause; opposition — the people who oppose that cause; risk — in spite of foreseeable danger the hero undertakes the cause; courage and commitment — the hero continues, despite knowing risk, out of commitment to said cause; death — the opponents kill the hero because of that person's commitment to the cause; and, finally, audience response — the death is commemorated and people may be inspired to pursue the same cause. The dead person may be explicitly labelled as a martyr.[1] Martyrs have inspired a cascade of ink, imagery, song and stories since the classical period, and continue to do so in our own time.[2]

Martyrdom is originally a religious concept. In the Western tradition, our understanding of what it means to be martyred derives largely from

George Gilbert is Lecturer in Modern Russian History at the University of Southampton, and Ben Phillips is Lecturer in Modern Russian History at the University of Exeter.

We would like to thank the four other authors for their excellent contributions, and the editors of SEER for their diligence and support in seeing the issue through to completion.

[1] Adapted from A. J. Wallace and R. D. Rusk, *Moral Transformation: The Original Christian Paradigm of Salvation*, New Zealand, 2011, p. 218.

[2] Important works on martyrdom include G. W. Bowersock, *Martyrdom and Rome*, Cambridge, 1995; Daniel Boyarin, *Dying for God: Martyrdom and the Making of Christianity and Judaism*, Stanford, CA, 1999; Elizabeth A. Castelli, *Martyrdom and Memory: Early Christian Culture Making*, New York, 2004; Brian Wicker (ed.), *Witnesses to Faith? Martyrdom in Christianity and Islam*, Aldershot and Burlington, VT, 2006; David Cook, *Martyrdom in Islam*, Cambridge, 2007.

Slavonic and East European Review, 102, 1, 2024   doi:10.1353/see.00001

the hagiography of the early Christian church, the *Acts of the Martyrs*, and from the theological parameters for martyrdom laid down by the Christian thinkers of late antiquity. The concept is not, of course, exclusively Christian: St Augustine's reverence for those who 'bore witness to the faith, [found] the world hostile and cruel, yet overcame the world not by defending themselves, but by preferring to die' recurs in all the major monotheisms.[3] Nor has it remained exclusively religious: since the seventeenth century, martyrdom has entered the realm of secular politics. In the ideological struggles that have shaped the modern world, all parties — from revolutionary and national liberation movements to the *anciens régimes* they challenged — have found meaning and value in the sacralized image of those who willingly lay down their lives for an imagined common cause. As the six contributions to this special issue of the *Slavonic and East European Review* demonstrate, Russia has been no exception to this pattern: indeed, a careful study of martyrdom in the Russian context may yield especially valuable insights into the general theme.[4]

The case studies explored in the articles that follow all focus on the final decades of tsarist rule in Russia (c.1881–1917). They are related not just chronologically but thematically, since all involve protagonists who were killed, or who suffered, for a political cause, and who were associated, in the main, with the revolutionary left. Writing on a variety of discrete but interrelated topics, and adopting a variety of methodological approaches, our contributors consider multiple aspects of martyr culture during the period in question, from interpretations and perceptions of leftist (and, in the case of George Gilbert's article, liberal) martyrdom in the public sphere to the role of gender dynamics, popular media and (after 1917) collective memory in shaping such martyrologies. In addition, two contributors consider the transnational reception of Russian martyr cults in case studies focusing, respectively, on Ireland and the United States. No contributions deal explicitly with religious martyrdom, which remained an object of popular fascination during the same period; several, however, point to the influence of religious (specifically Orthodox) culture on the

---

[3] St Augustine of Hippo, *The City of God*, XXII in Gerald G. Walsh and Daniel J. Honan (eds), *The Fathers of the Church*, no. 24, Washington DC, 1954, p. 451.

[4] A recent special issue of the Russian-language journal, *State, Religion and Church in Russia and Abroad*, explored the concept of martyrdom in a wide range of national cases and contexts: 'Muchenichestvo: ideia, kul´t, teoriia', *Gosudarstvo, religiia, tserkov´ v Rossii i za rubezhom*, 40, 1, 2022. For an insightful discussion of many themes raised in the pages that follow, see Simon Dixon, 'Reflections on Modern Russian Martyrdom', in Diana Wood (ed.), *Martyrs and Martyrologies*, Studies in Church History, 30, Oxford, 1993, pp. 389–415.

revolutionary underground, and thus on the hagiographical terms in which fallen 'freedom fighters' were celebrated.

The Russian martyr tradition, in its secular and political form, has of course a much longer history than discussed here. The religious sectarians of the mid seventeenth century were the first to die in the name of an idea that was open to interpretation in secular, as well as religious, terms: Old Believer (*staroobriadtsy*) martyrologies — those of the Archpriest Avvakum, Boiarynia Morozova and others — came to dominate the cultural memory of the Church Schism (*raskol*) for centuries to come.[5] In the eyes of later generations of populist and Soviet thinkers, Nikolai Novikov and Aleksandr Radishchev both figured in the development of a revolutionary tradition which included the Decembrist rebels of 1825. Their biographies provided ample material for mythmaking, seized upon, famously, by Pushkin, Gertsen and other writers.[6] Yet it is only with the emergence of more active and openly revolutionary opposition to the Russian monarchy at the end of the nineteenth century that one can speak of 'revolutionary martyrdom' — the core theme of these articles — proper. The preeminent representatives of the type were the terrorists of the People's Will (1879–80s) and, later, of the Socialist-Revolutionary (SR) Party (1901–20s), who willingly accepted, and in some cases seem actively to have sought, the gallows and Siberia as their fate. As the émigré publicist Sergei Stepniak-Kravchinskii — himself a terrorist of some renown — wrote in *Underground Russia*, his 1883 collection of 'sketches from revolutionary life':

[The terrorist] is noble, terrible, irresistibly fascinating, for he combines in himself the two sublimities of human grandeur: the martyr and the hero. He is a martyr. From the day when he swears in the depths of his heart to free the people and the country, he knows he is consecrated to death. He faces it at every step of his stormy life. He goes forth to meet it fearlessly, when necessary, and can die without flinching, not like a Christian of old, but like a warrior accustomed to look death in the face.[7]

[5] Perhaps the two most famous examples are V. I. Surikov's eponymous 1887 painting of Morozova under arrest, and the self-immolation scene at the end of Modest Mussorgskii's opera, *Khovanshchina*.

[6] See, for example, Ludmilla A. Trigos, *The Decembrist Myth in Russian Culture*, New York, 2009, and Daniel Beer, 'Decembrists, Rebels, and Martyrs in Siberian Exile: The "Zerentui Conspiracy" of 1828 and the Fashioning of a Revolutionary Genealogy', *Slavic Review*, 72, 3, 2013, pp. 528–51.

[7] Stepniak [S. M. Stepniak-Kravchinskii], *Underground Russia: Revolutionary Profiles and Sketches from Life*, 2nd edn, New York, 1883, pp. 39–40.

Several of the most enduring martyr-myths to emerge from Russia's revolutionary period were, indeed, connected with famous terrorists: two contributions to this collection (those of Sally Boniece and Ben Phillips) focus on noteworthy cases in point.

In all, four of the six articles in this issue focus chronologically on the 1905 revolution and its immediate aftermath. This is not coincidental, since the 'first Russian Revolution' would appear to represent a high point in the annals of revolutionary martyrdom. The dramatic upsurge in political violence that marked the years 1905–07, together with the unprecedented and wide-ranging civil freedoms granted by the tsarist regime in October 1905, created not just a superabundance of martyr-heroes, but a public sphere in which such figures, for the first time, could be openly commemorated and mythologized. Evidence for the widespread social resonance of martyrdom during this period is not hard to come by. Left-wing and liberal deputies in the First and Second State Dumas regularly called for a general amnesty for political prisoners, a demand echoed in popular petitions during the same period.[8] The activities of the newly-uncensored press and burgeoning publishing industry likewise attest to the public mood: book lists and newspaper columns during 1905–07 produced numerous hagiographies of dead terrorists and revolutionaries, whose mythologies were perpetuated, in turn, by oral and visual materials — songs, portraits and postcards — disseminated among the revolutionary crowd. In this context, defenders of the established order scrambled to disseminate counter-martyrologies of their own: perhaps the best-known example is the *Kniga russkoi skorbi* (*The Book of Russian Sorrows*, 1908–14), a fourteen-volume series published by the Union of the Archangel Mikhail and dedicated to the victims of revolutionary terror.[9]

Radical martyrologies and martyr cults attracted significant public interest not just within, but beyond Russia's borders. For large parts of the European and American public, which tended to see Russia as a backward and despotic 'other' (and therefore to condone the violent acts of the revolutionaries as an inevitable by-product of the struggle against tyranny and for universal liberal values), the image of the revolutionary martyr-hero was beguiling indeed.[10] Among the first notable examples is Vera Zasulich,

---

[8] Multiple examples are cited in Gregory Freeze, *From Supplication to Revolution: A Documentary Social History of Imperial Russia*, Oxford, 1988, pp. 277–93 and *passim*.

[9] One example is explored in George Gilbert, 'The Martyr Cult of Grand Duke Sergei Aleksandrovich', *The Russian Review*, 81, 2, 2022, pp. 265–83.

[10] For penetrating discussions of the international reception of Russian terrorism in the 1880s, see Michael J. Hughes, 'British Opinion and Russian Terrorism in the 1880s', *European History Quarterly*, 41, 2, 2011, pp. 255–77, and Lynn Ellen Patyk, *Written in Blood:*

who shot the governor-general of St Petersburg Dmitrii Trepov in 1878, only to be acquitted by a St Petersburg jury from a charge of attempted murder: she was held in high regard by parts of Russia's emerging civil society for her act, and her court appearances garnered considerable international media attention.[11] Numerous revolutionary terrorists who followed in later years — for instance, the leaders of the People's Will, Sofia Perovskaia and Andrei Zheliabov — gained notoriety and fame in parts of Europe as well as within the Russian Empire, their celebrity status bolstered later in the 1880s by the literary works of Stepniak-Kravchinskii and other revolutionary émigrés.[12]

In many cases, the reception of Russian martyr-cults abroad was shaped by domestic political concerns. One such connection emerges between our Russian radicals and the Irish terrorism that emerged after the Fenian Rising of 1867. Both in Russia and in Ireland there was a shared interest in the concept of martyrdom from radicals and rebels; chronologically, the 'martyr-terrorist' emerged in Russia and Ireland in the same era; and, finally, there is intriguing evidence that the two different cultures were in contact during this time. One contributor, Abby Holekamp, explores the position of both Irish Fenians and Russian nihilists in the European cultural imagination. As in the case of Russian radicals, being a terrorist in the Irish radical imaginary was not a negative quality: on the contrary, there was a moral imperative to struggle against unjust authority and bring salvation to the community left behind. In both contexts, radicals were fighting against a hostile oppressor. Irish examples proved alluring in the struggle against British rule, and a worldwide audience sometimes looked appreciatively at their struggle, including a large Celtic diaspora as well as publications aimed at a smaller audience in Ireland.[13] Their activities were

Revolutionary Terrorism and Russian Literary Culture, 1861–1881, Madison, WI, 2017, pp. 247–61. On revolutionary transnationalism more broadly, see Faith Hillis, *Utopia's Discontents: Russian Emigres and the Quest for Freedom, 1830s–1930s*, Oxford, 2021, and Ben Phillips, *Siberian Exile and the Invention of Revolutionary Russia, 1825–1917: Exiles, Émigrés and the International Reception of Russian Radicalism*, London, 2022.

[11] Ana Siljak, *Angel of Vengeance: The Girl Who Shot the Governor of St Petersburg and Sparked the Age of Assassination*, New York, 2008; Richard Pipes, 'The Trial of Vera Z.', *Russian History*, 37, 1, 2010, pp. 1–82.

[12] See Peter Scotto, 'The Terrorist as Novelist: Sergei Stepniak-Kravchinsky', in Anthony Anemone (ed.), *Just Assassins: The Culture of Terrorism in Russia*, Evanston, IL, 2010, pp. 97–126.

[13] Guy Beiner, 'Fenianism and the Martyrdom-Terrorism Nexus in Ireland before Independence', in Dominic Janes and Alex Houen (eds), *Martyrdom and Terrorism: Pre-Modern to Contemporary Perspectives*, Oxford, 2014, pp. 199–200. See also, D. George Boyce, '"A Gallous Story and a Dirty Deed": Political Martyrdom in Ireland since 1867', in Yonah Alexander and Alan O'Day (eds), *Ireland's Terrorist Dilemma*, Dordrecht, 1986, p. 14.

always controversial, and in Britain many were keen to stress differences between noble Russian terrorists and their Irish counterparts. Soon after the publication of Kravchinskii's *Underground Russia*, one newspaper claimed that it was 'absurd' to compare 'the deeds of Russian nihilists with those of Irish desperadoes'.[14]

The six articles that follow are connected, to varying degrees, by several key themes. The most obvious is the synthesis, within the Russian tradition of martyrdom, of secular politics with religious, or at least quasi-religious, conviction — a feature of Russian revolutionary culture to which scholars have previously drawn attention.[15] This synthesis can plausibly be traced to the aforementioned Church Schism (*raskol*) of the mid 1600s. The Old Believers and other religious sectarians of the seventeenth century were, of course, primarily martyred for their religious beliefs (i.e., their opposition to the liturgical reforms of the Patriarch Nikon). It is hardly a stretch, however, to conclude, as has one eminent historian, that their rebellion was not just religious but political in nature, inasmuch as it represented a rejection not just of the Nikonian reforms, but of an increasingly secularized and Westernized imperial state, and therefore constituted 'a rallying point for all those who objected to changes going on in the whole of Russia's political, economic and cultural life'.[16] It is unsurprising, then, that the revival of interest in the Schism some two centuries later was spearheaded by Populist intellectuals who seem to have regarded the Old Believers as, in a sense, their spiritual ancestors.[17] Revolutionary memoirs and other writings from this period contain numerous admiring references to the Old Believers: Vera Figner, for instance, wrote that the life stories of Avvakum and the Boiarynia Morozova 'struck me dumb when I first read them and stayed with me through all my long years in Shlissel´burg'.[18] In short, by casting themselves in the image of sectarian martyrs — as latter-day sufferers for a new, socialist faith — the revolutionaries of the nineteenth century drew a direct line from the Christian martyrological tradition to the anti-tsarist struggle.

[14] Quoted in Hughes, 'British Opinion and Russian Terrorism', p. 269.

[15] Perhaps the first to identify this trait was Sergei Bulgakov, in 'Geroizm i podvizhnichestvo: iz razmyshlenii o religioznoi prirode russkoi intelligentsii', *Vekhi: sbornik statei o russkoi intelligentsii*, Moscow, 1909, pp. 23–69.

[16] Geoffrey Hosking, *Russia and the Russians: From Earliest Times to 2001*, London, 2002, p. 169.

[17] Alexander Etkind, 'Whirling with the Other: Russian Populism and Religious Sects', *The Russian Review*, 62, 2003, pp. 565–88; Aleksandr Pyzhikov, *Grani russkogo raskola: tainaia rol´ staroobriadchestva ot semnadtsatogo veka do semnadtsatogo goda*, 2nd edn, Moscow, 2018.

[18] V. N. Figner, *Polnoe sobranie sochinenii v 6 tomakh*, Moscow, 1928–30, 5, p. 265.

Late imperial Russia was of course a deeply religious society, with rates of religious observance much higher than in many parts of Europe.[19] It is no coincidence, therefore, that political groups comprised mostly of convinced atheists nonetheless used imagery involving saints, sin, resurrection, faith and martyrdom. The reasons for this were twofold. Firstly, it reflected the backgrounds of many political activists, whose atheism was usually the unintended by-product of a devout religious upbringing: the well-known seminarians-turned-revolutionaries among the 1860s radical generation (*shestidesiatniki*), Chernyshevskii, Dobroliubov and others, are perhaps the best-known case in point.[20] Secondly, such images and symbols reflected a desire to connect with a wider popular audience, providing a readily accessible set of cultural codes and emblems with which the masses would likely be familiar. Maureen Perrie has shown how religious languages influenced the actions and identities of the SR Party, a group featured heavily in this collection (see especially articles by Phillips, Boniece and Green).[21] Yet the SRs were not unique in this respect: many other political groups, from the Bolsheviks to liberals, also drew on religious language and imagery and assessed related ideas of sacrality and faith in their own ways. The centrality of martyrdom to the cultural codes of what the historian Marina Mogil'ner, referencing Kravchinskii, has termed 'underground Russia' — that is, the broad cross-section of late-imperial Russian society that defined itself in opposition to the 'legal' state[22] — cannot be understood outside this context. Martyr status conferred moral credibility, integrity and commitment upon the subject, as they had given their life (or lives) for a cause that they believed in, or at least suffered greatly for in life. Martyr myths also had didactic value: the retelling and veneration of heroic deeds could help to ensure loyalty between the person or group in question and their followers and could also function as a statement of radical action, encouraging others to take up their banner.[23]

[19] See Gregory L. Freeze, 'A Pious Folk? Religious Observance in Vladimir Diocese, 1900–1914', *Jahrbücher für Geschichte Osteuropas*, 52, 3, 2004, pp. 323–40.

[20] A theme explored in Laurie Manchester, *Holy Fathers, Secular Sons: Clergy, Intelligentsia and the Modern Self in Revolutionary Russia*, DeKalb, IL, 2008.

[21] Maureen Perrie, 'K voprosu o "religioznosti" russkoi intelligentsii: religioznyi iazik u eserov-terroristov nachala XX veka', in B. A. Uspenskii (ed.), *Rossiia: Russkaia intelligentsiia i zapadnyi intellektualizm: istoriia i tipologiia*, Moscow, 1999, pp. 86–94.

[22] Marina Mogil'ner, *Mifologiia podpol'nogo cheloveka: radikal'nyi mikrokosm v Rossii nachala XX veka kak predmet semioticheskogo analiza*, Moscow, 1999.

[23] Mikhail Dolbilov, 'Loyalty and Emotion in Nineteenth-Century Russian Imperial Politics', in Jana Osterkamp and Martin Schulze Wessel (eds), *Exploring Loyalty*, Munich, 2017, pp. 17–43.

A second theme common to all the case studies featured here — echoing, among others, Claudia Verhoeven's pioneering work on the origins of revolutionary terrorism in Russia[24] — is that of 'modernity', broadly defined. Their 'underground' origins notwithstanding, revolutionary and radical martyr cults achieved a wider socio-cultural salience through the reception and mediation of a public sphere that, prior to the late nineteenth century, had been conspicuous in Russia by its absence. Indeed, the enthusiasm with which newspapers and journals, an increasingly literate public able to read them, and (after 1905) the public's elected representatives in the Duma picked up on and ran with the martyr theme illustrates a kind of symbiosis between 'legal' and 'underground' Russia that, somewhat paradoxically, could only fully take shape after the October Manifesto and the autocratic regime's concession of civic freedom.

Since the radical acts of the ancient Christians, martyrdom acts have always been public facing: they need an audience to be seen and believed. Nowadays information that can be accessed via the internet is key. Akil N. Awan discusses the 'hyperreality' of martyrdom, and how it functions in the new media environment. He describes the online community that surrounds radical Islamist martyrdom as '[a] cloistered yet highly immersive environment' which appeals immediately to the senses, with emotional messages, songs and music and arresting imagery, concerning its subjects.[25] Messages about the subjects and causes take hold in a new media landscape, with a specific set of symbols, cultural codes and images directed at a designated audience, affirming the acts of these radicals.

In our period, it was the printed word and associated images and symbols that were crucial to spreading martyrdom legends and events. The late nineteenth and early twentieth centuries were a time of growing popular literacy, and an increasingly vibrant press to match — a vibrancy that achieved new heights during and after 1905 with the near-total demise of censorship.[26] In this context, sensational acts of revolutionary violence, and the martyr-cults that often arose from such acts, made good copy for newspaper proprietors keen on boosting sales.[27] Radical groups, conversely,

[24] Claudia Verhoeven, *The Odd Man Karakozov: Imperial Russia, Modernity and the Birth of Terrorism*, Ithaca, NY, 2009.

[25] Akil N. Awan, 'Virtual Jihadist Media: Function, Legitimacy and Radicalizing Efficacy', *European Journal of Cultural Studies*, 10, 3, 2007, pp. 389–408, and 'Jihadi Ideology in the New Media Environment', in Jeevan Deol and Zaheer Kazmi (eds), *Contextualising Jihadi Thought*, London, 2012, pp. 99–119 (p. 110).

[26] See Jeffrey Brooks, *When Russia Learned to Read: Literacy and Popular Literature, 1861–1917*, Princeton, NJ, 1985.

[27] Louise McReynolds, *Murder Most Russian: True Crime and Punishment in Late*

did not operate through advertising or subscriptions, but these stories were a key part of their praxis, and revolutionary circles (*kruzhki*) developed their own reading habits: thus narratives of martyrdom featured heavily in many radical newspapers, journals and serial publications. These were usually aimed at a small audience of activists and a focus on their heroes became a core strategy for integrating followers into the causes and ideas of a group, with obituary columns and records of their deeds featuring prominently in their pages and stressing the necessity of sacrifice for the cause.

In short, although radicals primarily communicated with a small clientele of core supporters, in many cases these discussions reached a much larger audience, including — in the case studies discussed by Abby Holekamp and Alison Rowley — an international one. Graphic and sensationalized representations of martyrdom in the Russian and international press provided plentiful publicity for the revolutionary cause; at the same time, the notoriety such coverage afforded could prove to be a double-edged sword. In Rowley's assessment, whilst Russian anarchist martyrs were originally seen as heroes by sympathizers in the United States, continued association with spectacular revolutionary violence also alienated potential supporters and led to their cause becoming gradually less popular. Conversely, the Irish and Russian martyrs explored by Holekamp took up a prominent position in the terrorist nexus, and a place in the European cultural imaginary, eliciting different responses.

The centrality of the press aside, there were several other ways of disseminating key ideas. One was the picture postcard, printed in huge numbers in the late imperial period. Alison Rowley's article examines closely the cachet martyrs held as postcard subjects, though, intriguingly, this was unstable, with the violent and radical actions of the martyrs that featured on these cards discussed and debated.[28] Other forms of literature were equally important: to take one example, often the official publishing house for a political party or radical group would issue a commemorative pamphlet for a fallen activist which would explicitly discuss them as a martyr. The SRs did this for many of their most famous figures, including the terrorists Stepan Balmashev (1902), Ivan Kaliaev (1905) and Grigorii Gershuni (1908). The liberal martyrs featured were also subject to this technique, as we see with their 'in memoriam' books like the one issued

Imperial Russia, Ithaca, NY, 2013.
[28] See Laura Engelstein, 'Revolution and the Theater of Public Life in Imperial Russia', in Isser Woloch (ed.), *Revolution and the Meanings of Freedom in the Nineteenth Century*, Stanford, CA, 1996, pp. 337–43.

for the political leader and statesperson Sergei Muromtsev in 1910, which collated obituaries and featured an extensive overview of his life and work — both typical features of such texts. Other types of serial publications could record the activities of the martyr long after the act had taken place (Green). Finally, public events with a wide reach, including rituals, demonstrations and funerals, were crucial in the dissemination of martyr cults. Scholars have hitherto tended to focus on 'red funerals', i.e., the funerals of revolutionaries or non-revolutionary figures, such as the poet Nikolai Nekrasov, who were lionized by the radicals.[29] The focus here shifts slightly, with George Gilbert's article discussing funerals and demonstrations for liberal heroes from the years 1905 to 1910. Conversely, several articles (those by Boniece, Rowley, Phillips and Holekamp) look at a different type of event — spectacular examples of terrorist violence, which connects the dramatic image of the terrorist to the sympathetic figure of the martyr, and was carried subsequently in press narratives. In addition, a radical group could become the subject of its own retrospective mythologies, as Lara Green's study of the journal, *Katorga i ssylka* (Hard Labour and Exile) shows. In several cases, we assess private sources including diaries and memoirs that provide intriguing contrasts with the public-facing elements of the myths sketched above.

Contemporary gender norms loomed large in the construction, and dissemination, of revolutionary martyr-myths. Historically speaking, the social origins of the Russian revolutionary movement prior to the twentieth century lay not in the economic struggle of the overwhelmingly male proletariat for better working conditions (as in Europe), but in the struggle of the radical intelligentsia against the autocratic state. One immediate consequence of this was that women played a major role in revolutionary organizations from the 1870s onwards — in some cases realizing, as did Chernyshevskii's Vera Pavlovna, the ideals of freedom and gender equality within the revolutionary collective.[30] Thus many of the most famous revolutionary martyrs from the turn of the century — Sofiia Perovskaia, the Veras Zasulich and Figner, and Ekaterina Breshko-Breshkovskaia, to name but a few — were women. It would seem, moreover, that it was precisely these cases that resonated most with the public, both within and beyond Russia's borders. Based on a close reading of contemporary journalism and literature, Ana Siljak has argued that such individuals,

[29] Tom Trice, 'Rites of Protest: Populist Funerals in Imperial St Petersburg, 1876–1878', *Slavic Review*, 60, 1, 2001, pp. 50–74.
[30] For an overview, see Barbara Alpern Engel, *Mothers and Daughters: Women of the Intelligentsia in Nineteenth-Century Russia*, Cambridge, 1983.

by simultaneously embodying Victorian gender norms (modesty and chastity) whilst also appealing to contemporary tastes for melodrama and fascination, conformed to a 'beauteous terrorist' archetype.[31] The ways in which the gender dynamics of revolutionary struggle could, in turn, give rise to martyr-myths quite distinct from those that developed around male revolutionaries is examined here by Sally Boniece, whose subject, the SR terrorist Mariia Spiridonova, became in 1906 and afterwards symbolic of the anti-tsarist struggle — the feminized embodiment of the oppressed Russian nation, juxtaposed with a barbarous and masculinized autocracy.

Readers of these articles may well be struck, above all, by the plasticity of martyrdom in the Russian context: within the six case studies, we find the term 'martyr' applied to individuals who took their own lives, who died of natural causes, or who suffered various kinds of hardship for the cause, but relatively few who were 'martyred' in the conventional sense. Sally Boniece, for instance, explores 'the martyrdom of illness' in her study of Spiridonova — her struggles in life were interpreted as a form of self-sacrifice, and she had not died by the time that many SRs termed her as a martyr. Ben Phillips explores the case of Egor Sozonov, who assassinated the Interior Minister Viacheslav von Pleve on 15 July 1904: already considered a martyr to the cause for his imprisonment and exile, he achieved a second martyrdom through his prison suicide in 1910. Though they were distinct concepts, revolutionary tradition could accommodate both suicide and martyrdom, with the apparent death wish of the terrorists blurring the line between the two.[32] Indeed, as Phillips notes, one practice that left a mark in Russian cultural memory — including amongst the revolutionary left — was Old Believer self-immolation in the seventeenth century, which provided a template for martyrdom by suicide.[33] Meanwhile, Lara Green's article discusses how the editors of *Katorga i ssylka* sought to apply martyrdom as an interpretative framework to pre-revolutionary émigrés, whose sufferings in the name of the cause were — at first glance — hardly comparable to their comrades in prison and exile. All this points to an inclusivity with which the term was employed and, therefore, highlights the mediated and contested nature of the term: there were several available

---

[31] Ana Siljak, '"The Beauteous Terrorist": Russian Women and Terrorism in Literature at the Turn of the Century', in Carola Dietze and Claudia Verhoeven (eds), *The Oxford Handbook of the History of Terrorism*, Oxford, 2020, pp. 275–91.

[32] The key study is Susan K. Morrissey, *Suicide and the Body Politic in Imperial Russia*, Cambridge, 2006.

[33] See Thomas Robbins, 'Religious Mass Suicide before Jonestown: The Russian Old Believers', *Sociological Analysis*, 47, 1, 1986, pp. 1–20.

paths to martyrdom, with followers quite eager to afford a subject the label given the prestige it could offer to a cause. Moreover, martyrdom was not only an interpretative framework for a political death: it could be, in itself, a creative act and expression of subjecthood.

It is probably fair to say that Western scholars, like much of the Western public, have come in recent decades to associate martyrdom as a concept with religious (and especially Islamic) fundamentalism; such, at least, has been the major focus of most recent studies of the subject.[34] This collection, therefore, serves first and foremost as a timely reminder that political martyrdom has a much longer history. Indeed, since scholars now routinely trace the origins of modern terrorism and political extremism to late imperial Russia, a close study of martyr culture in the same historical context sheds important new light not just on the cultural histories of revolutionary Russia, but on the relationship between martyrdom and insurgent cultures more broadly. In addition, we must note that these articles — and all of us who have contributed herein doubtless wish it were otherwise — have a contemporary resonance all their own, since martyrdom remains a key feature of Russian opposition politics in our own time: in recent years, human rights abuses in Russian prisons and the incarceration of Aleksei Naval'nyi, Vladimir Kara-Murza and other high-profile oppositionists have created a new generation of dissident martyrs. We hope, therefore, that this issue and its contents will appeal not just to subject specialists but also those working outside the context of late imperial Russia, including scholars working on symbols, rituals, myth and political culture.

[34] In addition to works cited previously, see Rona M. Fields (ed.), *Martyrdom: The Psychology, Theology, and Politics of Self-Sacrifice*, Westport, CA, 2004; Jim Winkates, 'Suicide Terrorism: Martyrdom for Organizational Objectives', *Journal of Third World Studies*, 23, 1, 2006, pp. 87–115.

Liberal Funerals, Political Resistance and Sites of Martyrdom in the Late Russian Empire

GEORGE GILBERT

7 October 1910 saw the streets of central Moscow become host to a vast demonstration: the funeral of Sergei Muromtsev, formerly chair of the First State Duma (Russia's first parliament) in 1906 and a prominent member of the Constitutional Democrat (Kadet) party.[1] Muromtsev had died suddenly of a heart attack on 4 October. A leading name in liberal politics in late imperial Russia, Muromtsev was also widely associated with universities, the advancement of higher education, personal freedoms, civil rights and the liberation movement before the 1905 revolution. His funeral was a grand affair; starting with a group of sympathetic political figures including leading figures from the Kadet party gathering at his house, the procession in central Moscow drew tens of thousands of people — according to some estimates, perhaps over 100,000 spectators — bringing the streets of Moscow to a standstill. Many bystanders came to view the ceremonies, attracted by the chanting of the crowds. Students from Russia's higher educational institutes were also present.[2] The demographics were quite mixed: students — both men and women — were well represented, but the attendees also included many of the great and good of Russian civil society and the liberal intelligentsia, including figures from Muromtsev's Kadet party — Pavel Miliukov, Fedor Rodichev and Nikolai Gredeskul — who were all speakers at the graveside on 7 October. Their speeches

George Gilbert is Lecturer in Modern Russian History at the University of Southampton.

   The author would like to thank Peter Waldron, Matt Rendle, Erik van Ree, his colleagues in this special issue, and the two readers for *SEER* for their comments which have improved the article.

[1]   All dates provided are in Old Style, that is, using the Julian Calendar, which was 13 days behind the Gregorian Calendar, only adopted in Russia in 1918.
[2]   *Sergei Andreevich Muromtsev. Predsedatel´ pervoi gosudarstvennoi dumy*, Moscow, 1913, p. 16.

Slavonic and East European Review, 102, 1, 2024   doi:10.1353/see.00002

featured many of Muromtsev's political achievements, declaring that he had been a 'fighter for freedom' who had represented the best interests of a free Russia — a polity that was in a perilous position by 1910, with the muzzling of the State Duma from its heyday shortly after the revolution of 1905, and the encroachment of the government on what Muromtsev's supporters saw as precious rights and freedoms.[3]

The atmosphere at the funeral was relatively peaceful and there was no violence, but, as noted by perceptive observers, the large crowds demonstrating, and their songs, chants and messages showed that a fork in the road had been reached concerning Russia's future development. No less than the future of the Russian state was at stake here; would Russia evolve along the lines of a *Rechtsstaat* — a state based on the rule of law — or would Russia once again descend into a state where coercive force and arbitrary governmental authority were once again its guiding lodestones?[4] This question was a central dilemma of Russian liberalism, and Muromtsev's funeral prompted several dilemmas for those attending it as well as the following services: for some, his death was a 'tragedy' for Russia, so much was he personally associated with the causes of liberation and freedom.[5] Like other events, the funeral was a weathervane of public opinion, and potentially a harbinger of changes to come; more immediately, it was interpreted as a political demonstration by a host of observers on both the political left and right.

This article will provide a thematic analysis of three different political funerals, taking a comparative perspective concerning Muromtsev's funeral from 1910 and two significant examples that emerged amidst the tumult of the 1905 revolution — Lev Kupernik in Kyiv (Kiev) and Sergei Trubetskoi in Moscow. All three people were significant figures associated with key forces in Russian liberalism, including civil rights, legality, education and constitutionalism. The article will explore the circumstances behind these sites of resistance, and how these events reflected upon liberal ideologies of selfhood, individual rights, freedoms

---

[3]   One account can be found in the police archive collection dedicated to Muromtsev's funeral. Gosudarstvennyi arkhiv Rossiiskoi Federatsii (hereafter, GARF), f. 102, op. 119, 4-e d-vo, 1910 g., d. 315, l. 47, Telegram, to the director of the police department, Moscow, 8 October 1910. The events were extensively covered in the contemporary press: one example is *Vestnik evropy*, 11, 1910, pp. 342–48, 'Vnutrennee obozrenie: Pokhorony S. A. Muromtseva kak "priznak vremeni"'.

[4]   A classic question for the 'optimist' and 'pessimist' schools of thought concerning the development of late imperial Russia. One well-known statement is that of Richard Pipes in *Russia Under the Old Regime*, Harmondsworth, 1974, ch. 11: 'towards the police state.'

[5]   As expressed in a series of editorials of one leading liberal newspaper of the day: *Rannee utro*, 5 October 1910, p. 228; 6 October 1910, p. 229; 7 October 1910, p. 230.

and citizenship. They represented a growing liberal challenge to authority, which was part of a shared struggle — in every instance, liberal ideologies of civil rights, freedom and selfhood intersected with a radical vision of overthrowing the old order. An interpretative frame involves asking how these liberals were commemorated publicly — who supported them, what their main achievements or feats (*podvigi*) were, and to what extent these arenas became important sites of martyrdom. All three died of natural causes, but supporters could interpret their lives' work to improve Russian society as a form of self-sacrifice, and the term martyr (*muchenik*) emerged amidst a cluster of related concepts.[6] The politics of Russian liberalism have been much explored in the historiography of the late imperial period, but rarely in terms of the demonstrations created for its heroes and its potential to incite public unrest: most investigations explore the presence of liberals in the parliament or their key ideas. Drawing on a wide source base of newspaper records, contemporary reminiscences and archive material including personal collections and police records, the latter of which reveal much data concerning the size, composition and mood of the crowds, this article will explore the liberal tradition in protest and dissent, arguing that this was an important challenge to old regime Russia, and was also involved in the creation of a public, and specifically liberal, identity.[7]

Liberal protests and sites of dissent
Late imperial Russia was a society in which a repressive political environment co-existed with significant modernization in the economic and social spheres. This combination led to the occurence of several innovative means of political expression, one of which was the political funeral, a trend which became evident from around the late 1870s.[8] One outstanding analysis of the radical or 'red' funeral is offered by Tom Trice in his assessment of the funerals of the populist students Anton Padlewski and Nikolai Chernyshev in 1876–78, which drew huge crowds in the centre of St Petersburg. Both students had died from tuberculosis,

[6]   Olmo Gölz, 'The Imaginary Field of the Heroic: On the Contention Between Heroes, Martyrs, Victims and Villains in Collective Memory', N. Falkenhayner, S. Meurer and T. Schlechtriemen (eds), *Helden.heroes.héros*, *Special Issue 5: Analyzing Processes of Heroization. Theories, Methods, Histories*, 2019, pp. 27–38.

[7]   Dakota Irvin, 'Surveillance Reports', in George Gilbert (ed.), *Reading Russian Sources: A Student's Guide to Text and Visual Sources from Russian History*, London, 2020, pp. 110–27. In particular, I have drawn on materials located in the police collection in the Russian State Archive (GARF, f. 102).

[8]   Not only in Russia, as this trend could also be evidenced in nineteenth-century France, Germany, the Habsburg lands and Ireland. Robert Justin Goldman, 'Political Funerals', *Society*, 1984, pp. 13–17.

allegedly contracted whilst in confinement.[9] The political funeral afforded opportunities for demonstration quite aside from the political radicals, however. Literary figures were also celebrated; one was the poet Nikolai Nekrasov who died in January 1878 and became a model for the self-sacrificing intelligentsia. His funeral procession to Novodevichii Cemetery in central Moscow attracted 4,000 people: no less a figure than Fedor Dostoevskii delivered a eulogy calling Nekrasov the greatest Russian poet since Aleksandr Pushkin.[10]

Greater still was the funeral of the writer Ivan Turgenev, a figure associated by some observers with Russian liberalism's tendencies of moderate reform, engagement with influential ideas emanating from Western Europe and social criticism. His funeral on 27 September 1883 clearly worried the authorities in terms of its potential to incite unrest. As any reader of *Fathers and Sons* knows, Turgenev was no political radical, but his funeral had the potential to become a site of dissent, and, with the March 1881 assassination of Alexander II in recent memory, no chances were taken. Major newspapers received a circular from the Ministry of the Interior instructing that only official information about the funeral was allowed to be printed, forbidding any disclosure that such a communication had been received.[11] There were fears that radical literature would be distributed at the funeral site: the return of Turgenev's body from Paris and the procession from the platform of the Varshavskii railway station through to the Volkovo cemetery in central St Petersburg provided clear opportunities to become flashpoints for the many people who wished to attend. Many observers may have seen Turgenev mainly as a writer of beautiful prose, but, to some, he was something more: like Nekrasov and other contemporaries, he became a source of moral authority, with an influence separate from that of the Russian state. A speech delivered at a memorial service (*panikhida*) for him on 28 September by the priest N. P. Kladnitskii gives something of the flavour of his standing:

[9] Tom Trice, 'Rites of Protest: Populist Funerals in Imperial St Petersburg, 1876–1878', *Slavic Review*, 60, 1, 2001, pp. 50–74. An earlier example of radical protest was the funeral of the writer Nikolai Chernyshevskii. Daniel Beer, 'Civil Death, Radical Protest and the Theatre of Punishment in the Reign of Alexander II', *Past and Present*, 250, 2021, pp. 179–92.

[10] Konstantine Klioutchkine, 'Between Sacrifice and Indulgence: Nikolai Nekrasov as a Model for the Intelligentsia', *Slavic Review*, 66, 1, 2007, pp. 45–62.

[11] This detail is cited in Isaiah Berlin, *Russian Thinkers*, Harmondsworth, 1978, p. 262. For an official account of the funeral, see Aleksei Suvorin's newspaper, *Novoe vremia*, 27 September 1883, 2723, pp. 1–3, 'V den' pokhorona Turgeneva'. Additional documents can be found in *Byloe*, 4, 1917, pp. 146–56, 'Delo o pokhoronakh I. S. Turgeneva'.

Turgenev [was] on a par with the greatest modern poets! So, the glory of Turgenev is the glory of our motherland!... 'Eternal memory be to you from all of us, your compatriots, grieving for you, the most valiant husband of the Russian land!'[12]

A figure from the official Church praising a writer rather than a tsar is of interest; the funerals of both Nekrasov and Turgenev point towards the enduring importance of the intelligentsia — including students, members of Russia's gelatinous civic society and politicians — as society's moral centre.[13]

Turgenev's funeral became a model for liberal protest. Passions concerning his humanitarian and cultural contribution suggest why it became a site of dissent for a non-radical audience. This can prompt a consideration of the relationship between liberalism and radicalism, and their respective positions within a wider archaeology of protest in Russia. Liberalism — like other key political concepts — can be tricky to define in the Russian context, but many analysts agree on several key issues. Among these were the preservation or promotion of a *Rechtsstaat*; economic-social concepts including, most importantly, the principle of private property; an active political programme that sought change from the status quo ante; and — a twist unique to Russia — association with ideas and principles emanating from 'the West'.[14] These are the messages that supporters sought to communicate. In contrast to many Russian radical ideologies, liberalism lacked eschatological tendencies and preferred to ameliorate the state through reform rather than overthrow it through revolution. So it did not always appeal strongly to radical political activists.

---

[12] *Polnoe sobranie sochinenii I. S. Turgeneva v 12 tomakh*, vol. 1, St Petersburg, 1898, p. liii.

[13] The term is notoriously hard to define in the Russian context. See Martin Malia, 'What is the Intelligentsia?', in Richard Pipes (ed.), *The Russian Intelligentsia*, London, 1961, pp. 1–18. Contemporary observers noted the close link between Russia's student community (*studenchestvo*) and the changing moods of the intelligentsia at the outset of the twentieth century, whose leaders often maintained close links or worked in Russia's leading universities. N. Cherevanin, 'Dvizhenie intelligentsii', in L. Martov et al. (eds), *Obshchestvennoe dvizhenie v Rossii v nachale XX-go veka*, vol. 1, St Petersburg, 1909, pp. 272–76.

[14] There are many assessments of Russian liberalism. Among those informing this study are Richard Wortman, *The Development of a Russian Legal Consciousness*, Chicago, IL, 1976; Andrzej Walicki, *Legal Philosophies of Russian Liberalism*, Notre Dame, IN, 1992; Victor Leontovitsch, *The History of Liberalism in Russia*, trans. Parmen Leontovitsch, Pittsburgh, PA, 2012; Anton A. Fedyashin, *Liberals Under Autocracy: Modernization and Civil Society in Russia, 1866–1906*, Madison, WI, 2012. For a very recent assessment, see Paul Robinson, *Russian Liberalism*, Ithaca, NY, 2023.

Different traditions could intersect on occasion, which once again brings us back to the political funeral, an avenue that afforded opportunities for a variety of actors right across the political and social spectrum to contest their ideas in the public domain. These events often became 'sites of dissent' in old regime Russia. During the 1905 revolution socialist protests became a key feature of the empire's public environment; workers and socialist activists were celebrated in different parts of the Russian Empire in demonstrations that could take on significant proportions. Moscow-based socialists like the veterinarian Nikolai Bauman, as well as activists on the periphery, including in significant territories such as Ukraine, became the focus of huge protests that functioned as expressions of political opinion calling for the overthrow of the old regime. It should not be overlooked either that the funeral was also used by the political right in this time; funerals for murdered state servants or Romanovs like the tsar's uncle Sergei, who was killed by a terrorist bomb in Moscow in February 1905, became occasions to commemorate the heroes of autocracy, defending also concepts of Russian Orthodoxy and nationality.[15]

For our purposes it is the intersection between liberals and radicals which is most important, with these different traditions interacting in the public arena during the revolution of 1905 — both were present in rituals held in shared public space.[16] Protest, insurgency and martyrdom have usually been associated with radical tendencies in both Russian and non-Russian contexts; associating the protest nexus with liberalism might seem almost paradoxical, but several examples illustrate the history of liberal dissent and its cross-over with the radical tradition.[17] This article will argue that such traditions interacted in a shared defiance of the old regime, with their funerals and other services functioning as sites of defiance and insurgency. At the same time, an alternative challenge emerged to the regime based around key concepts of Russian liberalism, one that the authorities struggled at times to contain.

[15] For examples from the left and right respectively, see George Gilbert, 'Topographies of Protest in the Russian Revolution of 1905', *Slavonic and East European Review*, 100, 3, 2022, pp. 504–27, and 'The Martyr Cult of Grand Duke Sergei Aleksandrovich', *The Russian Review*, 81, 2, 2022, pp. 265–83.

[16] Laura Engelstein, 'Revolution and the Theater of Public Life in Imperial Russia', in Isser Woloch (ed.), *Revolution and the Meanings of Freedom in the Nineteenth Century*, Stanford, CA, 1996, pp. 314–47.

[17] Assessments of martyrdom often connect it to radical practices, such as the terrorism advanced by insurgent groups. A stimulating collection of essays is Dominic Janes and Alex Houen (eds), *Martyrdom and Terrorism: Pre-Modern to Contemporary Perspectives*, Oxford, 2014.

Place, space and people

The nineteenth-century events briefly sketched above suggest the enduring importance of the political funeral as a site of contestation for the Russian authorities. However, concerning the ongoing battle between regime and insurgents, the stakes were raised yet higher in the early twentieth century. An especially significant event was the 1905 revolution, which saw protests, strikes and demonstrations occur right across the empire, including in many recently industrialized areas to the south and west in areas like the Don Basin.[18] Throughout the year, a movement for constitutionalism emerged from Russia's liberal factions, and they were joined in their opposition to tsarism by more radical Social Democrats and Socialist Revolutionary Party (SR) forces who became involved in many strikes and disorders in both urban and rural settings.

The emergence of sites of protest occurred throughout the Russian Empire. To turn to our first example, Moscow was the second largest city in the Russian Empire at the end of the nineteenth century: according to the 1897 census, it had a population of just under one million. It had rapidly industrialized in the latter decades of the nineteenth century and boasted a large, skilled and quite well-organized urban workforce. It had a large student population — there was a prestigious university founded in 1755, a good number of technical schools and colleges, with many female students attending the Women's Higher Education Courses. Labour violence and unrest had emerged in Moscow even before the revolution of 1905, and it had a large and well-developed socialist movement including chapters from various Social Democrat groups. During 1905 it became a centre for working-class organization and political conflict, with massive strikes and demonstrations and many grass-roots political organizations emerging throughout the year.[19] In terms of liberal politics, Moscow had been one of the most politically progressive parts of the Russian Empire. It had hosted the Banquet Campaign in 1902, a movement for civil rights and liberal political activism, all of which exploded during 1904–05.[20]

---

[18] The standout general study on 1905 remains Abraham Ascher, *The Revolution of 1905*, 2 vols, Stanford, CA, 1988 and 1992. Useful essays can be found in Jonathan D. Smele and Anthony Heywood (eds), *The Russian Revolution of 1905: Centenary Perspectives*, London, 2005, and Felicitas Fischer von Weikersthal et al. (eds), *The Russian Revolution of 1905 in Transcultural Perspective: Identities, Peripheries, and the Flow of Ideas*, Bloomington, IN, 2013.

[19] Working-class politics is assessed in Victoria E. Bonnell, *Roots of Rebellion: Workers' Politics and Organizations in St. Petersburg and Moscow, 1900–1914*, Berkeley, CA, 1983. For Moscow in 1905, see Laura Engelstein, *Moscow, 1905: Working-Class Organization and Political Conflict*, Stanford, CA, 1982.

[20] Robert W. Thurston, *Liberal City, Conservative State: Moscow and Russia's Urban*

It was in this context that the funeral and demonstrations for Sergei Trubetskoi (1862–1905) took place. He was a Russian religious philosopher from the illustrious Trubetskoi family — his father was Prince Nikolai Trubetskoi, a co-founder of the Moscow Conservatory. Trubetskoi the younger was a professor of philosophy at Moscow University, with his credentials as a leading light of Russian liberalism further burnished by his membership of the discussion circle *Beseda* which played an important role in the liberation movement before 1905.[21] Like that of Muromtsev, his death was untimely; he died on 23 September from a brain haemorrhage whilst on a work trip in St Petersburg when rising radicalism, characterized by an active strike movement and political discontent from all quarters, was sweeping the capital.[22] Trubetskoi was a moderate liberal figure, but in the context of rising disorder and unrest during 1905, his death became a focal point for the urban revolution, uniting otherwise disparate groups. The funeral of Bolshevik activist Nikolai Bauman occurred in the same month and took on similar revolutionary implications to that of Trubetskoi, to which it was compared by some contemporaries. He was associated with emblems of Russian liberalism, including freedom, civil rights and political association. His undramatic death was not obviously heroic, but his work in life as a liberal activist was interpreted by supporters as selfless acts for the people (*narod*), by which was meant the masses of society. The 'martyr' had sacrificed himself for freedom and the greater good.[23]

On Sunday 2 October thousands of students, workers and members of St Petersburg society crowded round Trubetskoi's coffin at the Nikolaevskii train station. Reports from St Petersburg clearly show this gathering became a political demonstration, with students from St Petersburg University displaying the trademarks of radical protest in the crowd — red flags, placards and radical hymns for the deceased figure. Crowds of students passed along Nevskii prospect, pausing at the Kazan' Cathedral, then crossed the bridge to Vasil'evskii Island and the university. The doors to the university building were locked, and mounted police rushed towards the unarmed crowd, but several hundred people managed to enter the

Crisis, 1906–1914, Oxford and New York, 1987, ch. 1.

[21] For a biographical account, see 'Sergei Nikolaevich Trubetskoi', in V. V. Shelokhaev et al. (eds), *Rossiiskii liberalizm serediny XVIII–nachala XX veka*, Moscow, 2010, pp. 953–56. For analysis of the liberation movement, see Shmuel Galai, *The Liberation Movement in Russia, 1900–1905*, Cambridge, 1979.

[22] Trubetskoi's funeral is briefly assessed in Ascher, *Revolution of 1905*, vol. 1, *Russia in Disarray*, p. 212, and Engelstein, *Moscow, 1905*, pp. 95–96. See also, Samuel D. Kassow, *Students, Professors and the State in Tsarist Russia*, Berkeley, CA, 1989, pp. 269–70.

[23] *Moskovskie vedomosti*, 21 October 1905, 279, p. 3, 'Revoliutsionnyia pokhorony'.

building and gather in the auditorium. Most worrying for the authorities was that this meeting appeared unplanned, with a subsequent investigation suggesting that none of the major parties had been involved in organizing the meeting. With students and workers attending as well as members of the intelligentsia, the demonstration displayed a new sense of community across class ties and united disparate social groups.[24]

The funeral held the following day turned into a huge anti-government demonstration, with estimates suggesting crowds in the tens of thousands. A massive crowd including both workers and male and female students greeted the arrival of the coffin from St Petersburg. The events attracted a wide cross section of support, including students from the nearby Agricultural Institute; delegates from the Central Bureau of the Union of Unions; representatives from the *zemstva* (local councils); people from the Moscow chapter of the movement for Jewish equal rights; a group of lawyers from St Petersburg; students from the St Petersburg Spiritual Academy, and many others.[25] Joined by members of the intelligentsia as well as more revolutionary students, the procession united many disparate parts of the oppositional movement on Moscow's streets. These assembled in some of the central throughfares of the city; the Donskoi Monastery saw a large procession with crowds of 9,000 and 10,000 thought to be present, with workers and students both assembling on Kaluzhskaia Square in the city centre and carrying red flags to the monastery, where the internment took place and a variety of speeches were delivered.[26] The size, intensity and vocal nature of the crowds alerted a great many passers-by and put the watching authorities on high alert. The general context of Moscow during 1905 — working-class organization, political unrest and then the General Strike — was a backdrop for one of the biggest funerals in Russia's history of a politician who united radical and liberal onlookers in protest at the old regime. Violence at the funeral was another point of controversy.[27]

Lev Kupernik's funeral in Kyiv in October 1905 was another example of radical protest. Despite the great age of the city, much of Kyiv's urban

[24] GARF, f. 102.OO, op. 233a, 1905 g., 2 otd-e, d. 3, ch. 26, ll. 25–26, Report, office of the Governor-General of Moscow. This document is cited in Susan K. Morrissey, *Heralds of Revolution: Russian Students and Mythologies of Radicalism*, Oxford, 1998, pp. 112–13. A right-wing politician provides a similar account in Vladimir Purishkevich, *Materialy, po voprosu o razlozhenii sovremennogo Russkogo universiteta*, St Petersburg, 1914, p. 51.

[25] *Moskovskie vedomosti*, 4 October 1905, 263, pp. 2–3, 'Pokhorony kniazia S. N. Trubetskogo'.

[26] GARF, f. 102.OO, op. 233a, 1905 g., 2 otd-e, d. 3, ch. 32, ll. 78–79, Report, Ministry of Internal Affairs, office of the Governor-General of Moscow, 4 October 1905.

[27] Engelstein, *Moscow, 1905*, pp. 95–96.

infrastructure had developed relatively recently. During the last decade of the nineteenth century, some of the newly industrializing areas to the south and west of the empire had seen their populations grow threefold. According to the 1897 census, Kyiv had a population of around 240,000, and many of the new arrivals into the city joined the ever-growing urban workforce.[28] Kyiv, as a major centre in Ukraine in the southwest of the empire, had seen political radicalism prior to 1905. There were strong traditions of labour unrest and protest in the region: 1903 saw a General Strike, and up to 200,000 workers in Transcaucasia and Ukraine participated in a mass political strike in July and August. The strikes began in Baku but soon spread to other regions: July 1903 saw the 'Solidarity strike' in Kyiv, which was partly led by the committee of the Bolshevik journal *Iskra*. However, those involved went far beyond the local chapters of the illegal Social Democrat parties, with metal workers unaffiliated with any party playing a central role. In Kyiv and other areas of both Ukraine and Transcaucasia, strikes were combined with demonstrations, mass rallies and political meetings. Following this moment of unrest in mid 1903, city life gradually began to return to normal, but, according to Michael Hamm, continued insurgency led to a heightened, febrile atmosphere: a clash between Social Democrats and the authorities in Podil on 25 July 1905 led to many casualties, with 'Kiev [having] its own martyrs' of the workers movement following the violence dispensed by the authorities on crowds of demonstrators.[29] Adding into this context was ethnic unrest in a nationally, ethnically and religiously diverse region. In common with many other areas within the Pale of Settlement — where the vast majority of the empire's Jews lived — Kyiv witnessed a large pogrom in October 1905, adding to the cycles of violence, but, here, with an ethnic dimension.[30]

Like other cases assessed here, Kupernik did not have a dramatic death, but suffered a premature end, dying on 29 September from heart failure after a period of poor health. He did not have the national stature of Trubetskoi, but was a significant figure in Kyiv's developing civil society, a son of a distinguished family; his father Abraham (Avraam) was one of the most prominent lawyers in Russia, a trustee of Jewish charities in Kyiv and

[28] Assessment of Kyiv in this period can be found in Michael F. Hamm, *Kiev, A Portrait. 1800–1917*, Princeton, NJ, 1993, pp. 173–88, and Natan M. Meir, *Kiev: Jewish Metropolis: A History, 1859–1914*, Indianapolis, IN, 2010.

[29] Hamm, *Kiev*, p. 176.

[30] A detailed discussion of the Kyiv pogrom is in ibid., pp. 189–207. For analysis of the pogrom's impact on the Jewish community, see Meir, *Kiev: Jewish Metropolis*, pp. 122–30.

a prominent part of the Kyivan third sector. Later, Lev's daughter would become famous in twentieth-century Russia as a poet and biographer.[31] Lev worked as a lawyer in Kyiv, acquiring a strong reputation as a trial attorney, and his legal work became known more widely throughout the empire. He was also a keen contributor to the Russian liberal press, especially the journal *Voskhod*, often fulminating against the antisemitic tirades that appeared in the right-wing media. Though he converted to Russian Orthodoxy as an adult in order to marry a Russian woman, he was born into a prominent Jewish family and had high esteem amongst Jewish populations for his defence of the accused in the Blood Libel trial of Kutaisi in 1879, and he was a defender of Jewish self-defence groups standing trial following the Gomel pogrom of 1904.[32] He was thus closely associated with Jewish civil society, liberal politics and legal cultures in Kyiv, the city where he had spent most of his life. His undramatic death could not obviously be interpreted as a heroic one for supporters, but his feats in life including his extensive work in the legal sphere were interpreted as self-sacrificing.

Kupernik's funeral on 1 October 1905 appeared as a large demonstration in the urban centre amidst a period of high tension. The city had seen pogroms during the year, including in May, and the authorities interpreted the funeral — which turned into a large political demonstration — in the light of these events. Senator E. A. Turau, who compiled a long report on the anti-government 'unrest' in Kyiv, wrote as follows:

On 1 October, during the funeral, [Kupernik's] body was seen off by a large crowd of people, consisting mainly of young students and others among them. Wreaths with red ribbons were laid on the coffin, one had the inscription: 'To an honest citizen from the KKPSR' [the Kyiv Committee of the Socialist Revolutionary Party]. Along the route of the funeral procession, crowds sang 'The Marseillaise', and revolutionary speeches were made at the cemetery.[33]

---

[31] Kupernik's distinguished father is mentioned in ibid., pp. 74–75.

[32] Obituary in *Voskhod*, October 1905, 40, pp. 7–9, 'L. A. Kupernik'. There is a large literature on Jewish self-defence. Examples include Shlomo Lambroza, 'Jewish Self-Defence during the Russian Pogroms of 1903–1906', *Jewish Journal of Sociology*, 23, 1981, pp. 123–34; Inna Shtakser, 'Self-Defence as an Emotional Experience: The Anti-Jewish Pogroms of 1905–07 and Working-Class Jewish Militants', *Revolutionary Russia*, 22, 2, 2009, pp. 153–79; Stefan Wiese, '"Spit Back with Bullets!" Emotions in Russia's Jewish Pogroms, 1881–1905', *Geschichte und Gesellschaft*, 39, 4, 2013, pp. 472–501.

[33] *Materialy k istorii Russkoi kontrrevoliutsii*, vol. 1, *Pogromy po offitsial'nym dokumentam*, St Petersburg, 1908, p. 211; A funeral for 'Kopernik' [*sic*] is briefly mentioned in Hamm, *Kiev*, p. 186.

Though seldom remarked upon in secondary studies of Kyiv in this period, Kupernik's funeral was a sizeable affair and appeared as a radical event, uniting students and political activists from Jewish groups as well as people from local chapters of Social Democrat parties as well as the SRs. It was closely monitored by the authorities, their antennae finely tuned because of the various disturbances the city had seen in the past several months. Reports estimate around 4,000 numbered in the initial procession, with local politicians including well-known names such as the lawyer A. S. Gol´denveizer appearing amidst a crowd filing down Kreshchatyk and Aleksandrovskaia streets towards the Saint Sophia Cathedral. These were central spaces in Kyiv which gave the procession high visibility — many onlookers could see the crowds and hear the noise — some even joined in, which swelled the already substantial ranks.[34] The funeral was widely covered in the Kyivan press, especially in dailies that typically adopted a liberal line such as *Kievskaia gazeta* and *Kievskie novosti*. For many observers, Kupernik's advocacy of the cause of Jewish self-defence in life and his commitment to his local community in the form of civic activism and culture — he was a keen fan of opera and theatre and patronized several artistic societies — marked him out as an exceptional figure who represented the growing movement away from autocratic rule towards a different Russia, associated with peace, freedom and concepts of legality. His father's work as a lawyer during the Great Reforms of the 1860s gave this interpretation an additional cachet.[35] The crowd united many disparate elements: as well as the political groups, official religion was present — Kupernik's Orthodox background meant priests and clergy numbered among the procession which marched through Volodyrmyrska street on the way to Askold's Grave cemetery, where Kupernik was to be interred. This gave the procession and resulting demonstrations a curious, mixed social complexion, with religious figures, political activists and liberal figures from civil society forming a diverse crowd.[36]

Before turning to further thematic assessment, a few words on Sergei Muromtsev's funeral by way of comparison may be in order. Of the three funerals assessed this was the largest in scale by some distance, drawing enormous crowds (see Figures 1 & 2). The funeral on 7 October was the

[34] Reports on the funeral are in *Pravo*, 9 October 1905, 40, cols 3376–78, 'Khronika'. One can also find many documents in Kupernik's personal collection, housed in the Russian State Archive. GARF, f. 8420, op. 1, d. 6, l. 6, Clipping of *Kievskie novosti*, 2 October 1905. See also, in this file ll. 23–25, clippings from the newspapers *Kievskaia gazeta* and *Kievskie novosti*.

[35] GARF, f. 8420, op. 1, d. 6, l. 8, Clipping of *Kievskaia gazeta*, 30 September 1905.

[36] *Pravo*, 9 October 1905, 40, cols 3376–77, 'Khronika'.

first public demonstration of support for constitutional ideas since the dissolution of the First State Duma in 1906 — Muromtsev had convened this iteration. This gave the event a different contextual basis to our first two case studies. Whereas they coincided with the political insurgency of 1905, the Muromtsev funeral occured several years into the era of politics and parliament following the revolutionary year. Voluminous police records and wide discussion of the funeral in the contemporary press show the significance of the crowds in Moscow and the burial in Donskoe cemetery, widely interpreted as anti-government protests given Muromtsev's support for constitutional Russia.[37] Muromtsev had not been granted a state funeral, but large-scale civic demonstrations showed support for his ideas and were hard for the authorities to control. Intriguingly, demonstrations for Muromtsev were not confined to Moscow but occurred right across the empire: reports from St Petersburg, Kyiv, Kharkiv, Nizhnii Novogorod and other cities show that many people — particularly groups of students — held services and demonstrated in his honour. In some respects, the funeral was a return to the disquiet of 1905, revealing a restless and fragile empire.

Songs, messages, symbols
Trubetskoi's funeral in Moscow in 1905 was interpreted by many observers as a radical event. Students carried the coffin towards the Donskoe monastery in the lower Zamoskvorech´e district, and whilst the liberal presence was well represented by figures from the *zemstvo* and other associations, the semiotics of the event appeared to be radical. Red flowers and banners were held aloft by many members of the crowd, and though Social Democrat parties did not send representatives, many revolutionary anthems were chanted. Among these were 'Marsel´eza' ('The Marseillaise'), interspersed with a refrain of 'Vechnaia pamiat´´' ('Eternal Memory') — sung at the end of every Orthodox funeral — chanted by both students and clergy. The mixture of newer revolutionary anthems with the music of Orthodox religiosity was a curious feature of many protests seen during the revolution of 1905, of which this was one prominent example.[38]

Thematically, a commonality appears between Trubetskoi's passing and the death of Kupernik. Though Trubetskoi died of natural causes

[37] *Russkoe slovo*, 8 October 1910, 231, pp. 2–4, 'Pokhorony S. A. Muromtseva'; *Rech´*, 6 October 1910, 274, pp. 2–3, 'K konchine S. A. Muromtseva'.
[38] Susanne Ament, 'Russian Revolutionary Songs of 1905 and 1917: Symbols and Messengers of Protest and Change', MA thesis, Georgetown University, 1984, p. 22; Deborah Pearl, *Creating a Culture of Revolution: Workers and the Revolutionary Movement in Late Imperial Russia*, Bloomington, IN, 2015, ch. 4.

Fig. 1. Photograph of Muromtsev's funeral procession on Moscow's Theatre Square, 7 October 1910. *Venok na mogilu Sergeiia Andreevicha Muromtseva*, Moscow, 1910, p. 38. Collection of the National Library of Finland, Slavonic Library.

Fig. 2. Photograph of Muromtsev's funeral procession making its way from the city council to Moscow University on 7 October 1910. *Venok na mogilu Sergeiia Andreevicha Muromtseva*, Moscow, 1910, p. 71. Collection of the National Library of Finland, Slavonic Library.

rather than anything dramatic, his life's work in Russian universities and the liberation movement were understood to be a form of self-sacrifice. Hence, languages of martyrdom were evident here too; in this instance, it can be witnessed in the realm of music. Students chanted a popular revolutionary song heard at other radical funerals in the empire during 1905, 'Vy zhertvoiu pali v bor'be rokovoi' ('You, victims, who fell in a fatal struggle').[39] Trubetskoi was a moderate figure, but students, revolutionaries and others in the crowd made it clear that the event was an opportunity to contest the power of the old regime — red flags were widely apparent in the procession to the monastery. A Menshevik observer commented, 'it was not only a solemn funeral, but it was also the most grandiose political demonstration of that time'. Trubetskoi's association with concepts of legality and freedom set him apart from the dark iniquities of the old regime and led to his funeral becoming a major event in the annals of protest, with popular responses creating a martyrology around the dead figure.[40]

As William Nickell remarked in his study of Lev Tolstoi's death in 1910, memory politics in the late imperial period was contested as much on the pages of the printed press as it was on city streets.[41] Major publications began to interpret the meaning of Trubetskoi's death immediately after his passing. The daily newspaper, *Russkoe slovo*, one of the largest-circulating publications at the time, quoted Trubetskoi's own observations on the shifting political situation in the previous year in its obituary — 'the trial is coming', he had remarked. The editorial added:

the year that Russian society went through was a terrible, difficult year — terrible and difficult because, with incredible efforts and immeasurable sacrifices, we broke away from the past, were reborn, changed — and saw other people, too, reborn and changed.

The report concluded ominously that '[r]eturn to the past is impossible'.[42] Trubetskoi was a symbol of the change occurring across Russia, and, like other major figures, someone who had worked for the Russian land and

---

[39] GARF, f. 102.OO, op. 233a, 1905 g., 2 otd-e, d. 3, ch. 32, ll. 78–79, Report, Ministry of Internal Affairs, office of the Governor-General of Moscow, 4 October 1905; *Moskovskie vedomosti*, 5 October 1905, 264, p. 3, 'K pokhoronam kniazia S. N. Trubetskogo'.

[40] P. A. Garvi, *Vospominaniia sotsialdemokrata*, New York, 1946, p. 535.

[41] William Nickell, *The Death of Tolstoy: Russia on the Eve, Astapovo Station, 1910*, Ithaca, NY, 2010, pp. 133–35.

[42] The personal collection of Trubetskoi in the Russian State Archive contains many such reports. For one example, see GARF, F. 1093, op. 1, d. 45, l. 7, Clipping of *Russkoe slovo*, 5 October 1905.

people. Building on this idea of a man of the people, *Russkie vedomosti* published a letter from a Russian peasant, Seletskii, which compared the death of Trubetskoi to that of the 'tsar-liberator' Alexander II in 1881 and lamented his passing: 'to your great memory, a great citizen of the Russian land!'[43] At the other end of the social spectrum, no less a figure than Petr Struve wrote that his death represented an 'irreparable loss' for society; his work for Moscow University was irreplaceable: 'Glory to the memory of the fallen!'[44] This line of thought continued in later years. On 16 March 1908, a series of liberal politicians speaking at a meeting of the Student Scientific Society of Moscow University in memory of S. N. Trubetskoi speculated on his sacrifice to the cause of freedom in Russia and his contribution to wider knowledge. They spoke of their 'love, gratitude and reverence' for the deceased. Trubetskoi's martyrdom was the result of his work in life, with his diligent labour on questions of freedom widely interpreted as a form of self-sacrifice.[45]

Likewise, Kupernik's funeral saw the display of radical messages. The many wreaths laid in his memory at Askold's Grave in Kyiv bore red ribbons, and the coffin was carried to the grave site by students, held aloft, and strung with red banners. As for Trubetskoi, the music was a mix of Orthodox religiosity — accounts of the funeral and services remark on the use of 'Eternal Memory' — as well as revolutionary anthems like 'The Marseillaise' and the often associated 'Pokhoronnyi marsh' ('Funeral March').[46] Speeches were delivered by leading figures from Kyivan civil and political life. Among these were the lawyer Mark B. Ratner, a member of the Union for Equal Rights of the Jewish People and the Russian Social Revolutionary Party, and revolutionary political activist and community secretary Grigorii E. Gurevich, who commented on the wider contribution of Kupernik. One speech proclaimed 'Comrades! Citizens! Today we are burying a fighter for freedom!' Particularly of concern to watching authorities was how the year's political events had led to calls for a constitution — a diverse crowd had congregated in Kyiv which called for a new kind of society. A political solidarity was developing across ethnic and class lines, with many Jews and Christians mobilizing around the same banners, reflecting Kupernik's own pluralistic background. For some in the funeral crowd, tsarism was a 'despotism' for all citizens.[47]

[43] *Russkie vedomosti*, 9 October 1905, 264, p. 4, 'K konchine S. A. Muromtseva'.

[44] *Osvobozhdenie*, 18 October 1905, 78–79, p. 504, 'Kniaz´ S. N. Trubetskoi'.

[45] *Sbornik rechei posviashchennykh pamiati Kn. Sergei Nikolaevicha Trubetskogo*, Moscow, 1909, p. 58.

[46] GARF, f. 8420, op. 1, d. 6, ll. 22–22 ob., Clipping of *Kievskaia gazeta*, 2 October 1905.

[47] GARF, f. 102.OO, op. 233a, 1905 g., 2 otd-e, d. 1350, ch. 15, ll. 114–16, Report, Ministry

Following his interment at Askold's Grave, over which several of Kyiv's leading lights of liberal politics and civil society delivered speeches, part of the crowd left the cemetery singing revolutionary songs. Once the clergy and more moderate figures departed, the presence became more radical. Police monitoring the funeral remarked on the presence of 'Jewish youth' singing 'songs of a revolutionary character', including refrains of 'down with the autocracy, long live freedom, down with the police!'[48] At the same event, brochures and pamphlets of 'revolutionary content' were passed around: one police report suggested two members of a radical Ukrainian political grouping — Vladimir Gekhovskii and Vladimir Strashkevich — had distributed c.1,500 examples of printed literature calling for freedom and for the government to be overthrown.[49] As would be the case in Moscow several months later, Kyivan newspapers reported extensively on Kupernik's funeral, the resulting demonstrations and the crowd violence that followed. Concerning Kupernik's contribution, the speeches from individuals like A. S. Gol'denveizer were also reprinted extensively in the Kyivan press, couching his contribution in terms of self-sacrifice and even heroism — how he had 'given himself' to society and stood up for principle in his defence of Jewish self-defence groups in his long career as a 'citizen advocate'.[50]

Muromtsev's funeral five years later in 1910 took place in the context of a different national mood, but the symbols and semiotics likewise challenged traditional ideas concerning funeral practices. Although Muromtsev was not given a state funeral, large scale civic demonstrations saw widespread involvement of the clergy. Police reports of the event depict elements redolent of Orthodox religiosity: students in the crowd on the procession to the monastery sang 'Eternal Memory' and 'Sviatyi bozhe' ('O Holy God'). The demonstrations were also accompanied by priests.[51] However, the presence of the official Church at ceremonies for a prominent figure of Russian liberalism, as well as the non-religious content of some accompanying events, clearly irked certain observers. Observers on the political right — who well understood the mobilizational power of funerals — perceived such practices as irreligious or even blasphemous. They objected to the incorporation of religious elements, as with the funeral of renowned novelist Lev Tolstoi one month later. The far-right

of Internal Affairs, office of the Governor of Kyiv, 10 October 1910.
[48] GARF, f. 102.OO, op. 233a, 1905 g., 2 otd-e, d. 1350, ch. 15, ll. 99, 100, Encrypted telegrams circulated within the Kyiv police department's special section, 2 October 1905.
[49] Ibid., l. 100.
[50] GARF, f. 8420, op. 1, d. 6, l. 22, Clipping of *Kievskaia gazeta*, 2 October 1905.
[51] *Russkoe slovo*, 7 October 1910, 230, p. 3.

newspaper, *Russkoe znamia*, cited Muromtsev's funeral as a case where a 'Godless' person was unjustly given a church ceremony.[52] Elsewhere, the mass demonstrations were closely observed by the security services. One service held for Muromtsev at 3 pm on 6 October 1910 in the main hall of St Petersburg University — with the permission of the rector — was attended by many members of the university community. This followed a service held one day after his death at the same institution. Like the earlier service, the event on 6 October attracted many students sympathetic to Muromtsev's cause. By 1910 there were few public radical events of any kind, so liberal funerals could become especially attractive to those who desired to protest. A police report made note of the student leaders that attended this service and their various political associations: Nikolai Vasil′ev Appolonov — a Social Democrat; Shakskii — a Kadet; 'Karl' — an SR, and Apollonov II — listed merely (and contemptuously) as a 'progressive'. Overall, 1,000 students attended from a variety of St Petersburg's higher educational institutions. Though this was a peaceful demonstration, there was at times a 'revolutionary mood' in the crowd, with students again singing the Orthodox hymn 'Eternal Memory'. As well as religious songs, key messages of the liberal challenge again became apparent. Following the service, large numbers of students assembled outside St Petersburg University to hear a speech by the student Karl, which claimed that Muromtsev had been a fighter for citizenship and free rights — a language applied not only by liberals but also by political radicals like the SRs.[53]

The mixture of religious iconography with contemporary discussions of the liberal hero demonstrated that the traditional funeral service and associated rites of passage were becoming inverted and destabilized around this time.[54] The memory politics that followed his death showed that his image was contested. Particularly, observers on the political right objected to Muromtsev's presentation as a hero in the liberal media: not only was the use of religious rites objectionable, but he was supported by nefarious influences that sought to undermine the Russian Empire. The right-wing newspaper, *Zemshchina*, saw him only as a hero of the 'liberation movement' and 'Jewish press'. In typically vitriolic style, the article commented that his supporters had 'the blood of the faithful sons'

---

[52] Cited in Nickell, *The Death of Tolstoy*, p. 185.

[53] GARF, f. 102, op. 119, 4-e d-vo, 1910 g., d. 315, ll. 26–27, Police report, notes on the disorders in the capital, 11 October 1910.

[54] A variety of newspaper reports were collected in Muromtsev's personal archive following his death. One example is in GARF, f. 575, op. 1, d. 33, ll. 39–40 ob., Clipping of *Russkoe slovo*, 7 October 1910.

of the fatherland on their hands.[55] For Lev Tikhomirov, then editor of
the right-wing *Moskovskie vedomosti*, Muromtsev's funeral had been
brilliantly exploited by the revolutionaries; he reflected privately that
although Muromtsev had 'broken from the revolution' — shown by his
disassociation from more violent revolutionary tactics — it was certain
that, as in Trubetskoi's case in 1905, radical students would seek to exploit
the fallout from his funeral and try to force more radical change in
Russia.[56]

Crowd dynamics and violence

A notable feature of Trubetskoi's funeral was its radical character, and
how it saw violence between crowds of demonstrators and troops of
mounted police. On the day of the funeral, while professors eulogized the
dead rector at the Donskoi monastery, a crowd of around 2,000 students
gathered at the gates of the cemetery to listen to revolutionary speeches.
There was a radical mood and symbolism in this crowd — red flags and
red ribbons fluttered on poles, and speeches were interrupted by the
singing of 'The Marseillaise'. Cossacks gathered to confront this crowd of
students and violence ensued. The Cossacks mercilessly beat the students
with truncheons and whips — no fatalities were recorded, but several
students were injured in the ensuing violence, with a few receiving severe
facial injuries.[57] The violence against the crowds of students outraged
society — according to the Menshevik observer Petr Bronshtein writing
under the pseudonym P. A. Garvi, the 'indignation caused by this cruel
massacre was enormous in all sections of the population'.[58] Trubetskoi was
associated with memory of the liberation movement, and his funeral was
a moment of freedom of assembly and the right of expression which cut
across liberal and student society. The attack on students struck deeply at
liberals in the Russian establishment who sympathized with the students'
fate — the moment united many in liberal society, the intelligentsia and
members of the Russian student community (*studenchestvo*) who saw their
colleagues at the forefront of the authorities' attack. According to Laura
Engelstein, the authorities' use of violence at the funeral widely offended
a sense of justice and drew oppositional strands together amidst the white

---

[55] *Zemshchina*, 9 October 1910, p. 2, 'Vzmylennyi geroi'.
[56] 'Iz dnevnika L. Tikhomirova', *Krasnyi arkhiv*, 1, 1936, p. 178.
[57] Accounts of the violence are in GARF, f. 102.OO, op. 233a, 1905 g., 2 otd-e, d. 3, ch. 32,
ll. 78–79, Report, Ministry of Internal Affairs, office of the Governor-General of Moscow,
4 October 1905; *Moskovskie vedomosti*, 5 October 1905, 264, p. 3, 'K pokhoronam kniazia S.
N. Trubetskogo'; Garvi, *Vospominaniia*, p. 538.
[58] Ibid.

heat generated by the general insurgency in Moscow. This occurred around the time of the General Strike of 1905, which was followed by the Presnia Uprising in December.[59]

There was also violence at the funeral of Lev Kupernik. Similar trends can be evidenced to the funeral of Trubetskoi — after the demonstration at Askold's Grave, part of the crowd left the cemetery singing revolutionary songs. A group consisting mainly of students was met by a police squad. According to the report from the Kyiv chief of police, shots rang out from the crowd and stones were thrown, with troops responding by firing into the crowd. Several people were injured, and one young woman was killed — she was Jewish, and this aspect of her identity caught the interest of many radicals in the region, including Jewish Social Democrats.[60] Her death was reported in the local and national press, and outraged many in the local Jewish community. Following this, despite the best efforts of local police to deter students from meeting at Kyiv University, congregations of students gathered to honour her memory. The next day, hundreds of students entered the hall of the main building and staged a meeting. A police surveillance report estimated that around 4,000 were present inside and outside the university, with many chanting songs in her honour.[61] In this way, an intriguing martyrology developed following the funeral. Whilst Kupernik was claimed to be a hero, he had died of natural causes and was not widely termed a martyr by his supporters. But, in the cycles of violence that followed, the young woman — who is not named in accounts of the violence — became a symbol of arbitrary violence and tsarist brutality, leading to further demonstrations in central Kyiv through October that commemorated both the work of Kupernik and her own sacrifice. Her dramatic death was seen as a martyrdom and incited Kyiv's students, who congregated around the university building in the weeks following Kupernik's funeral. A police investigation was launched into her untimely death, but after a year this was terminated due to lack of sufficient evidence to conduct such an enquiry.[62] The atmosphere in the city remained tense for some weeks due in part to violence at the funeral.

---

[59] Engelstein, *Moscow, 1905*, pp. 95–96.

[60] There is a short file in the Russian State Archive collecting material concerning Kupernik's 'revolutionary funeral'. GARF, f. 124, op. 43, d. 1427, l. 1, Police report, n.d.; see also GARF, f. 102.OO, op. 233a, 1905 g., 2 otd-e, d. 1350, ch. 15, l. 116, Ministry of Internal Affairs, office of the Governor of Kyiv, 10 October 1910.

[61] *Pravo*, 9 October 1905, 40, cols 3376–77, 'Khronika'.

[62] GARF, f. 124, op. 43, d. 1427, l. 3, Prosecutor for the Kyiv judicial chamber, 11 January 1906.

In contrast to these two examples, the funeral of Muromtsev saw no violence but it was noted that it had a tense atmosphere — in other words, the potential for violence was apparent to those in attendance. The services seen for him across the empire were mostly autonomous — not organized by any political group but often the work of students who decided to mobilize in his honour at short notice. Like the funeral itself these were peaceful, but the worries of the authorities at what was occurring are apparent from reports, which show their own prejudices: one record on a service held for Muromtsev in Odesa described a 'political demonstration' and commented multiple times on the presence of Jewish students in the crowd.[63] The political right were aghast at his popularity and his status as a symbol of freedom and the hated era of politics and parliament, which writers of publications such as *Moskovskie vedomosti* observed with such dismay.[64]

Nevertheless, the life of Muromtsev was widely celebrated across the Russian Empire following his passing, and educational institutions became sites of mourning. On 11 October, a large demonstration at Kharkiv University held with the agreement of the university administration and rector attracted over 2,000 students. One student, Aleksei Pavlov, who delivered a speech celebrating Muromtsev's status as a professor, university rector and social activist, was greeted positively by the crowds. Muromtsev's role in the first Duma and his long-standing service to student issues in Russia were particularly praised. Like other services, this appeared to be directed, led by and mostly made up of students.[65] Intriguingly, the presence of industrial workers — who had played a key role in the demonstrations for some of the most intense activity seen during 1905 — was not widely commented upon, though some of the events were clearly aimed at mobilizing this group: one report of a service held at the Pokrovskii Monastery in Kharkiv on 10 October sent to then Minister of Education Lev Kasso described a crowd of around 300 students giving speeches, one of which finished 'Rise up, working people!'[66] Generally speaking, a contrast with Trubetskoi and Kupernik's funerals can be seen in the crowd composition, which here seemed to consist of the liberal

---

[63] GARF, f. 102, op. 119, 4-e d-vo, 1910 g., d. 315, l. 62, Telegram, Ministry of Internal Affairs, 9 October 1910.

[64] *Moskovskie vedomosti*, 8 October 1910, 'Moskva, 7 Oktiabria. S. A. Muromtsev i ego partiia'.

[65] GARF, f. 102, op. 119, 4-e d-vo, 1910 g., d. 315, ll. 104–104 ob., Report, head of the Kharkiv regional gendarmerie, 13 October 1910.

[66] Ibid., l. 148, Police report, to the Minister of Internal Affairs, L. A. Kasso, 11 October 1910.

intelligentsia and students, whereas the events in 1905 appeared to be more cross-class in nature, although students still played a vital role in terms of leading them, along with their presence at the demonstrations. Often it was radical youth that was most involved in the direction and dissemination of acts of violence, or resistance to the violent practices of the Russian state.

The liberal challenge

To return to a dilemma outlined at the start of this investigation, these events demonstrate the endurance of a public culture of liberalism. The status of Kupernik and Trubetskoi as liberal heroes of a changing Russia was undoubtedly at the forefront of their public commemoration. Tireless work in life was seen as self-sacrificing: Kupernik's supporters at the funeral claimed that they were burying a 'fighter for freedom', but at least as crucial was his status as a lawyer, citizen and defender of Jewish civil and legal rights.[67] Following his death, publications such as *Voskhod* were quick to claim him as a noble defender of exploited Jewry, seen in his defence of Jewish self-defence groups. The obituary claimed:

> when the task of civil freedom was seized before him, and among the whole of Russian society, he, with all the strength of his fiery nature, gave himself up to the new world.

Even his conversion to Orthodoxy as an adult 'did not alienate him from the Jewish masses'. His judgment was always 'open and honest', and he showed his closeness to his community by rushing to defend the 'heroes' of Gomel.[68] At the funeral itself speeches from fellow lawyers Iakov Gol'denveizer and Mark Ratner, as well as journalist A. I. Chagovets, speculated on his commitment to freedom and justice.[69] Legality had long been associated with traditions in nineteenth-century Russian liberalism, especially during the era of the Great Reforms from the 1860s, and Kupernik was part of this noble lineage. The presence of delegates from groups such as the All-Russian Union of Lawyers confirmed this. According to Ratner at his speech delivered at Askold's Grave, Kupernik was a friend of 'legal political freedom' who calmly fulfilled his political duty both to the country and people'.[70]

---

[67] GARF, f. 102.OO, op. 233a, 1905 g., 2 otd-e, d. 1350, ch. 15, ll. 114–16, Report, Ministry of Internal Affairs, office of the Governor of Kyiv, 10 October 1910.

[68] *Voskhod*, October 1905, 40, pp. 7–9, 'L. A. Kupernik'.

[69] GARF, f. 8420, op. 1, d. 6, ll. 23, 24, Clippings from *Kievskaia gazeta*, 2 October 1905.

[70] Ibid., l. 24.

Though he was a university rector and philosopher rather than a lawyer, Trubetskoi was similarly commemorated as one of the most steadfast defenders of freedom in Russia after his death. Like Kupernik, his supporters in the press, at the funeral and at subsequent services associated him with the best traditions of Russian learning, in part due to his professional background. Following his death newspapers including *Russkie vedomosti* published a large number of telegrams that they received: one from the association of Moscow-Kursk railroad workers described him as a 'fighter for freedom'; others from students described him as a saviour of the Russian university and an enlightened individual who had delivered a great service to Russian education.[71] Letters received by his widow Praskov´ia Vladimirovna show similar themes concerning a variety of topics, with several of these commenting on his heroism.[72] Alternatively, a communication from the head of Tsaritsyn City Council sent to Praskov´ia referred to his support for the Russo-Japanese War, claiming that the 'war gave birth to heroes'. Intriguingly, the liberal Trubetskoi had been a supporter of the Russo-Japanese War from the outset, which he regarded as a defence of Western civilization (represented by Russia) against a barbaric foe in the east.[73] It is curious that following his death he was widely commemorated as an anti-establishment figure, showing how meanings could shift and even become subversive depending on the political prerogatives of the day.

Trubetskoi and Kupernik both died in the most intense months of the 1905 revolution, and their funerals and services quickly became public events that challenged the old regime, taking on revolutionary implications. Though both were of undeniably liberal politics in the febrile atmosphere of 1905, they provided an obvious opportunity for protest for many with different political ideologies. Despite not sending delegates in any official capacity, in both instances Social Democrat activists attended the funerals and services. Muromtsev's commemorations were different in that they occurred in the non-revolutionary year of 1910, but, once more, political radicals were present. By this time there were virtually no public political funerals for any radicals, so such people were especially keen to utilize legitimate events to spread their political messages. For the autocracy, the

---

[71] *Russkie vedomosti*, 6 October 1905, 261, p. 4, 'Pamiati kn. S. N. Trubetskogo'.

[72] These are gathered in GARF, f. 1093, op. 1, d. 135, Letters, protocols and other documents addressed to P. V. Trubetskoi from social organizations expressing condolences concerning the death of S. N. Trubetskoi and honouring his memory.

[73] GARF, f. 1093, op. 1, d. 135, ll. 17–18 ob., Letter, Tsaritsyn city council to Praskov´ia Trubetskoi, 28 December 1905.

wider implications in terms of a challenge were obvious enough. Most of all, the events reanimated the ideals of the first State Duma, dissolved in 1906 after proving less pliant a body than some in government might have expected. For liberal contributors to publications such as *Russkoe slovo*, 'Muromstev stood as a living symbol, and this symbol was a symbol of the legendary first Russian Duma, a first and short-lived rising of Russian freedom'.[74]

For autocracy and its supports, the implications were clear — the events could result in the destabilization of society, harking back to an earlier time of revolutionary ferment. The status of the deceased was therefore dangerous, and comment gathered following his death, such as in the 1910 memorial book, *Venok na mogilu Sergeiia Andreevicha Muromtseva* (A Wreath on the Grave of Sergei Andreevich Muromtsev, 1910), which mobilized powerful imagery. In this book, Muromtsev was depicted as a hero and even a martyr, as in the speech delivered by the Kadet A. A. Manilov at the graveside: 'your majestic image of a citizen-fighter and teacher has become a worthy story.'[75] Destabilization was also a key theme from the political right, who saw funerals like that of Tolstoi's one month later as having negative consequences: the Tambov Governor Count Benkendorf wrote:

> Tolstoi's death, especially after the successful fuss with Muromtsev's funeral, will arouse in the Kadet-Jewish intelligentsia and the press a desire to make even more noise.[76]

From a very different perspective, liberalism's leaders noted the dilemma that the events raised concerning Russian statecraft. The Kadet leader Nikolai Gredeskul surmised that the funeral represented a bifurcation between state and society that could not be solved easily:

> Thinking about Muromtsev means thinking about Russia. To delve into the historical meaning of his funeral means to ascertain the abnormal and extremely dangerous state of our state organism. A state cannot be strong as long as it is split inside the way Russia is still split.[77]

---

[74] *Russkoe slovo*, 7 October 1910, p. 3, 'V konchine S. A. Muromtsev'.
[75] *Venok na mogilu Sergeiia Andreevicha Muromtseva*, Moscow, 1910, p. 44.
[76] 'Iz materialov o L. N. Tolstom', *Krasnyi arkhiv*, 4, 1923, p. 361.
[77] *Rech'*, 10 October 1910, 278, p. 2, 'Pokhorony Muromtseva'.

All three events show that a liberal lexicon of public dissent had emerged — an alternate discourse the regime could not control, touching on languages of freedom, citizenship, rights and legality. But Muromtsev's case exemplified an additional point concerning the fragility of the era of politics and parliament following 1906, with supporters widely noting how delicate these gains were. Followers of Muromtsev could console themselves that he had made a great contribution to Russia and his era. For his supporters in the press he was a key figure of his time and represented something more than trends in parliamentary politics. Though his death in autocratic Russia was tragic — society was far indeed from the ideal that he had worked for — his ideology had a longer-term impact. Fedor Golovin, the Kadet who had been chair of the second State Duma, wrote in *Utro Rossii* that 'death cannot destroy such people as Muromtsev. They live even after death, they live in those great ideas, whose preachers and ministers they were'.[78] One columnist, Gaiavata, wrote in *Kievskie novosti* on 7 October 1910: 'Muromtsev became more than a person: he became history.'[79] The leading Kadet Pavel Miliukov declared that Muromtsev was worthy of being honoured with a monument, but such was his contribution that he would be remembered widely in any event — he was, like Trubetskoi before him, both a 'hero and victim' of the liberation movement.[80] Such martyrological discussion of the politician following his death did not appear altogether uncommon — for many, he had become a hero, and his presence as a significant figure of political change represented wider flux and unrest in Russian society. His feats in the legislative chamber, as chair of a progressive institution, showed how Russia was and could be developing. His death cut short this era but represented a turning point for the state.

The emergence of Muromtsev's funeral and services as sites of mourning and resistance occurred shortly before the death of Lev Tolstoi. As in the case of Turgenev's funeral in the 1880s, these figures emerged as alternative sources of moral authority following their deaths. They were significant, non-regime people; the use of sacred images and the attendance of priests and the Church at the ceremonials held for such non-religious figures was contested in both instances; concerning both funerals, many of the resulting demonstrations held in the deceased's honour were spontaneous; and, for both the regime and observers on the right, they emerged as significant indices of the challenge to authority, denoting that the regime

---

[78] *Venok na mogilu*, pp. 102–03.
[79] Ibid., p. 123.
[80] Ibid., pp. 116–18.

could not fully control the streets or — perhaps more significantly — the media sphere.[81] From his Genevan exile Vladimir Lenin noted the importance of Muromtsev's funeral alongside Tolstoi's in ushering in a new age of instability:

> The death of Muromtsev, Chairman of the First Duma, a moderate liberal, a foreigner to democracy, evokes the first timid beginning of demonstrations. The death of Lev Tolstoi gives rise — for the first time after a long interval — to street demonstrations with the participation mainly of students but partly also of workers.[82]

Hence, the renaissance of the public funeral for Russia's great figures in this period was giving rise — however slowly — to a new era of dissent several years after the 1905 revolution had been quashed and authority restored. Autocracy had new challenges on the horizon.

Conclusion

Like revolutionary groups, liberals held political funerals and demonstrations, using these as a locus to challenge the status quo in old regime Russia. These three cases present some intriguing parallels and commonalities. In every event, the funeral and resulting services became sites of resistance, dissent and critique. Students were often in the vanguard of protest, continually criticizing the murderous character of tsarist governance.[83] Sometimes the nature of protest was obvious from the violent mood of radical crowds, but, at other times, the nature of dissent was more subversive. Particularly, these sites of liberal resistance posed a challenge to Russian autocracy that was profoundly modern, with the media environment a forum in which the memory politics of liberalism emerged clearly, in these cases based around key figures who had lived and died in an era of great change.[84] There was shared defiance at authority from both radicals and liberals in all events. Looking at the responses to Muromtsev's funeral following October 1910, we should be reminded that anti-tsarist feelings never went away after 1905, and, indeed, the plural

---

[81]   Nickell, *The Death of Tolstoy*, pp. 119–21.

[82]   *Rabochaia Gazeta*, 18 December 1910 <https://www.marxists.org/archive/lenin/works/1910/dec/18b.htm> [date accessed 16 November 2022].

[83]   This was evident too in protests surrounding the Lena Massacre of 1912. See Michael Melancon, 'Russian Society and the Lena Massacre of 1912', *Revolutionary Russia*, 15, 2, 2002, pp. 11–14.

[84]   Fedyashin, *Liberals Under Autocracy*.

nature of those involved in the protests — students, workers, liberals and radicals — reminds us that an anti-government consensus was apparent in the public sphere at this time.

What marked out liberals from their revolutionary counterparts was their central focus on Russian legality, a concept that had strongly emerged since the Great Reforms of the 1860s. The connection to legal philosophies of Russian liberalism, the advancement of learning and knowledge, and the desire for political reform was clear in every case, and attachment to concepts of civil rights drove resistance to Russian autocracy.[85] Although there was discussion concerning constructing monuments to the deceased at their sites, for a variety of reasons nothing emerged beyond standard graveside decorations, although Muromtsev was honoured with an impressive bust by sculptor Paolo Trubetskoi at the Donskoi monastery in 1912.[86] The true significance of these events is in the arena of comment and ideas — an unstable forum which the autocracy could not completely control. By the time of Muromtsev's death in 1910 the press was at a greater stage of development than several years earlier: there was more space for open debate of ideas, fewer restrictions on the press and more possibility to discuss and debate Russia's path in the media sphere — a key point in the case of all figures discussed.[87] The impact of major publications like *Russkoe slovo* and *Russkie vedomosti* in giving space for these ideas should not be underestimated.

All these events raised important questions concerning civil rights and the nature of freedom in an autocratic state. This was a key dilemma in the old regime, prompting a challenge from the liberal wing of society. During the 1905 revolution, an intellectual challenge emerged from liberalism, and this was still strong after public insurrection had been quashed. Whilst radical comment was pushed underground, liberal discourses were highly visible, with languages of freedom, rights and citizenship circulating in public, most of all via the printed press. Many commentators were figures from parties including the Kadets, sometimes active within the State Duma. Their views could intersect with the challenge coming from

---

[85] For work on civil rights, see essays in Olga Crisp and Linda Edmondson (eds), *Civil Rights in Imperial Russia*, Oxford, 1989. See also, Wortman, *Development of a Russian Legal Consciousness*.

[86] The possibility of a Kupernik memorial was discussed in *The Kiev Gazette*. See GARF, f. 8420, op. 1, d. 6, l. 24, Clipping from *Kievskaia gazeta*, 2 October 1905; Miliukov considered a tribute to Muromtsev: *Venok na mogilu*, p. 118.

[87] Caspar Ferenczi, 'Freedom of the Press under the Old Regime, 1905–1914', in Crisp and Edmondson (eds), *Civil Rights in Imperial Russia*, pp. 191–214.

other actors, who might share the same emblems of freedom and a desire to see Russia transform fundamentally. In an earlier period, groups of Social Democrats had become involved in phenomena like the Union of Liberation's Banquet Campaign in 1904–05. As Stephen Lovell states in his recent study of political rhetoric:

> Assemblies, committees, and associations across Russia were engaging in the civic ritual of conducting debate and passing resolutions in a liberal and 'democratic' vein. In a sign of things to come, worker and Social Democratic orators were muscling in on these liberal conclaves, above all in the unusually proletarian St Petersburg.[88]

The legacy of such intersections was strong. Trubetskoi's funeral in 1905 saw shared defiance from liberals and Social Democrats combine in a protest which quickly became a radical event, with crowds of students demanding change in Russia amidst a sea of red flags, violence and revolutionary song.

There was a simulacrum of radical activism and spirit with a liberal backing, yet the processes occurring were more than just a radical hijack of more moderate political ends. Different audiences recognized the lives of these liberal heroes as bound up not only with their own fates, but also that of the Russian Empire. The crowds supporting them were diverse — many young men and women from the student community and the liberal intelligentsia came together in 1910 in memory of Muromtsev. Funerals were especially important in forging a public liberal culture of dissent, with reformist 'martyrs' mourned especially due to their efforts in life, understood as a form of self-sacrifice. Their deaths in old regime Russia were interpreted as tragic, given the Russia that they had fought for had not emerged — this amidst the backdrop of increased state repression during and following the revolution of 1905. The liberal statesman Pavel Miliukov interpreted these deaths in such terms. Writing in 1935, he described Muromtsev's toil in trying to make the first State Duma work as a great act of self-sacrifice; he was a most memorable figure in the struggle for freedom in Russia: it was this service that would secure his position for posterity.[89] Liberal discourses of freedom, rights and citizenship surrounding such

[88] Stephen Lovell, *How Russia Learned to Talk: A History of Public Speaking in the Stenographic Age, 1860–1930*, Oxford, 2020, pp. 152–53.

[89] P. N. Miliukov, 'S. A. Muromtsev (K dvadtsatiletiiu konchiny)', *Poslednee novosti*, 17 October 1935, in P. N. Miliukov, *Russkii evropeets. Publitsistika 20–30-kh gg. XX v.*, Moscow, 2012, pp. 284–85.

protests endured throughout the final years of the old regime, but were
subsumed during the revolutions of 1917 to languages of socialist protest
that emphasized class struggle and the image of the worker. These became
part of a renewed lexicon of public, socialist protest — emerging around
the funerals of workers and revolutionaries, martyrs of insurrection and
change — and appealed widely to people across the empire, squeezing the
public space available to liberal discourse.[90]

However, this should not tempt us to overlook the important insights
that liberal protests from earlier years provide to us; indeed, the dilemmas
that liberalism raised did not go away. Perhaps it seems most fitting
to give the last word to a contemporary — in his own reflections on
Trubetskoi's contribution to Russian life, Muromtsev described him at a
1908 meeting as a 'citizen-philosopher, citizen-moralist and citizen-man'.[91]
Issues concerning citizenship, freedom of thought and the evolution of the
Russian state were not resolved by the imperial regime — the presence of
these sites of liberal dissent reveals a fragile, restless polity several years
before the cataclysm that would ultimately destroy it.

---

[90] One case was the funeral of Armenian revolutionary Vachagan Melik'ian in
Smolensk on 12 March 1917. See Michael C. Hickey, 'Discourses of Public Identity and
Liberalism in the February Revolution: Smolensk, Spring 1917', *The Russian Review*, 55, 4,
1996, pp. 615–37.
[91] *Sbornik rechei posviashchennykh*, p. 58.

An Ephemeral Look at Russian Anarchist Life in the United States

ALISON ROWLEY

'Anarchism gave the immigrants a sense of belonging, of
family, community, common ideals and aspirations,
which we desperately needed.'[1]
Russian-American anarchist Israel Ostroff

In May 1915, San Francisco resident Ernest Kundy received a picture
postcard from an unnamed correspondent. Published by the Detroit
branch of the Anarchist Red Cross, the postcard featured a depiction of
the Bloody Sunday massacre which sparked Russia's 1905 revolution and
served as one of the most important episodes in that country's history of
revolutionary martyrdom. By examining every aspect of the postcard this
article reveals, layer by layer, its connections to Russian anarchist life in
the United States and how notions of martyrdom continued to resonate
among those who had left the Russian Empire. In the process, the postcard
shows how using ephemeral objects as sources also helps to ensure a more
inclusive historical record, since the people who will be encountered in
the coming pages have factored very little in scholarly publications to
date.[2] The article begins by discussing the image on the front, explaining
how illustrations like the one here by Italian artist Fortunino Matania
were turned into widely disseminated postcards that spread revolutionary
messages well beyond the borders of the Russian Empire. While the French
and British postcards that commented on Russian disturbances have
received some scholarly attention, those that reached further afield, namely
to the United States, have not, so this article offers something new in that

Alison Rowley is a Professor of History at Concordia University, Montreal.

[1] Quoted in Paul Avrich, *Anarchist Voices: An Oral History of Anarchism in America*,
Edinburgh, 2005, p. 350.
[2] On ephemera and inclusivity, see Anne Garner, 'State of the Discipline: Throwaway
History: Towards a Historiography of Ephemera', *Book History*, 24, 1, 2021, pp. 244–63.

Slavonic and East European Review, 102, 1, 2024   doi: 10.1353/see.00003

regard as well.[3] Turning to the information on the back of the postcard, the
article next explores the history of the Anarchist Red Cross in the United
States and the role that it played in keeping recent immigrants connected
with their anarchist comrades still in Russia rather than encouraging them
to integrate into American society.[4] Then, the links between the sender's
handwritten message and an area of Chicago that features prominently in
histories of immigrant life, the settlement movement and the American
labour movement — Halsted Street — will be considered. Finally, the
connections between the recipient's family and a 1915 bank robbery in
California serves as a window into the history of the Russian anarchist
milieu on the West Coast of the United States, while also showing how
ultimately the trope of Russian revolutionary martyrdom fell out of favour
with the wider American public.

The image

Fortunino Matania (1881–1963) was nowhere near St Petersburg on 9
January 1905. Three years earlier, when he was but a young man of twenty,
Matania moved to London and found work with *The Graphic*, one of the
illustrated periodicals that were so popular at the time.[5] While his career
was briefly interrupted by a stint of national service in the Italian army,
Matania soon returned to his artistic work. The striking images that he
produced of the Russo-Japanese War on a freelance basis for the Italian
publication *L'Illustrazione* caught the attention of Clement Shorter, who
had founded the British illustrated weekly *The Sphere* in 1900.[6] Shorter
was sufficiently impressed that he offered Matania a permanent job as a
'black and white man'. These illustrators 'worked in a monochrome palette
known as "en grisaille" — a technique using white and grey shades of
gouache and watercolour to produce an image that would respond well
to printing processes' employed by magazine publishers at the start of
the twentieth century.[7] The images were superior in tone and contrast
to photographs, which had begun to appear in periodical literature in

[3]   See, for example, Alison Rowley, *Open Letters: Russian Popular Culture and the
Picture Postcard, 1880–1922*, Toronto, 2013, pp. 208–12.
[4]   For a brief historical overview of anarchism in Russia and the Soviet Union, see
Vladimir Cherniaev, 'Anarchists', in E. Acton, V. Cherniaev and W. G. Rosenberg (eds),
Critical Companion to the Russian Revolution, 1914–1921, London, 1997, pp. 221–30.
[5]   Biographical information about Fortunino Matania can be found in the introduction
to Lucinda Gosling, *Drawing from History: The Forgotten Art of Fortunino Matania*,
London, 2016.
[6]   Ibid., pp. 258–65.
[7]   Ibid., p. 4.

the 1890s but could not be duplicated with the same degree of clarity. In addition, slow exposure times meant that photographers were unable to capture scenes featuring dramatic action. In other words, it frequently fell to artists such as Matania to produce the images that defined current affairs for the European public in the early twentieth century.

Figure 1 shows how Fortunino Matania imagined the Bloody Sunday massacre, notably the moment when troops loyal to the autocratic government opened fire on a group of peaceful demonstrators who had hoped to present a petition to Emperor Nicholas II. As was the case with many of the images produced by illustrated weeklies across Europe in response to the event, the martyrdom of innocents in the crowd and the brutality of the episode were conveyed in dramatic detail. Such illustrations made it impossible to see tsarist soldiers, particularly the Cossacks, in heroic fashion, thereby undermining conventional conceptions of the military's protective purpose.[8] But the images also allowed revolutionary groups to soon control the narrative of what had happened and use it to garner support both within Russia and abroad by offering a damning critique of the Russian regime. Tobie Mathew's research into postcards at the time has found that many of the ones created to mark Bloody Sunday relied on images like Matania's, since the weeklies that published them could be easily purchased abroad and subsequently smuggled into Russia, where their illustrations were then pirated onto postcards. It did not matter if the images were accurate, because, as Mathew writes, they 'advanced the cause of violent insurrection, showing that the state would meet even peaceful protestors with blades and bullets'.[9] Moreover, such postcards, while illegal to produce for many months, were an important form of public discourse that spread across the Russian Empire without being challenged by a government that preferred to offer silence rather than its own commentary about the massacre. Indeed, even after the loosening of censorship rules following the release of the October Manifesto later in 1905, postcard manufacturers continued to rely upon images such as Matania's because these were, again to quote Mathew, 'readily available, familiar to the population, and cost nothing to commission'.[10]

---

[8] Christina Loder, '1905 and Art: From Aesthetes to Revolutionaries', Arts, 11, 2022, p. 13.

[9] Tobie Mathew, Greetings from the Barricades: Revolutionary Postcards in Imperial Russia, London, 2019, p. 285.

[10] Ibid., p. 461 n. 6.

Fig. 1. Postcard of Bloody Sunday massacre mailed to Ernest Kundy in 1915.
Author's collection.

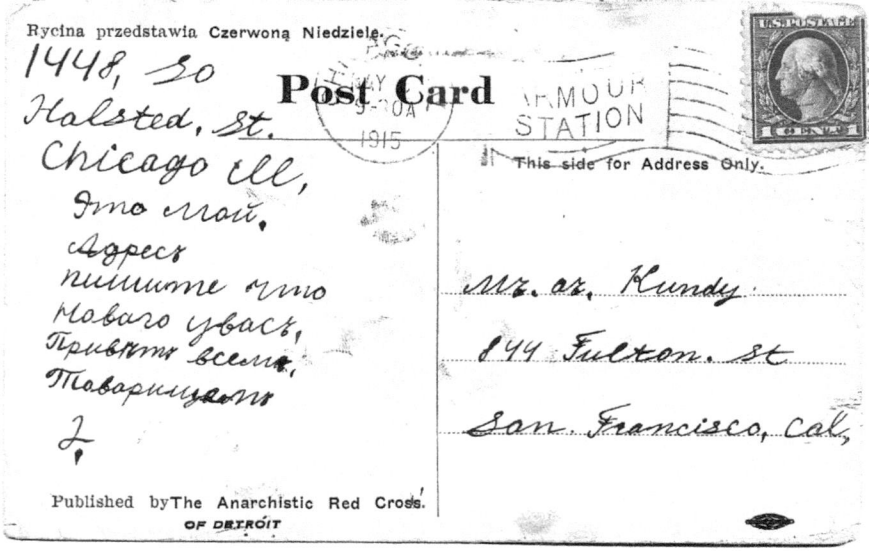

Fig. 2. Back of postcard mailed to Ernest Kundy. Author's collection.

The manufacturer

The power of Bloody Sunday was such that it continued to resonate for years after the event and far beyond the confines of Russia as well. Flipping our postcard over reveals several things about how it was made and how images such as these spread so widely (Fig. 2). At the top left-hand side, it says (in Polish) 'The figure presents Red Sunday'.[11] In the early twentieth century, Warsaw was one of the largest publishing centres in the Russian Empire as well as a city well-situated for smugglers who ensured that revolutionary literature was distributed widely.[12] Industrial workers in the Kingdom of Poland already had impressively high trade union and political party membership figures at the time of the 1905 revolution, and a full one-third of the strikes that occurred that year happened in this part of the Russian Empire.[13] It is also estimated that in Russian Poland more than 90 per cent of industrial workers participated in the strike movement in 1905, a figure that underscores the extent to which they had been radicalized.[14] Hence, it is not a stretch to believe that our postcard was manufactured in Poland, but instead of being sent eastwards like much revolutionary propaganda, it went in the other direction, all the way to the United States. The fact that three different fonts were used when the printed text switches to English is suggestive. 'Published by' indicates that either the original manufacturer or the middleman who exported the postcard knew that it could be destined for an English-speaking market, or they would have used French, Russian, German, or possibly a combination of those languages for that part of the text. But they left room for more information — in other words a specific seller — to personalize the postcard by inserting their name and, in essence, finish the sentence. In this instance, it was the Anarchist Red Cross which eventually did just that once the well-travelled postcard arrived in the United States, but in a final twist, it was not the biggest branch of that organization, but a smaller one in Detroit that also stamped its presence onto the postcard by inserting its name at the very bottom of the postcard.

Delving into these details means looking more closely at the history of Russian migrants to America in the years leading up to the First World War. The situation is complicated by the multi-ethnic composition of the

---

[11] In other words, Bloody Sunday. Thank you to my colleague Dr Erica Lehrer for translating the words in Polish for me.

[12] Beth Holmgren, *Rewriting Capitalism: Literature and the Market in Late Tsarist Russia and the Kingdom of Poland*, Pittsburgh, PA, 1998, p. 5.

[13] Robert Blobaum, *Rewolucia: Russian Poland, 1904–1907*, Ithaca, NY, 1995, p. 73.

[14] Ibid.

Russian Empire, which makes it difficult to categorize precisely many of those who left it. While the overall number of migrants stemming from the Russian Empire runs into the hundreds of thousands, it does not mean that all identified as Russian.[15] US census data from 1910, for example, records only 65,000 Russian-speakers in the country, although it is estimated that the figure grew closer to 100,000 by 1914,[16] and it is certainly possible that people lied, or selectively edited the information they provided, when answering the questions of the census takers, particularly if they held political beliefs that could get them into trouble with American authorities. It is worth remembering after all that in 1903 — two years after the assassination of President William McKinley — the US government passed the Anarchist Exclusion Act which barred foreign-born anarchists from coming to America; three years later, an additional piece of legislation prohibited them from obtaining US citizenship. However, it must be noted that the enforcement of these regulations was spotty. The government lacked a way to gather intelligence about anarchists and others deemed subversive until the Bureau of Investigation was created in 1908 and it took time for the new organization to find its legs so to speak. As historian Kenyon Zimmer points out, 'between 1903 and 1921, the United States excluded just 38 anarchists and deported few than half that number'.[17] Still, the fact that government measures proved unwieldy to implement did not remove the threat of possible arrest or deportation that always loomed over the heads of Russian anarchists living in America.

Life was also made more difficult by language barriers, which meant that those who arrived on American shores often found it difficult to make economic ends meet. In 1909, for instance, it is estimated that Russian workers in the US were paid an average of $2.06 per day, and some earned only half of that amount.[18] Meanwhile, American-born workers doing the same jobs were frequently paid at least double the wages that were given to immigrants. Unsurprisingly, then, many new immigrants from Russia gravitated towards membership in socialist and labour organizations. In

[15] Lazar Lipotkin suggests that 800,000 people of Russian origin arrived in the US between 1904 and 1914, but many of the places he lists they came from are today part of Poland, Belarus and Ukraine. Lazar Lipotkin, *The Russian Anarchist Movement in North America*, Edmonton, AB, 2019, p. 62.

[16] Paul Magocsi, *The Russian Americans*, New York, 1996, p. 46.

[17] Kenyon Zimmer, 'A Golden Gate of Anarchy: Local and Transnational Dimensions of Anarchism in San Francisco, 1880s–1930s', in C. Bantman and B. Altena (eds), *Reassessing the Transnational Turn: Scales of Analysis in Anarchist and Syndicalist Studies*, London, 2014, p. 110.

[18] Alison Behnke, *Russians in America*, Minneapolis, MN, 2006, p. 27.

1906–07, major cities such as New York, Philadelphia and Chicago saw vibrant groups emerge to cater to this community. Eighteen delegates, representing twelve such organizations, gathered for an initial congress in 1907.[19] The following year, Burevestnik (Stormy Petrel), the first Russian anarchist organization in the US, was founded in New York. It lasted three years and, alongside the socialist associations, laid the groundwork for the eventual establishment of the Union of Russian Workers, which will be discussed in greater detail below, in 1914. During the same years, Anarchist Red Cross (ARC) branches began to spread across the American urban landscape. The creation of ARC was a direct result of events in Russia. When the tsarist government decided in 1907 to use criminal proceedings to try anarchists, it deprived the defendants of certain rights and meant they could no longer receive material assistance from the political Red Cross, the group that had been assisting revolutionaries from various parties that opposed the government. In essence the Russian government forced anarchists to create their own organization to help comrades who ran afoul of the authorities, and undoubtedly the ongoing persecution that they faced solidified many anarchists' sense of being martyrs to the causes of political freedom and economic equality.

Fundraising was a crucial part of ARC activities from the very beginning. Once the New York branch was set up, it organized a successful benefit concert in 1908. The event spurred the ARC to grow in two ways: first, by establishing branches in other cities — Chicago in 1909 and Philadelphia in 1911, for example — and by encouraging members to develop a host of other activities to draw attention to the plight of prisoners, who were always cast as martyrs, in Russia. At the annual 'Prisoners' Ball' in New York, for instance, the evening's entertainments included *tableaux vivant* meant to depict scenes from the lives of people exiled to Siberia. The Chicago branch, which grew to 300 members by 1917, held a number of events in 1915, the year when our postcard was mailed from there.[20] Notices in a free local daily newspaper, *The Day Book*, show that a 'Prisoners' Ball', featuring scenes from Russian prison life, was planned for 6 March at the West Side Auditorium; that a fundraising picnic in Bowmanville Woods was organized at the end of May; and that a second ball to raise monies for Siberian political exiles was scheduled for 25 November.[21] Sometimes

[19] Lipotkin, *The Russian Anarchist Movement in North America*, p. 66.
[20] Boris Yelensky, *In the Struggle for Equality: The Story of the Anarchist Red Cross*, Chicago, IL, 1958, p. 29.
[21] See *The Day Book*, 3 March 1915, p. 29; *The Day Book*, 27 May 1915, p. 25, and *The Day Book*, 24 November 1915, p. 32.

ARC fundraising ventures directly referenced the events of 1905, thereby
showing the lasting importance of moments such as Bloody Sunday in
the minds of those who continued to oppose the Russian government
even from a continent away. For example, newspapers noted an event
in 1914, when a sizeable group of young Russian women 'invaded' Fifth
Avenue in New York to sell baskets of red carnations to commemorate the
anniversary of Bloody Sunday. The report indicated that nearly $1000 was
raised by the women.[22]

It is likely that our postcard was part of a more modest fundraising
endeavour — one inspired by the fact that revolutionaries of all stripes
began openly selling postcards in Russia to raise money during the 1905
revolution.[23] But the text on the back begs the question why the Detroit
branch of the Anarchist Red Cross felt the need to specifically insert its
claim to be the publisher of this postcard.

The population of Detroit grew rapidly in the first two decades of the
twentieth century as workers flocked to the city in response to Henry
Ford's promise to pay his workers $5/day for an 8-hour day. From a
relatively modest roughly 285,000 people in 1900, the city expanded to
hold just under a million residents by 1920.[24] A sizeable percentage of this
population (between 25 and 30 per cent) was foreign-born, with Russians
representing 3.18 per cent of the foreigners in 1900, 11.83 per cent in 1910,
and 9.4 per cent in 1920.[25] Again these figures have to be considered with
some caution since the chart they come from in Olivier Zunz's study of
immigrant life in Detroit categorizes Russians and Poles separately, but
he does not indicate what criteria were used to establish separate ethnic
identities for people who likely came from the same geographic region,
the Russian Empire. With that problem duly noted, what is clear is that
many of the Russian immigrants were Jewish, and they often lived in small,
but newly built, tenement houses owned by their German immigrant
neighbours.[26] At least half of Russian immigrants were unskilled, which
meant they did factory work or tried to make a living as street vendors.

---

[22] 'Russian Revolutionist Active Here', *The Sun* (New York), 2 August 1914, p. 41.
The story was picked up and reprinted in other newspapers as well. See, for example,
The Bangor Daily News (Bangor, Maine) on 8 August 1914, and *The Anaconda Standard*
(Anaconda, Montana) on 3 September 1914.

[23] Rowley, *Open Letters*, p. 203.

[24] Olivier Zunz, *The Changing Face of Inequality: Urbanization, Industrial Development,
and Immigrants in Detroit, 1880–1920*, Chicago, IL, 1982, p. 106.

[25] Ibid.

[26] Ibid., pp. 158, 160.

Their growing presence meant that a handful of organizations catering to the Russian community in Detroit sprang up as well. The Progressive Labour Club, which took a non-party stance, tried to unite the community by providing a facility in the middle of the city which hosted events such as public lectures and had a library.[27] Politically-speaking, however, Russians in Detroit remained divided. By early 1912, a social democratic group had been founded as well as a different association that supported the Socialist Revolutionary party in Russia. A few years earlier, a Relief Society for Russian Political Prisoners had been organized and it sent money to the Russian Political Red Cross. However, some Detroit residents were upset in 1912–13 when word reached them — first in the form of rumours, then via letters confirming the stories — that anarchists were not receiving monies from the collective funds.[28] That is what spurred the Detroit local of the Anarchist Red Cross into being and, while its members apparently did funnel some funds through the larger New York branch, members in Detroit also sent monies directly to Russia on their own initiative. It is highly likely that our postcard is a testament to exactly this independence that was being shown by the Detroit local.

The message
'1448 So. Halsted St. Chicago IL. This is my address. Write what is new with you. Hello to all the comrades.' This is the message our unnamed correspondent sent to Ernest Kundy in 1915. Apart from the fact that most of it is in Russian, which the vast majority of Americans would have been unable to read at the time, there is nothing particularly striking about the content, at least at first glance. It is only when one looks more closely at the message that things become more interesting.

It is reasonably safe to assume that the sender was Russian, or at least fluent in that language, given that the text does not contain grammatical errors and the handwriting shows no sign of hesitation or mistakes that have been corrected when it was written. The use of *'privet'* for 'hello' indicates a degree of informality in the exchange — since the word's meaning is closer to 'hi' — and it suggests that the sender and recipient were well acquainted. They could have been relatives, friends, or even members of the same political circle. That point is further underscored by the lack of a signature, something which created a closed loop between the correspondents. The absence implies that the recipient would recognize the handwriting of the

---

[27] Ibid., p. 186.
[28] Yelensky, *In the Struggle for Equality*, p. 32.

sender on sight and/or be expecting to receive word from them, but it also guaranteed the sender's anonymity should the postcard fall into the wrong hands, say of the police. Moreover, this decision not to sign the postcard also suggests that the sender is continuing to live as if he or she is still part of the revolutionary underground.

Then there is the intriguing fact that the brief sentence asks for greetings be passed along to 'comrades'. Used in revolutionary circles, including among anarchists, 'comrade' was a democratic form of address that became particularly popular in Russia after the February Revolution swept the Romanovs from power in 1917. As Orlando Figes and Boris Kolonitskii note, the 'term "comrade" was a badge of belonging to an inner circle of believers, a truly revolutionary self-identity. "Comrades" were the leading activists and cities of the revolution'.[29] Its appearance here lends credence to the notion that the postcard's sender was a Russian anarchist living in the United States.

The address provided — 1448 South Halsted Street in Chicago — does nothing to undermine that conclusion. Google Maps indicates that the house was 0.8 miles, in other words, no more than a fifteen-minute walk, from the Hull House settlement house. Established by progressive leaders Jane Addams and Ellen Gates Starr at the corner of Polk and Halsted Streets in 1889, by 1911 the settlement house had grown to encompass thirteen buildings. Its mission was to assist newly arrived European immigrants as they settled into life in the United States, and Hull House's location, which overlapped with Jewish, Polish, Greek, Czech and Russian neighbourhoods, made it perfectly suited to do just that.[30] By the turn of the century, so many immigrants inhabited the buildings along Halsted Street that part of it was, in fact, referred to as 'Migration Mile' by locals.[31] Addams was known for her long-standing support for Russian revolutionaries. She served on the executive committee of the American Friends of Russian Freedom, a society that had been revived as a lobby organization after the 1903 Kishinev pogrom garnered much anger in the United States.[32] Addams also hosted many celebrated revolutionary

---

[29] Orlando Figes and Boris Kolonitskii, *Interpreting the Russian Revolution: The Language and Symbols of 1917*, New Haven, CT, 1999, p. 61.

[30] John H. Macionis and Vincent N. Parrilo, *Cities and Urban Life*, 6th edn, Boston, MA, 2013, p. 315.

[31] Don Hayner and Tom McNamee, *Streetwise Chicago: A History of Chicago Street Names*, Chicago, IL, 1988, p. 50.

[32] Alison Rowley, 'Russian Revolutionary as American Celebrity: A Case Study of Yekaterina Breshko-Breshkovskaya', in Melanie Ilič (ed.), *The Palgrave Handbook of Women and Gender in Twentieth-Century Russia and the Soviet Union*, London, 2018, p. 9.

figures as they passed through Chicago. Anarchist Petr Kropotkin stayed for a week at Hull House in 1901 and delivered a lecture to the Chicago Arts and Crafts Society in one of its buildings. In January 1905, while on a successful speaking tour that raised thousands of dollars for the revolutionary movement, the 'Grandmother of the Russian Revolution', Ekaterina Breshko-Breshkovsksaia visited Addams at Hull House. And the following year, Socialist Revolutionary Grigori Gershuni stopped there for a few days as he journeyed across the United States, following his escape from Siberian exile. In short, Hull House was a welcoming place for those cast as victims of the Russian state, and Addams, who wrote the following in her 1930s autobiography, was among their biggest American supporters:

> Certain it is, as the distinguished Russian revolutionaries have come to Chicago, they have impressed me, as no one else even has done, as belonging to that novel company of martyrs who have ever and again poured forth blood that human progress might be advanced.[33]

In January 1915, in other words only months before our postcard (franked 'Armour Station') was mailed from this area of the city, Hull House served as the starting point for a demonstration — with some ties to the anarchist movement in the US — that turned violent. According to newspaper accounts, the incident began when police arrived at a meeting of the League of the Unemployed in the settlement house's Bowen Hall and attempted to stop a march that was due to follow the meeting. When the marchers, who did not possess the necessary permit from the city, refused to disband, the police resorted to using clubs against them. Things degenerated into a pitched battled between the police, some of whom were mounted on horses, and an estimated 1,500 unemployed men, women and children. During the thirty-minute melee, four young women — identified in newspaper accounts as Russian-Jewish girls but not in a way that indicated the labelling was intended to be pejorative in this instance — were seen carrying a large black banner with the word 'Hunger' written on it in large white letters; they were joined beneath the banner by Lucy Parsons who had been one of the featured speakers at the meeting.[34] Parsons was a well-known anarchist whose husband Albert had been hanged in 1887 for his role in the Haymarket Affair. Often referred to as the

---

[33] Jane Addams, *Twenty Years at Hull-House with Autobiographical Notes*, New York, 1930, p. 402.
[34] 'Women Help Slug Police; Bullets Fly', *The Chicago Tribune*, 18 January 1915, p. 1.

'Goddess of Anarchy', Parsons made speeches advocating propaganda of the deed, although she refrained from personally engaging in terrorism.[35] Ultimately twenty-one people were arrested and charged with inciting a riot, unlawful assembly, and parading without a license. Noted Russian anarchists Aaron Baron and his wife Fanya (née Grefenson) were among those arrested.[36] Bail was initially set at a whopping $1000 per person. Jane Addams intervened at this point and successfully raised enough money to free the six women who had been charged, but she was unable to pay the fees of the arrested men.[37] By the next day, *The Chicago Tribune* newspaper, whose coverage was decidedly pro-police, began to insist that the Industrial Workers of the World were also somehow involved in the riot.[38] Court proceedings vis-à-vis this event dragged out until the end of March 1915.

While this street brawl with police stands out, owing to its closeness in time and geographic proximity to our unnamed correspondent, it should be noted that there were other places in Chicago where Russian immigrants also came together, and they demonstrate the vibrancy of this community. In 1912, a small group that referred to itself as the 'Union of Russian Youth' opened a night school, and other cultural activities were organized by the 'Brotherhood of Russian Working People' between 1912 and 1914.[39] The social activities that the Chicago local of the Anarchist Red Cross planned as fundraisers in 1915 have already been mentioned earlier in this article. Finally, Chicago was home to a Russian section of the Industrial Workers of the World (IWW), which had more than three dozen members.[40] It too had connections to Halsted Street since 2422 North Halsted, which was 4.7 miles from the house where our postcard writer settled in 1915, served as the headquarters of the IWW from April 1933 to February 1970. Interestingly the same building housed the Alexander Berkman Fund for Aid to Imprisoned and Exiled Anarchists in Russia when it was founded following Berkman's death in 1936.

[35] Arlene Meyers, 'The Haymarket Affair and Lucy Parsons: 100th Anniversary', in D. I. Roussopoulos (ed.), *The Radical Papers*, Montreal, 1987, p. 35.

[36] In 1917 the Barons returned to Russia. Fanya was executed by the Cheka in 1921. Aaron, who spent years in Soviet prisons or exile, was executed in the late 1930s. See Paul Avrich, *The Russian Anarchists*, Oakland, CA, 2005, pp. 232–33, 245.

[37] 'Women Help Slug Police; Bullets Fly', *The Chicago Tribune*, 18 January 1915, p. 2.

[38] 'I.W.W. Faction Row Involved in Street Riot', *The Chicago Tribune*, 19 January 1915, p. 13.

[39] Lipotkin, *The Russian Anarchist Movement in North America*, p. 182.

[40] Ibid., p. 183.

The recipient

So far, the stories associated, however loosely, with our postcard have gone no further in a geographic sense than the American Midwest, but traces of a web of anarchist groups and communities (many of which included recently arrived Russian immigrants) are still apparent. The final section of this article — devoted to the recipient of the postcard, his wife and some of their acquaintances — shifts the narrative to the West Coast of the United States, notably to California where it turns out that Russian anarchists were just as active as their counterparts elsewhere. Obviously, any analysis of their undertakings is complicated by the fact that anarchist organizations were often secretive and conspiratorial in nature. Hence, they did not always issue membership cards or keep lists of members. Still, there is enough (admittedly often circumstantial) information for historians to speculate about their activities and show how their communities functioned.

Certainly, as articles by Choi Chatterjee and Krzysztof Wasilewski have shown, historians are on much firmer ground when it comes to addressing how the American public came to fear the episodes of terrorism that were associated with anarchists, and the labour movement more generally, in the years leading up to the First World War. Chatterjee's work on the image of Russians in American popular fiction demonstrates that many novels, plays and stories in magazines 'dwelt at length on the character of the revolutionary, the sinister male nihilist (Russian anarchist), and the equally sinister but infinitely more beautiful female *nihilistka*'.[41] While at times these portraits romanticized their exotic heroes and heroines, in other words continued to cast them as martyrs of a repressive government, that was not always the case. As the labour movement in the United States became more violent in its tactics, authors rethought their depictions of Russian revolutionaries so that their works jettisoned the more positive notion of martyrdom and instead 'offered crude caricatures of the anarchists as essentially violent, criminal, degenerate, undesirable aliens who were more often than not of Jewish origin'.[42] The press played a similarly important role in casting Eastern European immigrants, and anarchists in particular, not as heroic figures but as outsiders who were

---

[41] Choi Chatterjee, 'Transnational Romance, Terror, and Heroism: Russia in American Popular Fiction, 1860–1917', *Comparative Studies in Society and History*, 50, 3, 2008, p. 765.

[42] Ibid., p. 770. While undoubtedly this assumption was tinged with a strong dose of antisemitism, it is true that Jews were well-represented in the Russian anarchist movement. Historian Vladimir Cherniaev estimates that in 1907 roughly half of the 5,000 or so anarchists in the Russian Empire were Jews. See Cherniaev, 'Anarchists', p. 222.

seemingly incapable of embracing an 'American' way of life. As Wasilewski
writes:

> Based on the 'dangerous foreigner' stereotype then prevalent in American
> society, US newspapers ran a campaign in which even the slightest criticism
> of the country's economic or social system was deemed unpatriotic,
> treasonous, and foreign.[43]

These changes meant, of course, that the perceptions many Russians living
in America had of themselves, their revolutionary pasts, and their current
involvement in political movements that were designed to make the world
more equitable, now contradicted what was found in mainstream media.
Moreover, the evolution in attitudes is the backdrop to one of the most
important episodes of violence undertaken by industrial workers in the
decade prior to the start of the First World War: the October 1910 bombing
of the *Los Angeles Times* building. It is also where the next step in analysing
our postcard begins.

Harrison Gray Otis, the wealthy owner of the *Los Angeles Times*
newspaper, had no time or patience for the labour movement. Vehement
in his anti-union stance, Otis instead colluded with other members of
the California business elite to do everything possible to stop organized
labour from making any inroads in his city. His actions put him on a
collision course with labour leaders keen to improve the lives of workers
— many of whom were recent immigrants to the United States — through
unionization. Not surprisingly then, the most visible symbol of Otis's power
and influence became a target for terrorists. In the previous four years,
across the country, more than 200 construction and building sites had
been bombed; many of these terrorist attacks were funded and executed by
the International Association of Bridge and Structural Iron Workers (IW)
union.[44] After a trial which garnered much media attention, IW secretary-
treasurer John J. McNamara and his brother James B. McNamara were
convicted for their parts in the bombing of the *Los Angeles Times* building,
which had led to the deaths of more than twenty people.

Also convicted was one of the supporting cast members, so to speak,
in the bombing: a man named David Caplan. A Polish Jew, Caplan, along
with his wife and two children, settled in the anarchist Home Colony

[43] Krzysztof Wasilewski, 'The Image of Immigrants as Anarchists in the American
Press, 1886–1888', *Hungarian Journal of English and American Studies*, 23, 2, 2017, p. 371.

[44] Lew Irwin, *Deadly Times: The 1910 Bombing of the Los Angeles Times and America's
Forgotten Decade of Terror*, Guilford, CT, 2013, p. xi.

on Puget Sound in Washington state after leaving the Russian Empire.[45] Eventually the Caplan family moved to San Francisco, where its patriarch soon became immersed in the city's political life. Caplan's apartment became a place for socialists, anarchists, indeed free thinkers of all kinds, to congregate. As journalist Lew Irwin put it:

> [the] small group that gathered at David Caplan's San Francisco home represented fixtures of radical politics of the day: a coterie of international agitators bent on overturning American capitalism and replacing it with an idealistic workers' utopia by any means.[46]

Caplan was one of two men who provided logistical support to the bombers, J. B. McNamara and Ortie McManigal, who were responsible for destroying the headquarters of the newspaper. When police searched Caplan's apartment, they found clippings about labour topics from Russian newspapers as well as part of a card with the words 'Russian Progressive Society, S.F.' on it.[47] Ultimately, Caplan was convicted of second-degree manslaughter; he went on to serve seven years of the ten-year prison sentence that he was given in San Quentin.[48] There is no evidence that he ever returned to his San Francisco residence. That apartment — located at 1641A Fulton Street — was a scant 0.7 miles, or roughly eight city blocks, from 844 Fulton Street, where the recipient of our postcard lived in 1915.

Reading about the struggle for labour rights and unionization in California, it quickly becomes clear that the 400 miles separating Los Angeles and San Francisco were no impediment to the movement of both people and ideas. Instead, these flowed freely between the two metropoles, with leaders from San Francisco's more advanced labour movement often visiting Los Angeles to spur on their counterparts in that city. San Francisco was home to a notably vibrant and ethnically diverse anarchist movement as well. The roots of that community stretched back to the 1880s, and police officials estimated that it numbered 500 people by 1908.[49] After the 1905 revolution drove many new immigrants to the American West Coast, the number of Russian-born residents in San Francisco grew dramatically — from 1,500 in 1900 to 5,800 people only twenty years later.[50]

---

[45] Ibid., p. 62.
[46] Ibid., p. 64.
[47] Ibid., p. 153.
[48] Ibid., p. 334.
[49] Zimmer, 'Golden Gate', p. 100.
[50] Kenyon Zimmer, *Immigrants Against the State: Yiddish and Italian Anarchism in America*, Chicago, IL, 2015, p. 89.

That growing presence was quite visibly associated with anarchism as well. For example, in 1906, two Russian-Jewish anarchists opened the city's first vegetarian restaurant, and over the next few years, Yiddish-speaking immigrants established first the Freedom (Frayhayt) Group and then the Radical Branch of the Workmen's Circle.[51] Later, in 1915, Alexander Berkman settled in the city; he then founded *The Blast*, an English-language organ meant to unite the disparate radical groups involved in California's labour movement the following year.

By far the most important development, however, was the creation of the Union of Russian Workers of the United States and Canada (UORW). Founded by 1908 in New York by anarchists who had fled the tsarist crackdown that followed the failed 1905 revolution, the association initially advocated for open and armed warfare against the state, both in Russia and the United States, before gravitating towards anarcho-syndicalism and stronger ties to the Industrial Workers of the World (IWW) within a few years. Very quickly more than a dozen branches of the UORW were established and a congress to organize a federation of them was held in Detroit in early July 1914. There 596 people, representing two dozen organizations, adopted a series of resolutions to guide the activities of the UORW.[52] These included supporting the economic struggles of American workers via strikes and other labour disturbances, as well as promoting efforts to deepen the knowledge of Russian workers and organizing the training of anarchist propagandists to do just that in Russia and the US. Soon 'People's Houses' set up by the UORW were providing free classes on an array of topics — from English to mathematics to Marxist and anarchist theory — to union members. Overall, the federation eventually encompassed approximately fifty local chapters, whose estimated total membership varied between 4,000 and 10,000 people.[53] San Francisco had a UORW local — its meetings were held in a house on San Bruno Avenue — and its members had a good working relationship with the Russian-language branch of the city's IWW Mixed Local 173.

These details are important because when Russian anarchist Gregory Chesalkin died in a shoot-out with police in San Francisco in September 1915, he did so with an Ironworkers union membership card in his pocket and a UORW membership card — from the Seattle local — among his

---

[51] Kenyon Zimmer, 'Revolutionaries by the Bay: Immigrant Anarchists in San Francisco, 1880s–1930s', *Journal of the West*, 53, 3, 2014, p. 27.

[52] Lipotkin, *The Russian Anarchist Movement in North America*, p. 73.

[53] Andrew Cornell, *Unruly Equality: U.S. Anarchism in the Twentieth Century*, Oakland, CA, 2016, p. 35.

personal effects.[54] There are no immigration records indicating when Chesalkin arrived in America, so it is impossible to be sure that this was his real name or if he was living under an assumed identity. Once he was living in California, however, Chesalkin began to use the name George Nelson and, during the first few months of 1915, he was employed as a licensed jitney cab driver by a man named Jules Finburd. Finburd, who spoke to the media after Chesalkin's death, characterized his employee as:

> a rabid anarchist who took every occasion to air his views on defying all forms of organized government. He preached his doctrines of defying government authority whenever he had an opportunity to address his countrymen in San Francisco.[55]

At some point in the year, Chesalkin moved with his friend William Juber to Los Angeles, where they began to room with one of Juber's childhood friends, William Calish. Chesalkin and Juber also decided to rob the Boyle Heights branch of the Home Savings Bank and brought a third man, Charlie Butoff (who police were never able to find) into the plan. The trio apparently selected their target because it was in a quiet neighbourhood and, after watching the area for several days, the robbers, who were armed with four guns, struck on 20 August 1915.[56] They obtained more than $2000 from the bank before fleeing the scene in a car; their get-away was not entirely clean, however, since Juber sustained a gunshot wound to one of his arms.[57]

Police soon traced Chesalkin and Juber back to San Francisco, where they arrested the latter. After confessing to his involvement in the robbery, likely in the hopes of obtaining medical treatment for his now infected arm, Juber agreed to lead the authorities to the boarding house where Chesalkin was hiding. However, things did not go as intended since Chesalkin was not taken quietly into custody; instead, a six-hour armed standoff with dozens of police officers ensued. Caught in the melee was an innocent bystander named Hugh MacBeth (the proprietor of the rooming house), who eventually died of a gunshot wound. Chesalkin also sustained

---

[54] 'Nelson Union Ironworker', *The Los Angeles Times*, 13 September 1915, p. 9, and 'Second Life Paid in Bank Bandit Fight', *The San Francisco Examiner*, 14 September 1915, p. 3.
[55] 'Dead Bandit is Bared as an Anarchist', *The San Francisco Examiner*, 15 September 1915, p. 10.
[56] 'Bank Bandits Not Romantic', *The Los Angeles Times*, 17 September 1915, p. 12.
[57] 'Deny Coercion; To Try Robber', *The Los Angeles Times*, 28 September 1915, p. 12.

a number of wounds, and he eventually chose to kill himself rather than surrender to police.

The exploits of Chesalkin and his comrades were far from celebrated in the newspapers that covered the robbery. *The Eugene Guard* in Oregon referred to the men as a 'ring of Russian criminals' in one headline, while the two major San Francisco newspapers consistently used the word 'bandit' when discussing Chesalkin.[58] Unsurprisingly, *The Los Angeles Times* — the newspaper whose headquarters had been bombed only three years earlier — was scathing in its coverage of events. At one point, the paper emphatically declared in a headline that the 'Bank Bandits [are] Not Romantic'.[59] William Juber, wounded in the robbery but denied medical treatment unless he confessed and agreed to help the police catch his compatriot, was consistently labelled as 'yellow', meaning cowardly, in the newspapers.[60] Clearly, the days when the public could see Russian revolutionaries — especially those who had settled in the United States and apparently continued to act against state and business interests — as martyrs were gone. Now, it was Hugh MacBeth, the murdered bystander, who received public sympathy and was martyrized.

As the days passed and the authorities tried to unravel the complexities of this case, they brought in Professor Frank Damenstein, who had worked as an official police interpreter before, to analyse the papers left behind by Chesalkin, since these were largely in Russian, meaning the officers were unable to read them themselves. Damenstein's opinions were then quoted widely in contemporary newspaper accounts, and these lent further credence to the impression that the robbery was an anarchist undertaking. Damenstein let reporters know that he had examined 130 to 150 letters and notes, as well as a diary, but that — just like our postcard — none of these materials was signed or contained the names of individuals, something he suggested was highly suspicious.[61] Damenstein also concluded that the use of certain (unspecified) phrases, as well as what looked like codes in the correspondence, led him to believe that 'the man had been a Siberian convict, thoroughly drilled in criminal work'.[62]

---

[58] 'Ring of Russian Criminals says 'Frisco Police', *The Eugene Guard*, 16 September 1915, p. 2; 'Girl's Photo is Found on Dead Bandit', *San Francisco Chronicle*, 13 September 1915, p. 4; 'Dead Bandit is Bared as an Anarchist', p. 10, and 'Crime Codes Bare Life of Dead Bandit', *The San Francisco Examiner*, 16 September 1915, p. 3.

[59] 'Bank Bandits Not Romantic', p. 12.

[60] See, for example, 'Proclaim Him Real "Yellow"', *The Los Angeles Times*, 18 September 1915, p. 13.

[61] 'Crime Codes Bare Life of Dead Bandit', p. 3.

[62] 'Ring of Russian Criminals Says 'Frisco Police', p. 2.

San Francisco police also sought a formal identification of Chesalkin's body. That led them to Mrs Anna Kundy, the wife of our postcard recipient, who was brought to the morgue along with her son and an unnamed lodger. Anna Kundy told police that Chesalkin had rented a room from the family in either late February or early March 1915; the duration of his tenure there was three to four months, meaning it overlapped with the arrival of our postcard in May.[63] Part of the time he spent living with the Kundys, Chesalkin was joined by an apparent girlfriend, Reva Sopanoff — another person for whom there are no US government records — and his future bank-robbing comrade-in-arms William Juber. Indeed, it was right after the short Juber visit that Chesalkin left for Los Angeles and the pair embarked on the robbery.

Having introduced quite a cast of characters in the previous few paragraphs, it is time to look more closely at their personal histories. Freedom of Information requests for all of these people came up empty, but traces of their lives can be found in census returns, immigration documents, and military records that are available through Ancestry.com. Chesalkin's main accomplice William Juber, for instance, entered the United States at the port in New York City on 18 May 1909, according to the Declaration of Intent that was filed for him with the Bureau of Immigration and Naturalization. Born in Odesa, possibly in June 1886 (other documents give 1884, 1887, 'about 1888' and 'about 1890' as his date of birth), Juber formally renounced his allegiance to Nicholas II and the Russian government upon arrival in America and swore in his statement that he was not anarchist. The US Army Register of Enlistments shows that Juber joined in the army in 1909. A private in an infantry unit, he saw service in the Philippines before being honourably discharged in 1912. Juber told police detectives in San Francisco that, after leaving the military, he 'owned a chicken ranch in Montana for several months and worked in car shops in Wallace, Idaho, Seattle and Tacoma'.[64] He apparently met Chesalkin in Seattle in 1914.

At the time of Juber's arrest, he was living with a Russian Jewish woman, Bella (sometimes Beila) Ganoplski. The couple were officially married on 28 February 1925, in other words eight months after Juber was paroled from prison. Bella Juber was roughly a decade younger than her husband, with her 1942 Declaration of Intent saying that she was born in Kremenezug, Russia (present-day Kremenchuk in Ukraine) on 31 December 1894. Kremenchuk at that time had a sizeable Jewish community, with Jews

[63] 'Second Life,' p. 3.
[64] Ibid.

accounting for 47 per cent of the city's population by 1897.[65] Given the large number of pogroms that swept across southern Ukraine, down into the Crimean Peninsula, in the early twentieth century, it is not surprising that the family, particularly if members of it had become radicalized at some point, decided to leave the Russian Empire. In addition, Kremenchuk was reasonably close — about 160 km — to Ekaterinoslav (present-day Dnipro in Ukraine), which was a major centre of Russian anarchism in the first decade of the twentieth century, and the city had a well-established rail link with Odesa, another hotbed of anarchism at the time.[66] Bella, her brother and their parents entered the United States in Galveston, Texas, in mid 1912. The family settled in the Portland, Oregon area and it is unclear exactly when or how her relationship with Juber began, but they remained married until Juber died in 1941.

William Calish (Vladimir Kalishus), who briefly shared rooms with Juber and Chesalkin in Los Angeles but who was ultimately cleared of any involvement in the bank robbery, arrived in the US on the same ship, the *Pennsylvania*, as Juber in May 1909. And like Juber, Calish was born in Odesa — on 1 April 1884 to be precise. In Los Angeles, Calish worked as a painter and lived with the woman who would become his wife in January 1916. Mary Calish, who at various points in her life used the names Mania Calish, Mania Shugal, Mania Siegal and Mary Sigol, was similarly called in for questioning concerning the Los Angeles bank robbery and cleared by the police. She may have known Bella Juber when they were girls in Russia since she too was born in Kremenchuk, although she was two years older; like Bella's family, Mary's also left for the United States in 1912. In later years, census records show the Calishes took in a lodger, Adrian Popoff, likely to help cover the costs of the mortgage on the house census records show they bought some time between 1920 and 1930. Born in Saratov in 1888, Popoff had arrived in America in 1907 and worked as a painter.

Anna Kundy, the woman who identified Chesalkin's body, was born Anna Maltochanoff somewhere in Russia in the 1880s. Her death record states 3 February 1880, but census records also give her year of birth as 1882 and 1885. She arrived in the US in 1909 — the same year as Juber and Calish. Her husband Ernest was the odd man out of this group of people. He was born in Königsberg, Germany in September 1886 rather than in Russia, and he worked as a musician in an orchestra rather than as a

[65] 'Kremenchug', *Jewish Virtual Library* <https://www.jewishvirtuallibrary.org/kremenchug> [accessed 8 January 2023].

[66] Charters Wynn, *Workers, Strikes, and Pogroms: The Donbass-Dnepr Bend in Late Imperial Russia, 1870–1905*, Princeton, NJ, 1992, p. 156.

labourer. Despite the fact that Anna had been using his last name for years, Kundy's 1917 draft registration card listed him as single; it also does not refer to their son, the boy who accompanied Anna to the morgue in 1915. However, it does appear that the pair eventually married in 1924. While it is unclear exactly when they moved to 844 Fulton Street, city directories indicate they stayed at that address until 1918, when they moved to 573 Scott Street.

The information contained in the last few paragraphs fits well with how historians have described the contours of everyday anarchist life in the United States at the turn of the twentieth century. Most immigrant anarchists lived in working-class neighbourhoods. They preferred to live alongside people who originally came from the same part of the world and who spoke the same language, as familiarity brought a sense of stability and community.[67] In addition, '[m]ost anarchists lived as monogamous couples raising children together, although', as historian Andrew Cornell writes, 'many chose not to legally marry, rejecting the idea that either a church or government should regulate their emotional bonds'.[68] It was also quite common to find single men living as boarders with anarchist families.

With that said, there are also distinctly Russian elements to the life stories just provided. The connections to the port city of Odesa — where Juber, Calish and supposedly Chesalkin were born and lived prior to leaving the empire — are noteworthy. Odesa was one of the first places where anarchism sprouted in Southern Russia in 1905, and the activities of anarchists were particularly violent at this time. Odesa was home to a 'battle detachment', established by the Chernoznamentsy (the Black Flagists), which subjected merchant vessels docked in the city's port to 'expropriations'.[69] The city's anarcho-syndicalists set up another 'battle detachment,' which eventually robbed a train and a bank; the monies that were obtained were then used to buy weapons and a printing press.[70] It was not until the end of 1906, when Minister of the Interior Petr Stolypin had a state of emergency firmly in place, that the violence began to die down. The restoration of peace stemmed, in part, from the jailing and charging the government's political opponents for their crimes. In Odesa, an estimated 167 anarchists, or people deemed anarchist 'sympathizers' were put on trial in 1906–07. As Paul Avrich notes, the 'list contains a fairly

[67] Cornell, *Unruly Equality*, p. 25.
[68] Ibid, p. 25.
[69] Avrich, *Russian Anarchists*, p. 47.
[70] Ibid., p. 62.

equal proportion of Russian, Ukrainian, and Jewish names. The ages [of those on trial] were mostly nineteen to twenty-two. Of those tried, 28 were executed and 5 escaped from jail'.[71] What Avrich does not go on to reveal is how many of those young anarchists opted to leave Russia in the wake of the failed revolution, in other words, the path likely chosen by the people connected to our postcard.

Conclusion

History does not remember or celebrate the people who made up the Kundy family's circle of acquaintances. These were not anarchist luminaries who have left memoirs and paper trials for scholars to follow, nor have they been sought out by oral historians keen to capture their experiences for posterity. Instead, apart from a smattering of census documents, an obituary or two, and a few newspapers articles about a bank robbery that was soon forgotten, all that remains is our postcard. Still, its value is immense since it clearly demonstrates the transnational nature of the Russian revolutionary movement and the desire of émigrés to feel that they remained an important part of it. As each aspect of this ephemeral piece of cardboard is examined, what emerges is a spider web of stories about the lives Russian anarchists carved out for themselves in America. Given what they likely endured during the 1905 revolution, it makes perfect sense for a postcard featuring an image of the Bloody Sunday massacre to resonate deeply with them and, hence, be used in correspondence, even though popular culture in their new country of residence no longer viewed Russian revolutionaries as martyrs once anarchist violence became a regular feature of American life. Other details of the postcard allow us to see the continued engagement of Russian immigrants with politics in the world they left behind as well as their desire to help those who shared the same political beliefs, no matter what messages they were being given by the mainstream press in the United States. We also learn of the organizations that they set up to fight for a better standard of living for all workers in their new country, and the lengths to which they were willing to go to achieve those goals. Finally, their need for both community and secrecy is evident. Russian anarchists living in the United States were right to be worried about their uncertain status, since their host government grew much more concerned about their beliefs and activities as the First World War progressed and it became more likely that the US would be drawn into the conflict. Anti-radical provisions were strengthened in the Immigration

---

[71] Ibid., p. 68 n. 120.

Act of 1917, meaning that immigrants 'found to support anarchism could thereafter be deported at any time, regardless of how long they had lived in the country'.[72] Deportations did occur, notably during the 1919–21 Red Scare, and it is estimated that more than 10,000 immigrants were forced to leave the country.[73] In addition, in November 1919, Attorney General Mitchell Palmer sent agents to raid Union of Russian Workers premises in a dozen cities, including New York and Detroit. These raids led to the detention of more than a thousand suspected radicals — people just like this article has been discussing. However, truly extending the narrative beyond 1915 — when our postcard was mailed and received — is beyond the purview of this article. It would also need lightning to strike twice in the sense that another postcard like the one analysed here would have to turn up for sale on eBay or be found in a box of papers at a garage sale. Still, one never knows what ephemeral treasure might pop up in the future and all one can do is keep looking.

[72] Cornell, *Unruly Equality*, p. 62.
[73] Ibid., p. 75.

Nihilists, Fenians and Revolutionary Martyrdom in Transnational Context

ABBY HOLEKAMP

IN June 1880, a pro-nationalist Dublin newspaper found itself in the position of having to defend the recently formed National Irish Land League against 'odious' rhetoric that equated its organized opposition to Ireland's landlord system to Russian nihilism. 'It is quite true', the unnamed journalist admitted, 'that, occasionally, there have been words used by unaccustomed orators which ought not to have been used in addressing an Irish audience. There have been two or three allusions of a favourable kind to Nihilism, and some other talk of the sort'. However, these allusions were deemed to be no cause for alarm as they amounted to nothing more than 'simply wanton and windy rhetoric — sounding brave and bold, gusty and tempestuous as a winter's storm, and passing lightly as a summer zephyr'. The Land League, it was stated, endorsed neither 'Nihilism' nor 'the Communism of the Continent'.[1]

What triggered *The Irishman*'s strong reaction to rhetoric tying the Land League's aims and actions to those of Russian nihilism? How can we understand such a dismissive response from a newspaper that was typically *more* radical than any of the Land League's aims — which were themselves quite distant (both geographically and ideologically) from those of the Russian Empire's revolutionaries?

Founded in August 1879 by the well-known Irish nationalist Michael Davitt, the Land League itself had a narrowly defined goal of nonviolently organizing against landlordism.[2] However, the League was born of a

Abby Holekamp is Mellon Assistant Professor of Russian and East European Studies at Vanderbilt University, Nashville, Tennessee.

[1] 'The Land League', *The Irishman*, 5 June 1880. At this time, *The Irishman* was the official paper of Fenianism in Ireland.
[2] The League was founded in Castlebar, Co. Mayo, as the National Land League of

Slavonic and East European Review, 102, 1, 2024

doi:10.1353/see.00004

temporary consensus among competing factions of Irish nationalists and was by no means an ideologically unified organization.[3] Furthermore, the League's local offshoots were even less subject to oversight than its main committee, which led to the expression of a wide variety of viewpoints in its name (or in the name of Irish Fenianism more broadly).[4]

The Irishman's journalist ultimately 'advis[ed] the avoidance of topics and language that are not relevant to the case of the politics of our country'.[5] However, I assert that the very existence of this newspaper article in fact makes the opposite argument: Russian nihilism, as it was (mis)understood by various historical actors, *was* relevant to the case of Irish politics. In this context, so-called Russian nihilism became a trope that could — and did — function as a form of shorthand in explaining what Fenianism was or was not. As a result, such tropes bolstered what Lynn Ellen Patyk has called 'a subtle and intricate feedback loop between art and life' in the genealogy of modern terrorism.[6] Thus, the creation and evolution of this kind of trope was a mediated, multidirectional process. It was a process that, in turn, broadened the array of possible meanings of a term like 'nihilism'.

As we will see, studying this process illustrates how broader interrelated concepts such as political violence and political martyrdom were mediated across explicitly transnational contexts. In fact, their shifting historical meanings are difficult to understand *without* considering this transnational

Mayo; it was re-organized as the National Irish Land League in Dublin in October 1879.

[3] The League's president, MP and longtime nationalist leader Charles Stewart Parnell, advocated a deliberative approach of nonviolent action. He hoped that once the land issues at hand were suitably resolved — ideally without alienating the landholding classes — landlord and tenant would be able to unite behind the political cause of home rule for Ireland. Other members of the League's 54-person committee held more overtly revolutionary views and goals. For a brief summary of these variable goals, see S. J. Connolly (ed.), *The Oxford Companion to Irish History*, New York and Oxford, 1998, pp. 296–97.

[4] An example of this kind of rhetoric: at a meeting held to protest an eviction in Castlejordan, Co. Meath, about a week before the aforementioned article was published, *The Irishman* noted that 'Mr. Thomas Brennan, who was received with cheers, supported the motion. In the course of his speech he said — [...] No doubt they would be told that these were very revolutionary ideas, and, as their respected chairman said, they would be accused of preaching Communism from the platform. Well, he did not know whether he was preaching Communism or not (no), but if it were Communism to say that the earth was made by God for the people, and that the people had as much right to the ground as they had the free air of heaven, or to the water that coursed through the beautiful rivulets that he passed by on coming there that day, then he was a Communist and he gloried in the avowal (cheers)'. 'Land Meeting in Meath', *The Irishman*, 29 May 1880.

[5] 'The Land League'.

[6] Lynn Ellen Patyk, *Written in Blood: Revolutionary Terrorism and Russian Literary Culture, 1861–1881*, Madison, WI, 2017, p. 11.

circulation. This article uses a case study of the surprisingly dense web of rhetorical connections between the seemingly unconnected Russian and Irish revolutionary movements to demonstrate this crucial facet of the history of revolutionary movements. I have previously written about the blurred boundaries 'between art and life' in the case of 'nihilists' and French print culture; here I show that this phenomenon was not unique to the French context.[7] By probing the contours of the transnational information ecosystem that shaped European political and cultural imaginaries in the second half of the nineteenth century, we see how Russian nihilism was indeed relevant to Irish politics.

Whereas in relation to ecology, the popularization of the ecosystem concept led humans to re-examine their relationship to the environment, I invoke it here to embark on a re-examination of how we think about the creation and circulation of information in a historical context. It is a concept that privileges interconnection and integration in analysing processes of knowledge production.[8] By situating the uses of a concept clearly within the context of its information ecosystem, and by identifying and analysing authorship, transmission medium and circulation, we can begin to make connections among diverse cultural outputs that might otherwise remain obscured.[9]

This approach is especially useful in a study of Russian revolutionary movements because both terrorism and martyrdom require easily legible publicity to succeed. Terrorism researchers Alex P. Schmid and Jenny de Graaf have argued that acts of political violence can and should be read as 'a kind of violent language', and 'without communication, there is no terrorism'.[10] Martyrdom too — whether religious or political — requires

---

[7]   Abby Holekamp, 'Who Are Vera and Tatiana? The Female Russian Nihilist in the Fin de Siècle Imagination', *Representations*, 150, 2020, pp. 1–31.

[8]   My thinking on the concept of the ecosystem and its history in the field of ecology was shaped by Frank Golley, *A History of the Ecosystem Concept in Ecology: More than the Sum of the Parts*, New Haven, CT, 1996.

[9]   Scholars of Russia and the Soviet Union such as Katerina Clark, Michael David-Fox and Jeffrey Brooks have previously invoked the idea of the ecosystem to describe, in different but related ways, cultural change and continuity over time. Despite their differences, all three intuitively tap into the idea of culture as a holistic system with interdependent parts that evolve in tandem. See, for example, Katerina Clark, *Petersburg, Crucible of Cultural Revolution*, Cambridge, MA, 1996, pp. ix, 1–28; Michael David-Fox, *Revolution of the Mind: Higher Learning Among the Bolsheviks, 1918–1929*, Ithaca, NY, 1997, pp. 190–91; Jeffrey Brooks, *The Firebird and the Fox: Russian Culture under Tsars and Bolsheviks*, Cambridge, 2019, pp. 1, 51.

[10]   Alex P. Schmid and Janny de Graaf, *Violence as Communication: Insurgent Terrorism and the Western News Media*, London, 1982, pp. 9, 1.

an analogous kind of communication. It too is, as Dominic Janes and Alex Houen have asserted, 'a social formation'. Therefore, it is not surprising that 'a crucial place in the history of martyrdom is occupied by mediated forms', such as hagiographies.[11] Scholars of terrorism in various historical periods and places have similarly emphasized the importance of the mutually generative myth-making relationship between media, its readers and (would-be) terrorists themselves. In mid to late nineteenth-century Europe, it was the mediation of the rapidly expanding public sphere on which this generative feedback loop hinged.

It is true that there were no Russians intimately involved in the Irish cause (nor vice versa). But even as *The Irishman* article's author attempted to downplay the relevance of nihilism to Ireland, he plainly acknowledged its appeal, asserting that:

> [the] very remoteness of the thing may tempt men of imagination to refer to it by a far flight of fancy — if there was but a possibility of its approach they would be reserved and reticent. [...] This shows that the thing apprehended by some is so utterly remote — so completely beyond our horizon, and the horizon of popular desire — as to be no danger, nothing more than a fantastic phantom.

A temptation from the imagination, a flight of fancy, a fantastic phantom — the language used to describe nihilism here rendered it innocuous, inchoate and difficult to grasp or define in this remote context. Once again equating multiple '-isms', the author's final conclusion was that in Ireland, 'Communism is a Chimera'.[12]

The Irishman's conclusion, and in particular, the journalist's use of the term 'chimera', presaged a complaint about terminology that a former Russian revolutionary would pen several years later. In 1886, Lev Tikhomirov, who was living in Paris at the time, published an influential book titled *La Russie politique et sociale*, which dedicated a full appendix to his thoughts on the 'nihilist' problem. (A two-volume English translation was published in London in 1888 as *Russia, Political and Social*.)[13] At this point in his career, Tikhomirov felt that 'nihilism' had always been something of a chimera. Its very creation as a concept was the product of

---

[11] Dominic Janes and Alex Houen, 'Introduction', in Janes and Houen (eds), *Martyrdom and Terrorism: Pre-Modern to Contemporary Perspectives*, New York and Oxford, 2014, p. 4.

[12] 'The Land League'.

[13] L. Tikhomirov, *Russia, Political and Social*, trans. Edward Aveling, 2 vols, London, 1888.

the kinds of flights of fancy chronicled by our Irish journalist. In his book's appendix, Tikhomirov noted that:

> To be sure, the intellectual movement in Russia, as elsewhere, can give rise in certain individual cases to some ridiculous, silly manifestations, lending themselves to caricature, some possibly even criminal. It is precisely from these particular cases that nihilism was composed, uniting them without any reason whatsoever into one single idea, despite the fact that they were in no way united in reality. Thus in nature there are creatures who have tails, others with lizard scales, still others with a tiger's paws and claws, others still with wings. When you bring all of these attributes together in a dragon, you have before you a creation of your imagination, not a real being. This is exactly how nihilism was created. But if the dragon plays a convenient role in tales used to frighten children, it has no place in natural history. In a serious study of Russia, nihilism as a doctrine or a particular trend similarly can have no place.[14]

Here Tikhomirov described a physical chimera — an imagined dragon that was an amalgam of scales, claws, wings and other assorted parts borrowed from other, actually existing beasts. Figuratively, of course, a chimera is an illusion of the mind, an impossibility. Although in different ways and about different topics, Tikhomirov and the unnamed Irish journalist both invoked the deleterious role imagination played when it came to explaining or understanding the contours of contemporary revolutionary movements.

I borrow the metaphor of the chimera to suggest that *fin de siècle* European mass media discourses around a host of concepts associated with terrorism formed their own chimera, in both senses of the word. Metaphorically, a chimera is an illusion — it is completely false. Mythologically, the chimera has a lion's head, the body of a goat and a serpent's tale — it is an imagined assemblage of *real* creatures. Thus, like Tikhomirov's dragon, these concepts become agglomerative because the related terminology was used interchangeably and allusively, albeit not always (or even often) in an intentional way.

If, for example, a French police report on Russian émigré activity in Paris used the words 'nihilist' and 'anarchist' completely interchangeably, that does not necessarily mean that the officer who wrote it was making a political point or was even consciously blending these terms.[15] Such

---

[14] Lev Tikhomirov, *La Russie politique et sociale*, Paris, 1886, pp. 534–35. My translation.
[15] Multiple examples of this phenomenon can be found in the Archives Nationales de

slippages were common in a variety of published genres and point to characteristics of the second sense of the word chimera: the role of a transnational political imaginary in how terrorism, political martyrdom and their adjacent concepts and terms were understood, blended into Tikhomirov's 'one single idea' and applied in discourse. It also reminds us that there was no one 'true' definition of terms like nihilism or Fenianism in this historical context. If we consider media about Russian revolutionaries as an especially foundational part of a discursive chimera of terrorism in *fin de siècle* Europe, we can see that what seems like an issue purely of haphazard terminology is actually an issue of meaning that requires closer examination.

In the pages that follow, we will delve more deeply into the concepts of political violence and martyrdom in this time frame by entering into the information ecosystem in which they were circulating. In particular, we will focus on ideas of and about Irish Fenians and Russian nihilists as they appeared in English-language newspaper reporting in the early 1880s and in two foundational texts of political martyrdom in the Irish and Russian contexts respectively: *Speeches from the Dock*, compiled by Alexander Martin Sullivan and Timothy Daniel Sullivan, and *Underground Russia*, written by Sergei Stepniak-Kravchinskii. Ultimately, we will arrive at the shocking 1882 Phoenix Park murders in Dublin, a galvanizing event that tightened nihilism's chimeric discursive grip on how political violence and martyrdom were represented and seen.

The discursive chimera and its information ecosystem
This discursive chimera existed and evolved within an information ecosystem that was peculiar to the era and inextricable from it. As will be shown, it is within this ecosystem that the slippery nature of terminology is enabled. We have already seen that for Lev Tikhomirov the word 'nihilist' was strongly chimeric and therefore had no place in meaningful discussions about his homeland. However, his position on terminology contrasted sharply with that of another revolutionary turned publicist-in-exile, Sergei Stepniak-Kravchinskii, known to the European public by his pen name, Stepniak. Stepniak, as we will see, embraced the term 'nihilist' and all that it came to stand for — regardless of accuracy. While the role of émigrés in explaining/promoting Russian revolutionary political goals

France, Paris, F/7/12519 and F/7/12520/A. These files contain police surveillance conducted on various Russian émigré groups — particularly those deemed 'anti-tsariste' — in France from 1881–1914.

abroad has been well documented, it is essential to place these activities in conversation with other contemporary revolutionary currents in the final decade of the nineteenth century in Europe (and, to some extent, the United States) because that is how their writings and other outputs were experienced by those who engaged with them. They were, importantly, part of this broader information ecosystem whose parts acted on one another rather than operating in isolation. This dynamic in turn changed the meanings of Russian revolutionary martyrdom, though, as we will eventually see, not in the ways one might expect.

Tikhomirov and Stepniak both had revolutionary bona fides. Stepniak fled the Russian Empire in 1878 after stabbing the chief of gendarmes, Adjutant General Nikolai Mezentsev, in St Petersburg. Tikhomirov, for his part, had been active in the populist 'going to the people' campaign of the 1870s, and was a member of the Executive Committee of the People's Will. Because of this, the 1881 assassination of Tsar Alexander II forced him into hiding, and he emigrated to Switzerland in 1882. Tikhomirov's diaries show that in emigration, his political views began to change. He eventually repudiated his revolutionary past in an 1888 Russian-language pamphlet with the straightforward title *Pochemu ia perestal byt' revoliutsionerom* (Why I am No Longer a Revolutionary), which would enable him to return to Russia with a full pardon from Tsar Alexander III.[16] Stepniak, on the other hand, never repudiated his past (though he was always publicly coy when asked about Mezentsev). His subsequent career as a sympathetic interpreter of Russian nihilism for Western audiences brought him name recognition and influence, especially in Britain.

As other scholars have pointed out, the meaning of the word 'nihilism' itself had always been ambiguous.[17] Russian writers like Belinskii, Gertsen and Turgenev did dabble in philosophical themes adjacent to nihilism in their writings in the 1840s and '50s, and Turgenev, of course, is generally credited with introducing the nihilist persona to the wider reading public in his 1862 novel, *Fathers and Sons*.[18] However, nihilism's most precise

[16] L. A. Tikhomirov, *Vospominaniia*, Moscow, 2003; L. Tikhomirov, *Pochemu ia perestal byt' revoliutsionerom*, Paris, 1888. For more of an overview of Tikhomirov's ideological evolution, see Aleksandr Repnikov and Oleg Milevskii, *Dve zhizni L'va Tikhomirova*, Moscow, 2011; for a narrower look at Tikhomirov in emigration, see Abbott Gleason, 'The Emigration and Apostasy of Lev Tikhomirov', *Slavic Review*, 26, 3, 1967, pp. 414–29.

[17] For example, Abbott Gleason, *Young Russia: The Genesis of Russian Radicalism in the 1860s*, Chicago, IL, 1983, pp. 70–73, and Michael Confino, 'Révolte juvénile et contre-culture: les nihilistes russes des "années 60"', *Cahiers du monde russe et soviétique*, 31, 4, 1990, pp. 489–537.

[18] For a summary of these philosophical themes, see Victoria Frede, 'Nihilism', in Caryl

expression is usually attributed to the writings of the critic Dmitrii Pisarëv, who famously identified himself — for a period of time — with Turgenev's nihilist Bazarov.[19] Nevertheless, in the opening sentence of his 1882/3 book, *Underground Russia*, Stepniak gave credit to Turgenev, declaring that he has 'rendered himself immortal by a single word': nihilism.[20] Stepniak also criticized inaccurate use of the term 'nihilist', but nonetheless continued to use it in recognition of the meanings it had taken on outside of Russia (and perhaps the titillation it caused). As his *Underground Russia* was going to press, Stepniak wrote a letter to the Executive Committee of the People's Will in Russia in which he outlined his thinking on why such a book should be published, invoking the denialism typified by the piece in *The Irishman* cited above:

> Europe has its own affairs, its own troubles, and up to now it has been interested in 'nihilists' more as a rare and wondrous beast, more as an amusement, as a kind of curious gladiatorial combat. It does not recognize in them any particle of itself, and we have to hammer and keep hammering away at one point, so that we can hammer it into their skull that our contemporary terrorists are the men of '93 and '89 in France to whom all Europe gives pride of place.[21]

Stepniak was not the first to propose such an approach. In London in the spring of 1880, Lev Hartman, who had recently escaped extradition from France to Russia for his role in the November 1879 assassination attempt against Alexander II, proposed creating an English-language newspaper called the *Nihilist*. The newspaper would be used to raise funds for the revolutionaries, so the 'most important thing is that the tone and characteristics of the articles conform to the English spirit'. In a letter to a colleague, Hartman further observed that '"Nihilist" is a word that interests the West and hence it is desirable to use it' for the newspaper's name in order to attract readers.[22] Although this project never materialized,

Emerson, George Pattison and Randall E. Poole (eds), *The Oxford Handbook of Russian Religious Thought*, New York and Oxford, 2020, pp. 152–68.

[19] Dmitrii Pisarëv, 'Bazarov', in Ivan Turgenev, *Fathers and Children*, trans. and ed. Michael R. Katz, New York, 2009, pp. 193–215.

[20] Stepniak, *Underground Russia*, London, 1883, p. 3.

[21] Cited in Peter Scotto, 'The Terrorist as Novelist: Sergei Stepniak-Kravchinsky', in Anthony Anemone (ed.), *Just Assassins: The Culture of Terrorism in Russia*, Evanston, IL, 2010, p. 106.

[22] Hartman quoted in Dioneo [I.V. Shklovskii], 'V emigratsii', in A. A. Titov (ed.), *Nikolai Vasil'evich Chaikovskii*, vol. 1, Paris, 1929, pp. 174–75. Translations from Donald J. Senese, *S. M. Stepniak-Kravchinskii, The London Years*, Newtonville, MA, 1987, pp. 23–24.

Hartman's thought process is indicative of the hold this terminology had over the way Russia was imagined at this time.

In *fin de siècle* Europe, the political imaginary was fuelled within the information ecosystem by a blurred boundary between fact and fiction, a prominent feature of the rapidly expanding mass media landscape that shaped the wider information ecosystem. As one scholar of the French press has written of this time period, 'the journalism of the imagination play[ed] a role as important as news journalism' in shaping the content of this new media landscape.[23] In the British context, literary scholars such as Barbara Arnett Melchiori have noted the web of connections between popular Victorian 'dynamite novels' and press coverage of actual 'dynamite outrages'. In this formulation, a 'dynamite novel' is one in which the plot revolves around the activities of revolutionaries of various stripes, though of course writers often did not differentiate among them. As Melchiori put it, 'a bomb is a bomb, it explodes or not, and either way it can often make a story'.[24]

In a broader context, novels that engaged with themes of terrorism were part of the wider interest Victorian fiction took in social 'questions'. Fiction writers' and readers' interest in the people who would perpetrate this kind of political violence — whether Russian nihilists, Irish Fenians, anarchists from Italy or Germany or others — was one manifestation of a very real sense of anxiety about impending and inscrutable violence committed by unseen malefactors. The protagonist of Henry James's 1886 novel, *The Princess Casamassima* — an English bookbinder drawn into a terrorist plot — invoked the dark imaginings of the moment while summarizing this feeling succinctly: 'Nothing of it appears above the surface', he says, 'but there's an immense underworld people with a thousand forms of revolutionary passion and devotion'.[25]

In this regard, the case of the Fenians is illustrative. Fenianism first developed among Irish immigrants in the United States after various setbacks experienced by Irish nationalist groups in the 1840s. In 1858, some of the veterans of the failed 1840s movements met in Dublin to found a secret group called the Irish Republican Brotherhood (IRB), which soon became synonymous with Fenianism. Starting in the late 1870s, some members of the IRB started collecting money for a 'Skirmishing Fund', much of which came via fundraising subscription efforts by émigré newspapers catering

---

[23] Michael Palmer, *Des petits journaux aux grandes agences: Naissance du journalisme moderne, 1863–1914*, Paris, 1983, pp. 26–29.

[24] Barbara Arnett Melchiori, *Terrorism in the Late Victorian Novel*, London, 1985, p. 8.

[25] Henry James, *The Princess Casamassima*, London, 1987, p. 492.

to the large population of Irish emigrants to the United States (giving it an interesting transnational dimension quite different from the transnational dimension of the nihilists' activities). As with the term 'nihilist' there is some ambiguity to the label 'Fenian', and there has been some scholarly debate as to whether those referred to as Fenians would have used the term to self-describe.[26]

Skirmishing in Britain began in earnest in 1881. In the first half of that year, a bombing killed one person at Salford Barracks near Manchester, an explosive device failed to detonate at Mansion House in London, barracks were bombed in Chester and Liverpool, and 'disguised explosives' were found aboard multiple ships (the SS *Malta* and SS *Bavaria*) also in Liverpool.[27] Further attacks on train stations, Scotland Yard and the London Underground occurred, with the campaign culminating in what the press called 'Dynamite Saturday' on 24 January 1885, when Irish conspirators detonated bombs at the Tower of London, the House of Commons and in Westminster Crypt.[28] While Fenian-planned bombings in Britain did not end in 1885, they did dramatically decrease in frequency, in part because the US government finally started to crack down on what one American newspaper described as the ability of US-based Fenians 'to discuss their nefarious plans in public without further marks of rebuke'.[29] Taking a longer view of the history of the Irish 'question', this so-called 'skirmishing campaign' from 1881–85 was not typical but instead represented a 'break with the insurrectionary tradition' of Irish nationalism from 1867–1916.[30] However, its impact on media representations was much longer lasting than the campaign itself.

As has been noted, the development of mass media was a crucial factor in the advent of 'modern' terrorism and therefore the historical context of that development is essential to any discussion of the history of terrorism. As Carola Dietze asserted in a recent historiographical overview of histories of terrorism, '[t]errorism as a specific tactic of political violence was invented when spectacular violence was combined with mass media reporting to

---

[26] See Niall Whelehan, *The Dynamiters: Irish Nationalism and Political Violence in the Wider World, 1867–1900*, Cambridge, 2012, pp. 7, 25; Owen McGee, *The IRB: The Irish Republican Brotherhood, from the Land League to Sinn Féin*, Dublin, 2007, and M. J. Kelly, *The Fenian Ideal and Irish Nationalism, 1882–1916*, Woodbridge, 2006.

[27] Shane Kenna, *War in the Shadows: The Irish-American Fenians Who Bombed Victorian Britain*, London, 2014, pp. vii–viii.

[28] Ibid., pp. 205–08.

[29] Cited in ibid., p. 216.

[30] Whelehan, *The Dynamiters*, p. 1.

address a mass public'.[31] This combination catalysed in the middle of the
nineteenth century. Although the technological changes that allowed mass
media to develop rapidly were not the only important factor in how our
discursive chimera of terrorism, nihilism and martyrdom developed and
spread, these changes to the European media landscape did occur at the
same time as an increase in certain (sometimes new) forms of political
violence, involving the dynamic interplay of 'dynamite, international wire
services, mass media sensationalism, and consumer capitalism'.[32] In the
case of Britain specifically, we can note a combination of the abolition of
newspaper stamp and paper duties that led to a sharp drop in newspaper
prices in the early 1860s, the subsequent creation of news agencies like
the Press Association (1868) which helped especially provincial papers
gather and distribute news more efficiently, and the steady increase in the
number of miles of both telegraph and railway lines. To give an example
of how quickly certain publications grew: the *Illustrated London News* —
one the first papers created to appeal to a mass readership — increased
in circulation from about 67,000 in 1850 to 123,000 by 1855 alone.[33] By the
end of the century, the highest circulation newspapers and magazines in
Britain were printing around one million copies of each issue. (It should
be noted here that the periodical industry in Ireland was generally much
smaller than in England and, though robust, remained so throughout the
nineteenth century.)[34] Thus, in this time of political instability and change,
there were concurrent economic and technological developments that
facilitated transnational communications and connections as never before.

In Britain, some of the aforementioned Victorian novels featured Russian
nihilists who, as Melchiori noted, were portrayed as romantic figures
deserving of sympathy. This contrasted sharply with Victorian novels
featuring Irish radicals who were painted as ordinary criminals devoid of

---

[31] Carola Dietze, 'The Invention of Terrorism in Nineteenth-Century Europe, Russia,
and the United States', in Carola Dietze and Claudia Verhoeven (eds), *The Oxford
Handbook of the History of Terrorism*, New York and Oxford, 2022, p. 187. Dietze greatly
expands on this argument in her monograph, *The Invention of Terrorism in Nineteenth-
Century Europe, Russia, and the United States*, trans. David Antal, James Bell and Zachary
Murphy King, London, 2021.

[32] Dietze, *The Invention of Terrorism*, p. 12; Lynn Ellen Patyk, 'Remembering "The
Terrorism": Sergei Stepniak-Kravchinskii's "Underground Russia"', *Slavic Review*, 68, 4,
2009, p. 767.

[33] Richard D. Altick, *The English Common Reader: A Social History of the Mass Reading
Public, 1800–1900*, 2nd edn, Columbus, OH, 1998, pp. 391–96; Graham Law, 'Distribution',
in Andrew King, Alexis Easley and John Morton (eds), *The Routledge Handbook to
Nineteenth-Century British Periodicals and Newspapers*, London, 2016, pp. 56–59.

[34] Elizabeth Tilley, 'Periodicals in Ireland', in ibid., p. 208.

the lofty ideals of the nihilists. Some of these differences of representation could be explained by press coverage of actual political violence and the relationship between fact and fiction in popular media. As newspapers and novels were the two main sources of information for both the authors writing these books and the reading public in general at this time, it can be legitimately argued, as Melchiori did, that newspaper coverage had a substantial effect on the way Victorian novelists imagined different sources of political violence. Simply put, access to information enabled by the rapidly changing media landscape shaped writers' perspectives and thus had a substantive impact on their material output. As we will see, the British media panic over the Fenian skirmishing campaign does not make sense outside that context and that of the Victorian cultural imaginary around Russian nihilism — an imaginary shot through with acts of terror and invocations of martyrdom. Bringing the Irish case alongside the Russian one is an effective means by which to grasp the outsized role that Russian revolutionaries played in the European imagination. It was a role that shaped the discursive chimera of terrorism and must be understood as a key component of the broader cultural imaginary around political violence in the second half of the nineteenth century.

Paradoxical press
As already noted, the Fenian 'skirmishing' campaign began in earnest in early 1881. About two months after the Salford Barracks explosion, the assassination of Tsar Alexander II on 13 March (N.S.) in St Petersburg set off weeks of breathless press coverage around the globe. In the United States, newly elected president James A. Garfield was shot in July by an assassin who believed he had helped with Garfield's election victory and therefore was owed a job by the administration; Garfield died of an infection caused by his wounds in September. The confluence of these events in the first half of 1881 brought the discursive chimera of terrorism to the forefront of the collective imagination in Europe. On top of these acts of violence, there were other seemingly related events that occasioned uneasy press coverage, including an International Anarchist Congress that took place in London at the end of July, during which delegates including the prominent figures Petr Kropotkin, Errico Malatesta and Louise Michel debated so-called 'propaganda of the deed'.

The concurrence of the beginning of the skirmishing campaign and the apotheosis of the campaign to assassinate the tsar meant that Fenians and nihilists were written about simultaneously. Immediately after the

Salford Barracks explosion on 14 January — in which one person was killed — newspapers began to mention Fenians and nihilists in tandem. The fear of an impending 'union of Nihilists and Fenians', as one Lancaster newspaper put it in 1882, turns up as a recurring theme in the English press throughout the first half of the 1880s.[35] The two groups were also brought together metaphorically, as in a January 1881 satirical article in *Punch* titled 'Our New Bogeys', that began: 'One is called a Fenian; the other a Nihilist'. The article proceeded:

> The Fenian is the most dreaded as he is a Home or domestic demon. He causes water pipes to burst, the Thames to overflow, and the gas to burn badly; he creates the fogs to choke and blind us, and the mud to spoil our clothes. He corrupts cabmen and makes them abuse and overcharge us, he makes servants insolent, and theatrical attendants rapacious.

On the other hand, the *Punch* writer continued:

> The Nihilist is a foreign demon, with a curious passion for clockwork. He is credited with many offences of which he is probably not guilty. [...] and he and his and his brother Bogey, the Fenian, have caused Volunteers to look sharply after their arms, and the policemen after their truncheons.[36]

Satire only works when it is grounded in reality, and this piece succinctly summarized some very real anxieties in Britain about terroristic activities.

The inspiration supposedly went both ways: that same month, the same paper reported on a 'telegram from Vienna' about the nihilists' new programme. 'They are now bent on provoking an agrarian revolution in Russia, modelled after the proceedings of the Irish Land Leaguers', the reporter wrote. 'They threaten more especially to carry out a systematic series of secret murders of Russian landlords.'[37] However, another recurring theme in the press was the idea expressed in 1896 by an English journalist who had worked in Russia, that it was unbelievable that nihilists would have 'any connection whatsoever' with the Fenians, in part because

---

[35] 'Union of Nihilists and Fenians', *Lancaster Gazette*, 7 June 1882. It is noteworthy that this piece was published not long after the Phoenix Park murders.

[36] 'Our New Bogeys', *Punch*, 22 January 1881, p. 34.

[37] *Manchester Evening News*, 16 February 1881. In reality, at least from the Russian side, there was not a lot of interest in Fenian activities at this time, though Derek Offord has located one 1880 letter written by Andrey Zheliabov that, in his words, 'commended the example of the Fenians (and [Charles] Parnell)'. Offord, 'Political Terrorism in Russia in the 1880s: The Fenian Lesson', *Irish Slavonic Studies*, 5, 1984, p. 27.

nihilists perceived Irish radicalism as 'mainly composed of creatures 'with a price'.[38] The aforementioned 'Dynamite Saturday' explosions in 1885 that injured several bystanders inspired numerous unfavourable comparisons in the London press between, as the *Times* put it, the 'cowardly' Irish 'dynamite fiends' deemed responsible for the seemingly random attacks and 'the Nihilists and Anarchists of the Continent' whose 'designs are at least intelligible', if also deserving of condemnation. Stepniak, interviewed by the *Pall Mall Gazette*, supposedly denigrated these blasts as 'mere baby work' and 'stupid, objectless, directed against no particular individual, furthering no great cause'.[39] (Of course, the Irish political project as a whole *was* discernible to those willing to pay attention.)

In this press coverage, then, we see two prominent, coincident themes that were seemingly at odds with each other. On one hand, there was the thought that a union between nihilists and Fenians made perfect sense, and on the other, the idea that nihilists operated on a much higher level than the amateurish Fenians and would never deign to associate with them. Furthermore, these two threads not only coincided, but they also seemed to entangle and pull against each other to a significant degree in journalistic writing from these years. A limited but compelling sample of both themes can be found in the English press from 18 March 1881 — five days after the assassination of Alexander II and two days after the incendiary device was discovered at Mansion House in London. Before the Irish-American perpetrators of the Mansion House attempt were arrested in the following weeks, many newspapers asked if there was a connection between the tsar's assassination and the event that the *Portsmouth Evening News* rather dramatically termed 'The Dastardly Outrage at the Mansion House'.[40] Several publications thought it possible and lent this idea varying levels of credence. On the more sober end of things, the *Times* wrote that while it was 'hardly possible not to imagine a connexion between the crime which was perpetrated in St. Petersburg on Sunday and the mysterious attempt to cause an explosion at the Mansion House on Wednesday night', it also seemed that this 'connexion, however, if it exists at all, must be a very remote one. The Nihilists of St. Petersburg are far more accomplished adepts in the science of outrage than the clumsy contrivers of the attempt on the Mansion House'. The *Times* concluded its coverage in this issue of the paper by cautioning readers

[38] 'Nihilists and Invincibles', *Huddersfield Chronicle*, 21 September 1896.

[39] Citations from Melchiori, *Terrorism in the Late Victorian Novel*, pp. 24, 27–28.

[40] 'The Dastardly Outrage at the Mansion House', *Portsmouth Evening News*, 18 March 1881.

that 'there is no occasion for a general alarm, and still less for anything like a panic. But there is no doubt that science has lately put very powerful weapons into the hands of the secret foes of society', including those who would be 'clumsy imitators' of actual revolutionaries.[41]

At the other end of the spectrum, on the same day, the London correspondent for the *Manchester Courier and Lancashire General Advertiser* announced that there was indeed reason to believe that the incident at Mansion House 'was the joint work of Fenianism and Nihilism'. This correspondent then continued with a completely fictitious, conspiracy-laced backstory that seems not to have appeared in other publications:

> Indications have come to light recently of a *rapprochement* between these two elements of mischief. Seeing that they had a common object in view — the spread of terrorism — their respective agents here are said to have joined ranks, and entered into a pledge to help one another by all possible means. As a portion of this program, they have been sending menacing letters to people of position and influence, sometimes written in broken English, sometimes in the Hibernian dialect. Most of these threaten to blow up 'somebody or something', and all are illiterate to such a degree that there must have been an assumption of ignorance on the part of the writers.[42]

Such an invented scenario might well have come straight out of the pages of a 'dynamite novel'. Nevertheless, the prevailing view doubted that there was a connection to Russia because the plot had been so clumsily attempted. The idea that the Fenians were less technically skilled than the Nihilists was also a trope in newspaper reports. After the Mansion House incident, the *Huddersfield Daily Chronicle* scoffed that:

> The idea that 15 lbs. of coarse blasting powder placed in an open spot would have blown up the official residence of the Lord Mayor is of course ridiculous. The perpetrator may have thought that such a quantity of explosive material would have destroyed the building, but if he did, he could not have been a conspirator skilled in the sense that the Russian Nihilists have proved themselves to be by their many ingenious efforts to kill the late Emperor.[43]

---

[41] *The Times*, 18 March 1881.
[42] *Manchester Courier and Lancashire General Advertiser*, 18 March 1881.
[43] *Huddersfield Daily Chronicle*, 18 March 1881.

As another paper put it when speculating on what the Fenians might do next, 'the chief safeguard' against a future attack by a 'hypothetical Hibernian' who 'might get into the Speaker's Gallery' was that 'a Fenian is not a Nihilist but a cowardly animal, who, if he has no respect for other people's lives, takes very good care not to imperil his own'.[44] If Fenians were bumblers and cowards, then, did that make them more or less dangerous than nihilists? It was hard to know, though they were certainly not exalted as martyrs to a worthy cause. To be sure, the above example represents an extreme in terms of density of references and comparisons, due to the temporal proximity of the Mansion House explosion to the assassination of the tsar. But it also clearly represents the thematic tensions that ran throughout late Victorian print culture, and vividly exemplifies the discursive chimera of terrorism.

The print culture of revolutionary martyrdom: 'Speeches from the Dock' and 'Underground Russia'
Within European media in this time frame, the terms terrorist/terrorism and martyr/martyrdom figured frequently in discussions or stories about nihilists/nihilism. As the editors state in the introduction to a 2014 essay collection on these topics, martyrdom and terrorism 'have histories that are interlinked in fascinating and important ways', even though the scholars who have approached the cultural histories of these concepts have typically studied them as separate entities.[45] Yet, in representations of Russian nihilism, they are especially strongly connected.

For example, on 23 April 1881, the *London Evening Standard* published an article that sought to capture the mood among the Russian so-called 'nihilists' after the regicides had been executed on April 15. It cited heavily from a recently published piece from a Parisian daily, *Le Voltaire*, supposedly written by a Russian correspondent in St Petersburg — a certain 'Piotr Merskoff'. Merskoff focused especially on the posthumous status of Sophia Perovskaia, one of two women arrested for the murder and the only one to be executed (the other, Gesia Gel'fman, was pregnant, and her death sentence was commuted after she gave birth that autumn). As was standard for the way in which the Western European press operated in the late nineteenth century, many regional newspapers reprinted adaptations of this story during the following days.[46] The article claimed that:

---

[44] *Sheffield Daily Telegraph*, 19 March 1881.
[45] Janes and Houen, 'Introduction', p. 1.
[46] Versions of it appeared in at least 28 other English-language newspapers. A full list of the dates and papers in which I have been able to find versions of this story is as

Sophia Perowska [sic] has been elevated into a sort of St. Agnes. Her life has been written in the form of a religious romance, in which the most extraordinary virtues are attributed to her. She is worshipped as a martyr, and the nihilist faithful regard the clothes she wore and the ringlets which were cut from her head as so many religious relics. These objects have been distributed as talismans among the leaders of the party.

The article's writer went on to link this supposed propensity for making martyrs ('this species of dreamy mysticism') to 'the national temperament' of Russia. Because of this temperament, 'criminals who are constantly sent to the gallows are easily transformed by the popular imagination into heroes and martyrs, and their lives are surrounded with a help of legend which works on the mind of the masses'.[47] Of course, people were not actually hoarding Perovskaia's hair to use as talismans, and there was no *inherent* characteristic that predisposed Russians toward martyrology.

However, it is clear that this predisposition for martyrology was a received idea about Russia. While the author(s) of this article formulated a particularly striking and unequivocal correspondence between Russian revolutionaries and religious martyrs, that comparison was, in fact, common in Western media in the 1880s and beyond. Furthermore, as evidenced by the way in which this article was adapted and reproduced in the British press, we can see that it was an image that seems to have resonated with producers and consumers of contemporary mass media. Even more than a full year after the execution, the language being used in the press about martyrdom was remarkably stable, down to the anecdotes about the distribution of Perovskaia's clothes and hair, which were generalized as emblematic of a broader affective posture. 'A form of

follows. On 25 April, it appeared in the *Eastern Morning News, Northern Whig, Manchester Courier, Belfast Morning News* and the *Liverpool Echo*. On 26 April, it appeared in the *Staffordshire Sentinel, Dublin Daily Express* and the *East Anglian Daily Times*. On 27 April, it appeared in the *Buxton Herald* and the *Hartlepool Daily Mail*. On 28 April, it appeared in the *Banbury Advertiser* and the *Sutton Journal*. On 29 April, it appeared in the *Merthyr Telegraph and General Advertiser for the Iron Districts of South Wales*. On 30 April, it appeared in the *West Somerset Free Press, Jersey Independent and Daily Telegraph, Newcastle Guardian, South London Press, Staffordshire Sentinel* (again), *Rutland Echo and Leicestershire Advertiser, Sheerness Guardian and East Kent Advertiser, Potteries Examiner, Bridlington Free Press, Stroud Journal, Weston Mercury, Trowbridge Chronicle* and the *Hinckley News*. The *North Devon Journal* carried it on 5 May, and the *Times of India*, on 18 May.
[47] 'Russian Affairs', *London Evening Standard*, 23 April 1881. The original version of this article appeared in the Paris paper *Le Voltaire*. Piotr Merskoff, 'La Situation en Russia', *Le Voltaire*, 23 April 1881.

religious worship, too, keeps alive the flame' of nihilism, wrote the London *Times* in September 1882:

> [It] has its martyrs, its relics, and its shrines. [...] Photographs of Sophia Perovskaya [*sic*], bits of her prison dress and hair, are still kept sacred and shown with bated breath, while for hundreds of votaries the Semenovsky-square [*sic*], in which she was executed, has become a holy place.[48]

It is worth pointing out here how durable these kinds of images were in the British press. While writing in September 1906 about the case of accused terrorist Maria Spiridonova, a correspondent for *The Times* also described his strategy for enduring the interminable lengths of his visits to provincial Russians' homes: 'On such occasions, when gravelled from lack of matter in conversation, I profess eager interest in photographs and ask to see "the album".' Thus, he claimed to have 'discovered' that in families with student sons or '*Kursistka*' daughters,

> it ordinarily happens that 'the album' *par excellence* is a collection of photographs of — assassins. [...] The last album that I saw was the cherished possession of a damsel of 'sweet seventeen'. She called it her 'pantheon'. On the first page was a photograph of a painting which was entitled 'Prove thyself worthy', and which represented a girl thrusting into the hands of her lover a revolver with which he was to go forth and — assassinate. The second page was adorned with a sketch of a Roman in whom I was supposed to recognize — Brutus! Then followed photographs of Kalayeff, who assassinated the Grand Duke Serge, of Sozonoff, who assassinated Plehve, and of many others — assassins all...[49]

The correspondent's satirical tone presents a comedic inversion of the stories from 1881 — which in and of itself is indicative of a change in certain Western European attitudes toward Russian political culture around this time — but it nevertheless represents a continuity in the portrayal of revolutionary martyrdom in a Russian context, all the more notable given the dramatic political upheavals in Russia that occurred in between.

Irish Fenianism developed its martyrology earlier than Russian nihilism.[50] This was thanks to both contemporary events and to active

---

[48] *The Times*, 27 September 1882.
[49] 'Russia Revisited', *The Times*, 19 September 1906.
[50] In the sense of martyrology, the primary precursor to the nihilists would be the Decembrists, punished for their failed uprising against Russian autocracy in 1825, though they were not spoken about in the same way as Fenian precursors appear to have been.

claims made to a revolutionary lineage stretching back to the 1790s. In both aspects a single book was foundational: *Speeches from the Dock*, a compilation that sprang from a series of events that took place in 1867.

In the early part of that year, the acting leader of the Irish Republican Brotherhood, Thomas J. Kelly, spearheaded a short-lived and unsuccessful armed insurrection that came to be known as the Fenian Uprising. Several months later, a group of Fenians in Manchester attempted to spring Kelly and one of his collaborators from the prison van that was transporting them from a court appearance back to the jail. During the commotion of the rescue attempt, an English policeman was shot and killed (and both imprisoned Fenians escaped). Five men — four of whom had been part of the rescue attempt but none of whom had fired the shot that killed the policeman — were arrested and tried for the policeman's murder. Three of those men — William O'Meara Allen, Michael Larkin and William O'Brien — were hanged at the jail in Salford on 23 November 1867. Those three men 'were instantly transformed' into the 'Manchester Martyrs'; a commemorative funeral procession for the men (who had not been allowed a proper burial and were typically represented as devout Catholics) was held in Dublin in early December and attracted a crowd of 50,000 people.[51]

It was quickly obvious that the significance of the Manchester Martyrs reached beyond the small number of Irish nationalists who were members of the IRB or identified with Fenianism.[52] Kelly had been prescient when, after the failure of the Fenian Uprising, he urged his comrades to take heart: 'Did not Christianity commence by defeats? Did it not, like us, water the ground with the blood of its martyrs?'[53] *Speeches from the Dock* was published immediately after the events of November–December 1867, and it set speeches made by the Martyrs during their trial alongside those of a host of the most prominent Irish nationalists of decades past, such as Wolfe Tone and Robert Emmet. Its compilers were two brothers named Alexander Martin and Timothy Daniel Sullivan. Both were MPs and newspaper publishers who were nationalists but who were also critical of the 'physical force' tactics promoted by the IRB. However, they clearly saw the potential the Martyrs had for the Irish movement as a whole. *Speeches*

[51] Owen McGee, '"God Save Ireland"': Manchester-Martyr Demonstrations in Dublin, 1867–1916', *Éire-Ireland*, 36, 3–4, 2001, p. 43.

[52] Gary Owens, 'Constructing the Martyrs: The Manchester Executions and the Nationalist Imagination', in Lawrence W. McBride (ed.), *Images, Icons and the Irish Nationalist Imagination*, Dublin, 1999, pp. 18–36.

[53] Cited in Guy Beiner, 'Fenianism and the Martyrdom-Terrorism Nexus in Ireland before Independence', in Janes and Houen (eds), *Martyrdom and Terrorism*, p. 203.

from the Dock went through twenty-three editions in Ireland by the time it saw its first American edition in 1878; it was constantly in print and updated well into the twentieth century. In relation to the popular image of men like the Manchester Martyrs, scholars generally agree that 'no single book was more influential'.[54]

I have already mentioned Stepniak's 1882/83 book, *Underground Russia*, which compiled profiles and sketches by Stepniak of various Russian revolutionaries, many of whom he counted among his friends. His name recognition and influence — especially in Britain, where he moved in 1884 — was catalysed in large part by this one publication. *Underground Russia* began its life as a series of columns 'from a Russian patriot' in an Italian newspaper, but after it was published as a stand-alone volume in Italian, it was quickly translated and published in English and several other European languages, including Dutch, French, German, Hungarian and Swedish.[55] As with *Speeches from the Dock*, the popularity of *Underground Russia* helped codify particular ways of speaking about their respective revolutionary movements — though the two volumes' intended audiences and rhetorical styles differed in important ways.

In his own work, Stepniak described the Russian revolutionary ethos in religious terms similar to those used by the European press to discuss Perovskaia; Stepniak too told his readers that the 'tendency to become excited even to fanaticism, about certain things which would simply meet with approval or disapproval from a man of Western Europe' was an inherent characteristic of the 'Russian mind'.[56] Stepniak also explicitly called the figure of the Terrorist (he always capitalized its first letter) a martyr.[57] For all of that, in the preface to the second edition of his novel *The Career of a Nihilist*, Stepniak asserted that as both a 'witness of and participator in' the nihilist movement, his goal as a first-time novelist was 'to show in the full light of fiction the inmost heart and soul of these humanitarian enthusiasts, which whom devotion to a cause has attained the fervour of religion, without being a religion'.[58]

As was noted earlier, Stepniak reluctantly embraced the term 'nihilism', but this was because he felt that if he could build on received representations

---

[54] McGee, '"God Save Ireland"', p. 53; Beiner, 'Fenianism and the Martyrdom-Terrorism Nexus', p. 206.

[55] Cited in Scotto, 'The Terrorist as Novelist', pp. 104–05.

[56] Stepniak, *Underground Russia*, p. 6.

[57] Ibid., p. 40.

[58] Stepniak, *The Career of a Nihilist: A Novel*, 2nd edn, London, [1901], p. ix. Cited in James W. Hulse, *Revolutionists in London: A Study of Five Unorthodox Socialists*, Oxford, 1970, p. 41.

of revolutionary Russia, which came in large part from novels, he could show Europeans that a 'nihilist' was not a 'rare and wondrous beast' but rather, consonant with the revolutionary traditions of which Europeans were proud and therefore deserving of the public's support. According to the reports of his contemporaries, Stepniak's strategy seemingly worked. The éminence grise of anarchism Petr Kropotkin recalled that Stepniak's writings 'made a deep impression' on the English reading public. He remembered a lecture tour he took of the English provinces during which 'everyone' was asking him about one of Stepniak's recently published essays. 'Everyone read this essay, everyone suffered through it, everyone asked: "Is this really possible in Russia?" and concluded: "If I were in Russia, I would also be a 'nihilist' (i.e., a terrorist)."' He wrote that he had heard this final phrase 'thousands of times, from the calmest Englishmen, men and women: politicians known to the whole world, scientists whose names are repeated with reverence — people of all political parties and of all classes'.[59]

The Russian Marxist Lev Deutsch echoed this in his recollection of *Underground Russia*'s impact as 'a kind of revelation [...] for the Western European public'. They had imagined Russian revolutionaries as:

> fearsome conspirators who took oaths of loyalty and obedience to the leaders of their secret organizations on daggers, revolvers and dynamite, and then committed the most terrible crimes [...] in the imagination of Europeans, the Russian revolutionary was analogous to Carbonari, or even to a member of the Camorra or the mafia.

However, after reading Stepniak's book, they instead saw 'intelligent young men and young women appeared before European readers, although "somewhat carried away", but undoubtedly honest, selflessly giving themselves to what they consider just'. Even 'the most sceptical reader, the strictest critic' had to admit that Stepniak's representations were 'imbued with deep truth and sincerity'. In fact, Deutsch asserted, even those who, like himself, knew the people described in Stepniak's books personally 'must admit that Stepniak managed to give surprisingly truthful and accurate images' of them in his profiles.[60]

---

[59] 'Vospominaniia P. A. Kropotkina', in S. M. Stepniak-Kravchinskii, *Sobranie sochinenii, Chast'* 1, ed. S. A. Vengerov, St Petersburg, 1907, p. 23. The essay in question was titled 'Poor No. 39'.
[60] Lev Deich, *S. M. Kravchinskii*, Petrograd, 1919, p. 41.

While *Underground Russia* received a substantial number of positive reviews in the Western press, some took issue specifically with Stepniak's evocation of faith and religion. One unnamed correspondent, supposedly reporting from St Petersburg, complained that the book 'undertakes not only the bold task of whitewashing anarchic and revolutionary movements in general, but also the more difficult one of making their leaders pass before the spectator in the guise of martyrs or of saints'. He did concede that though 'Stepniak's heroism is a mock kind of thing at best, [...] his pictures of Nihilists are in a high degree vivid and realistic'. In the final analysis, he concluded that 'so long as the reader fancies he is perusing the life of a saint all goes appropriately, and it is only when he remembers the overdrawn picture is of an assassin that he arrives at anything like an adequate knowledge of the possibilities of Nihilist martyrology'.[61] As for determining whether a revolutionary individual should be seen as a saint or an assassin, that is, a 'good' nihilist or a 'bad' one, the *New York Times* called up the words of Stepniak himself:

Anybody, taking a good look at him, would say: 'There's a man overflowing with good nature; a warm-hearted, sympathetic fellow. He cannot be a Nihilist'. But that is the very sort of man to make a good Nihilist, according to the definition which Stepniak himself gives, for, as he puts it, the Nihilist is a man who, touched by the suffering of his people, feels impelled to espouse their cause and to make a martyr of himself, if needs be, to right their wrongs. He may do very bad things, but he does them because he is a very good man.[62]

How does all of this compare with *Speeches from the Dock,* which predated *Underground Russia* by some fifteen years but very much existed alongside it, given its protracted publishing history? First, *Speeches from the Dock* was explicitly for Irish readers. As its compilers wrote in the introduction:

We live under a government which claims to be just, liberal, and constitutional, yet against no other government in Christendom have the same number of protests been made within the same space of time. Not Poland, not Hungary, not Venetia, can point to such an unbroken succession of political martyrs.[63]

[61] 'The Martyrology of Nihilism', *The Globe*, 7 February 1883.
[62] 'Nihilist Stepniak Here', *New York Times*, 31 December 1890.
[63] T. D., A. M. and D. B. Sullivan, *Speeches from the Dock*, Providence, RI, 1878, p. 12.

Given that the collected speeches are those of 'the men who fill the foremost places in the ranks of Ireland's political martyrs', readers 'ow[ed] it to the brave men whose patriotism is attested in the addresses comprised in this volume, that the memory of their noble deeds shall not pass away, and that their names shall remain enshrined in the hearts of their countrymen'.[64] In contrast, Stepniak's target audience was clearly a non-Russian one; *Underground Russia* began with a lengthy explanation of what nihilism *actually* was, and Stepniak also emphasized 'the influence of Europe' and the uninterrupted 'communion of ideas between Russia and Europe' on the development of Russian revolutionary ideas throughout his introductory chapters.[65]

A second noticeable difference was how martyrdom is gendered in each work. Unlike the figures profiled by Stepniak, only men were included in *Speeches from the Dock*. This points to important differences in how martyrdom — and revolutionary activity in general — was gendered. We have seen how the European press discussed Sofia Perovskaia, and Stepniak's work struck a similar tone. Despite being 26 years old at the time of her execution, she was 'girlhood personified', beautiful, fond of children and an excellent nurse, he wrote. Yet she was also 'one of the most dreaded members of the Terrorist party [...]. What Titanic force was concealed under this serene appearance?' He also noted that regardless of how one felt about nihilism in general, one had to admit that 'there was one question in which Nihilism rendered great service to its country. It was the important question of woman. Nihilism recognized her as having equal rights with man'.[66] The subject of gender in Irish vs. Russian revolutionary movements deserves its own article but suffice to say that the 'woman question' was not part of the vocabulary or framing of any type of Irish nationalism at this time. For an example, we can look to the Ladies' Land League, which was active in 1881 and 1882 and carried out the work of the Irish National Land League after it was banned and its (male) leadership imprisoned. In 1881 the *Saturday Review* declared that 'revolutionary jargon in the mouths of women degenerates into unbecoming but harmless prattle'. Later that year, *The Times* summed up its attitude toward the Ladies' Land League with what one scholar has characterized as the 'dominant view' in the British press at the time: 'When treason is reduced to fighting behind

---

All citations in this article from *Speeches from the Dock* are from this 23rd Dublin edition/ first American edition.

[64] Ibid., p. 11.
[65] *Underground Russia*, p. 13.
[66] Ibid., pp. 115–16, 8.

petticoats and pinafores, it is unlikely to do much mischief.'[67] The views of some male Land Leaguers were apparently not too different from those of the British press. Anna Parnell, the sister of Charles Stewart Parnell who was tasked with steering Land League activities while its male leadership was in prison wrote in her memoirs that trying to regulate the hostile and disorganized conduct of the men in the Land League 'was enough to make the stoutest heart quail'.[68] For his part, Michael Davitt (who was among the imprisoned League leadership) presented a view of the Ladies' Land League that was closer to Stepniak's representation of women like Perovskaia and Zasulich.[69] Women like Anna Parnell, Davitt wrote, were 'in certain emergencies, more dangerous to despotism than men. They have more courage, through having less scruples, when and where their better instincts are appealed to by a militant and just cause in a fight against a mean foe'. He too attributed an inherent feminine quality to the willingness of such a woman to sacrifice herself to a 'just cause', though unlike Stepniak he did not emphasize the contrast but rather the harmony between her exterior appearance and her interior resolve:

> The fight was to save the homes of Ireland — the sacred, domestic domain of woman's moral supremacy in civilized society, while the enemy was the system which had ruined tens of thousands of Irish girls, morally and otherwise, in evictions and in consequent misery and wrong.[70]

More directly related to the skirmishing campaign, one trope that appears (especially in the American press) is that of 'Bridget', the single female Irish émigré working as a domestic servant who, as a collective, was bankrolling Irish political violence with her donations.[71] Niall Whelehan's study of Fenian political violence in transnational perspective describes how these women were represented as, on the one hand, the backbone of Fenian fundraising efforts, without which skirmishing would not have

---

[67] Cited in Michael de Nie, *The Eternal Paddy: Irish Identity and the British Press, 1798–1882*, Madison, WI, 2004, pp. 242–43.

[68] Anna Parnell, *The Tale of a Great Sham*, ed. Dana Hearne, Dublin, 1986, p. 90.

[69] Margaret Ward, *Unmanageable Revolutionaries: Women and Irish Nationalism*, London, 1995, pp. 13–14, 17.

[70] Michael Davitt, *The Fall of Feudalism in Ireland; or, The Story of the Land League Revolution*, London, 1904, p. 299.

[71] Demographically, it is worth noting that 'Irish immigration to the United States was distinctive for its equal sex balance. Irish women migrated in much higher proportions than their European counterparts and many left home unmarried'. Whelehan, *The Dynamiters*, p. 234.

been possible, and on the other, as dim-witted dupes being taken advantage of by 'perfidious patriots' who were stealing their money for hopeless endeavours. Thus, in his words: 'Paradoxically, Bridget was both victim and villain.'[72] There is no neat equivalent to this Bridget in the Russian context.

A final major difference between *Speeches from the Dock* and *Underground Russia* was the literary aspirations — or lack thereof — of each volume. As Peter Scotto has pointed out, even in its planning stages, Stepniak was attuned to the novelistic nature of his material; as he wrote in a letter to his wife, Fanny, at the end of 1881, *Underground Russia* 'will make really good material for a future historian or novelist'.[73] Stepniak did indeed publish a novel titled *The Career of a Nihilist* in 1889, which — as was common for novels about 'nihilists' published in this era — was reviewed and evaluated not necessarily for its literary qualities but rather for the information it could impart to readers. A typical recommendation noted that while it was a work of fiction, it was nonetheless 'very instructive' for 'anyone who wishes to understand the Russian question [...] for it is the best and most vivid picture of the innermost thoughts and feelings of the men and women who devote their activity and their lives to the cause of their country'.[74] Indeed, after Stepniak's death, his friend (and subject of one of the profiles in *Underground Russia*) Vera Zasulich noted that Stepniak's dedication to explaining 'nihilism' a European audience meant that he was prevented 'from concentrating on the literary activity that gave him pleasure and where, probably, he could have achieved a lot'.[75]

On the other hand, the Sullivan brothers promised that in the pages of their book 'little more will be found than a correct report of the addresses delivered, under certain peculiar circumstances, by the group of Irishmen whose names are given on the titlepage'.[76] Although the book does contain journalistic passages written by the Sullivans that provide necessary context for the speeches, it is indeed the speeches that are emphasized — typically without additional analysis. Historian Guy Beiner has noted that though they were nationalists, the Sullivans had been critics of physical force nationalism. However, after the execution of the Manchester

---

[72] Ibid., pp. 234, 236.
[73] Cited in Scotto, 'The Terrorist as Novelist', p. 105. See also, E. Taratuta, *Podpol'naia Rossiia: sud'ba knigi S. M. Stepniak-Kravchinskogo*, Moscow, 1967, pp. 49–93.
[74] *Free Russia*, 1, June 1890, p. 20.
[75] Vera Zasulich, *Vospominaniia*, Moscow, 1931 <http://az.lib.ru/z/zasulich_w_i/text_1919_vospominania.shtml> [accessed 21 May 2023].
[76] *Speeches from the Dock*, p. 8.

Martyrs, they 'came to recognize the popularity of pro-Fenian sentiment and its marketing potential', eventually leading to the creation of *Speeches from the Dock*, which, as we have seen, was extremely successful.[77]

Ultimately, the differences between these two works represent an example of the different yet similar roles constructions of martyrdom in the Irish and Russian contexts played as elements of a broader, dynamic and complex information ecosystem. The comparison between the two revolutionary movements became even more acute in the spring of 1882, when a particularly shocking pair of murders set off a renewed blurring of terminology.

The Phoenix Park murders and the tightening of nihilism's discursive grip
On the evening of 6 May 1882, the newly appointed chief secretary for Ireland, Lord Frederick Cavendish, and the under-secretary for Ireland, Thomas H. Burke, were stabbed to death while walking home through Dublin's Phoenix Park. The Phoenix Park murders, as they came to be called, were carried out by several members of a small breakaway IRB group called the Invincibles. They had formed to advocate — and practise — political assassination as a revolutionary tactic. Leaving the scene of the Phoenix Park crime, the perpetrators made sure to notify the press of their actions. '[One of them] went to the *Express* newspaper office. The card he put in its mailbox (and those of the *Irish Times*, *The Irishman*, and the *Freeman's Journal* the following day), claimed responsibility for the murders. It read: "Executed by order of the Irish Invincibles".'[78] Nationalist leaders like Parnell and Davitt quickly denounced the murders, but the killings outraged English public opinion at a crucial moment when Prime Minister William Gladstone had been close to dropping a series of coercive laws that had characterized England's rule over Ireland since the 1833 Suppression of Disturbances Act. The murders thus forced Gladstone to reverse course, much to the chagrin of Parnell.

Coverage of the Phoenix Park murders in the English and Irish press again demonstrated both the outsized role of the nihilist in the European imagination and Irish ambivalence towards it. For example, the Fenian-aligned *Irishman* — recipient of one of the Invincibles' calling cards — explicitly distanced itself from the murders by reminding readers that not only had the paper 'week after week, during many months [...] been

[77] Beiner, 'Fenianism and the Martyrdom-Terrorism Nexus', p. 205.
[78] Julie Kavanagh, *The Irish Assassins: Conspiracy, Revenge, and the Phoenix Park Murders That Stunned Victorian England*, New York, 2021, p. 157; 'The Phoenix Park Murders', *The Times*, 19 February 1883.

incessant in reprobating assassination', but also by insisting that the Irish cause was not to be confused with anything Russian. Ireland's 'cause was exceptional, pure and sacred: not to be confounded with Continental plots, not to be dragged down with bloody hands to the soiling slough of Russian Nihilism'.[79] At a meeting convened in suburban Dublin to discuss the murders, the *Irish Times* quoted one participant as declaring that:

> Other nations should see that the Irish people were loud in their detestation and protestation against this dreadful crime which was thoroughly un-Irish. It was a crime Nihilistic in its object, which [was] totally opposed to the designs and aspirations of the people of this country.

Therefore, he believed, the crime had to have been 'committed by some foreign desperadoes'.[80] Foreign European papers also made strikingly similar comparisons, as reported in the Anglophone press. 'A deed which in all respects resembles the Nihilist crimes in Russia', wrote one Austrian newspaper; the French *Journal des Débats* claimed the crime surpassed any previously perpetrated by Nihilists.[81]

In English and Irish unionist press coverage, it was not uncommon to see references to 'Irish Nihilists' or 'Irish Nihilism' in the aftermath of Phoenix Park.[82] 'Like their foreign exemplars, [they] are determined to work by terror', asserted the *Birmingham Daily Post*.[83] On the other hand, a unionist paper like the Dublin *Daily Express* opined that not even a Russian Nihilist would have stooped so low as to 'shed [...] the blood of a perfectly inoffensive gentleman' such as Lord Cavendish. The *Shields Daily News* took that idea even further and opened its coverage of the Phoenix Park murders with the statement that they 'transcended in turpitude' even the 'the foulest of the foul deeds perpetrated by the Russian Nihilists'. While popular outrage over the murders is not surprising, the fact that the reference point for the heinousness of these events was so frequently (and specifically) nihilism speaks to its discursive grip. The *Shields Daily News* clearly felt it was being generous when it noted the power this comparison

[79] 'Ireland and Assassination', *The Irishman*, 13 May 1882.

[80] 'The Blackrock Township', *Irish Times*, 11 May 1882.

[81] *Irish Times*, 9 May 1882; 'Foreign Opinion on the Murders in Dublin', *St. James's Gazette*, 8 May 1882.

[82] See, for example, 'Reception of the News at Home and Abroad', *St. James Gazette*, 8 May 1882; 'The Murders in Phoenix Park, Dublin', *Morning Post*, 9 May 1882; 'News of the Day', *Birmingham Daily Post and Journal*, 8 May 1882, and the *Daily Express* (Dublin), 8 May 1882: 'English Radicalism denounces its officials. Irish Nihilism murders them.'

[83] 'News of the Day', *Birmingham Daily Post and Journal*, 8 May 1882.

must have had over the imaginations of the perpetrators of the crime themselves:

> Irish malcontents have not the same excuse for outrage as the Russian, since no such grinding political oppression is or ever has been in modern times exercised in Ireland, as that under which all subjects of Russia groan. But we will waive this consideration, and suppose that some Irishmen may in their own minds conceive themselves to be suffering under the same intolerable tyranny as the Russians or the Poles.[84]

At this point, clearly, no one considered the Invincibles — five were eventually hanged and a further eight imprisoned for the crime — to be martyrs for an Irish cause. They were never included in the later editions of *Speeches from the Dock*.[85]

Why was there increased reference to so-called Irish Nihilism in the case of the Phoenix Park murders? The obvious difference is that they were successful as assassinations, whereas most of the acts of 'skirmishing' violence did not do significant damage to their targets (though they did harm or kill bystanders in some cases). The murders also differed from 'skirmishing' in other quantifiable ways, one of which was the weapon used to enact the violence: the notable skirmishing incidents of the preceding year were enacted with dynamite, whereas the Phoenix Park assassins had used surgical knives. This aspect of the attack, in combination with its brazenness (Cavendish and Burke had been attacked in daylight), seemed to be what increased the comparisons to nihilists. While Alexander II was killed with explosives, some high-profile acts of Russian political violence had been carried out with knives, notably Stepniak's slaying of Mezentsev. In his memoirs Tikhomirov somewhat snarkily discussed how Stepniak and the other revolutionaries who planned the murder of Mezentsev had specifically wanted to attack him with a knife because it was deemed more 'correct' than using explosives or a gun. (He further claimed that Stepniak wanted to behead Mezentsev with a sabre, but that this idea was quickly abandoned because Stepniak was not tall enough to achieve the necessary angle.)[86] Despite the fact that it took seven attempts for Russian revolutionaries to assassinate Alexander II, something about the seemingly

---

[84] 'The Dublin Tragedy', *Shields Daily News*, 9 May 1882.
[85] See for example, T. D., A. M. and D. B. Sullivan, *Speeches from the Dock, or Protests of Irish Patriotism*, new edition, ed. Seán ua Ceallaigh, Dublin, 1945.
[86] 'The circle [of revolutionaries] already had little faith in revolvers, and the dagger seemed more correct [*vernee*]'. Tikhomirov, *Vospominaniia*, pp. 157–60.

efficient brutality of a knife attack called to mind the Russian case. This is evidence of our discursive chimera again. While Russian political violence was neither more efficient nor more brutal than other contemporary strands of terrorism, and no more likely to employ knives, by 1882 it had nevertheless become the *ne plus ultra* of terrorism in Victorian print culture.

Conclusion

A few years after the publication of *Underground Russia*, a conservative British journalist named William Earl Hodgson privately published a small pamphlet titled *A Night with a Nihilist* (complete with skull and crossbones gracing the top of the title page).[87] In it, he described his efforts to arrange an invitation to a meeting with 'S—' (i.e., Stepniak) at the house of writer and Fabian Society co-founder Edward R. Pease. Hodgson was disappointed by his sight of Stepniak:

> He was not an ideal nihilist at all. He was not a slender, fierce-visaged person of lean and hungry look, in the restlessness of whose small sharp eyes you could catch an indication of dire intent to stab you, or to poison you, or to explode you.

Rather, Stepniak 'seemed to be a man thoroughly capable of enjoying a good dinner'. Hodgson was even more taken aback when Stepniak told him that 'we are not Nihilists' at all; though 'we don't object' to the 'nickname given to us by the thick-headed Saxon'. He nevertheless listened to and reported on Stepniak's thoughts on the situation in the Russian Empire, and by the end of the pamphlet, he has reasoned that there is truth in the 'nihilist' stance; a man as worldly and sagacious as Stepniak was 'not likely to become passionate over a figment'.[88]

This article has argued that *fin de siècle* European mass media discourses around a host of concepts associated with terrorism formed a discursive chimera that did in fact make many commentators passionate over what were essentially figments, to borrow Hodgson's turn of phrase.

---

[87] There is little biographical information about Hodgson available, but he wrote for a wide variety of popular publications, including the *Morning Post*, the *Pall Mall Gazette*, *Cornhill Magazine*, the *Daily Mail* and the *Spectator* — most often on the topic of angling. W. Earl Hodgson, *Trout Fishing*, London, 1904, pp. xiv–xv.

[88] W. Earl Hodgson, *A Night with a Nihilist*, Cupar, 1886, pp. 6–8, 18. It is worth noting that I could not find any equivalent account of someone being disappointed when a Fenian they met did not live up to the physical stereotypes they had in mind.

To a deliberate extent, I have taken a global approach to the examination of two European revolutionary traditions, in the spirit of one recent definition of global history as a perspective that looks at 'parallel and simultaneous processes in different arenas and the probability of their synchronization'.[89] While Russian and Irish revolutionaries were not linked by shared goals or networks, they were very much linked in and by the popular imagination of producers and consumers of print culture. Imagined connections like the 'union of Nihilists and Fenians' feared by several newspapers in the early 1880s in turn shaped the very real meaning(s) of concepts like terrorism and martyrdom. This is because these connections were all part of a broader information ecosystem made up of parts that did not operate in isolation but rather acted on one another, sometimes with surprising consequences.

Hodgson — who portrayed himself as a staunch political conservative in his *Night with a Nihilist* — ultimately concluded that 'the Nihilists are aglow with the same spirit that would send the British Tories into rebellion' if Britain was threatened with autocracy.[90] This language very much echoes that of the letter Stepniak addressed to the People's Will Executive Committee before the publication of *Underground Russia*: if Europeans understood that so-called nihilists were 'the men of '93 and '89 in France to whom all Europe gives pride of place', they would whole-heartedly support the Russian revolutionary cause. The popular image of the terrorist and the popular image of the martyr could, depending on the specific historical context, become two sides of the same coin. To observe this helps underscore an important and revealing aspect of information transmission and transformation: that rather than obscuring meaning, disagreements or confusion or slippage over language can actually create it.

While Stepniak never hid the fact that he embraced the label of nihilism despite his agreement that it was inaccurate terminology, it was more conservative Russian commentators like Tikhomirov who were the keenest to point out the ironies of British commentary like Hodgson's. Tikhomirov transcribed in his diary a May 1890 letter he received from the self-styled 'M.P. for Russia', Olga Novikova, who was a prominent fixture in the London émigré colony: 'The cursed Stepniak stirs up everyone and everything in England against everything that is dear to Russia. Just woe,

[89] Matthias Middell, 'Introduction: European Perspectives in Global History? Recent Development in Practicing Global History across the European Continent', in Matthias Middell (ed.), *The Practice of Global History: European Perspectives*, London, 2019, p. 1.

[90] Hodgson, *A Night with a Nihilist*, p. 19.

woe.'[91] The conservative newspaper editor Mikhail Katkov criticized the English media's seemingly tight embrace of Stepniak as an authoritative voice on all things Russian. In an 1885 article for his paper, *Moskovskie vedomosti*, he castigated recent articles in English publications such as the *Westminster Review* that had positively cited Stepniak's writings as the last word on Russian affairs. With his characteristic grandiloquence, Katkov accused both the English press and the English reading public of engaging with Russia in bad faith due to their own taste for spectacle over substance:

> Is it possible to utter the kind of absurdities about Russia that are usually told by indiscriminate [*beskontrol'nye*] travellers about some tribe in Central Africa? The British have every opportunity to know exactly what is happening in Russia, through their embassy, their consuls, through English subjects who have been living with us for a long time, through many of their compatriots who deliberately came to Russia for a thorough long-term study of its life, and finally, even through the more serious 'special correspondents' of their newspapers. But news received through these more or less reliable means is obviously not to the taste of the English public and the English journalists who conform to that taste. They prefer to fraternize with a gang of murderers who fled Russia...[92]

In the crescendo of his article, Katkov wondered how the English would react if, 'in our newspapers, we not only published 'sketches' [*etiudy*] about England written by Irish dynamiters [*dinamitchiki*], but also coordinated our way of acting with regard to England to these very "sketches"?' He concluded:

> They would raise loud shouts of protest and condemnation, just as they condemn the American press, which places the articles of American Fenians in its columns. And the Irish, who are fighting for the faith, nationality [*natsional'nost'*], and economic well-being of their motherland, deserve in any case more credence [*doverie*] than the 'practical nihilists' like 'Stepniak', who recognize neither nationality, nor state, nor property, nor laws, nor any obligations of conscience and honour whatsoever.[93]

---

[91] Tikhomirov, *Vospominaniia*, pp. 448–49.
[92] M. N. Katkov, "'Slabost' Rossii," iavstvuiushchaia iz proizvedenii angliiskikh "dzhentl'menov pechati" i razoblachenii "mistera Stepniaka'", *Moskovskie vedomosti*, 226, 17 August 1885 <http://az.lib.ru/k/katkow_m_n/text_1885_slabost_rosii.shtml> [accessed 24 May 2023].
[93] Ibid.

This was something of a party line for conservative Russian journalists and publicists, both inside the country and in emigration, and was particularly noticeable in the British press. In a piece for the *Pall Mall Gazette*, Olga Novikova also explicitly invoked the irony of English discourse about terrorism in Russia in relation to the English position on Ireland:

> It was not long ago, however, that supreme disdain was displayed whenever Russian dynamitards were discussed. We Russians were dogmatically advised to listen to the voice of such men as Krapotkin [*sic*] and Stepniak. 'Only tyranny', exclaimed some uninvited judges, 'could breed Nihilism'. [...] But now you almost all talk and write like sensible Russians. The moral efficacy of dynamite must really be great. It has not secured Home Rule, but it has converted Englishmen to Russian views of the subject of murder and assassination.
>
> Theoretically, England's policy in Ireland is Russian. [...] A few years ago English liberals used to say that if Nihilists blew up railway trains in Russia the one specific was the grant of a Constitution. Nowadays, when an Invincible stabs a Minister, instead of granting a new Constitution, they suspend the old one.[94]

Of course, neither Tikhomirov, nor Katkov, nor Novikova were notable advocates for the cause of Irish nationalism in and of itself. Stepniak expressed sympathetic views toward the Irish cause but he also downplayed the revolutionary potential of Irish political violence; he wrote in early 1882 that there was 'no need to resort to violence' in the Irish case 'precisely because the free expression of the individual is not suppressed by violence' under British law as it was in the Russian Empire.[95] This (mutual) lack of understanding was ultimately — paradoxically — a generative one. Because of this agglomeration of concepts and terminology, these seemingly unconnected movements were fused into a discursive chimera that irrevocably shaped what the reading public knew — or thought they knew — about terrorism and martyrdom at the end of the nineteenth century.

[94] 'Madame Olga de Novikoff, née de Kiréef', 'The Russianization of England — I', *Pall Mall Gazette*, 15 January 1885.
[95] Cited in Taratuta, *Podpol'naia Rossiia*, pp. 32–33.

The Martyrdom of Illness: Mariia Spiridonova in Siberian Imprisonment, 1906–17

SALLY A. BONIECE

In the summer of 1906, Mariia Spiridonova, the controversial twenty-one-year-old Socialist Revolutionary (SR) assassin lauded by the opponents of autocratic tsarism and demonized by the tsar's supporters, was transported with five other convicted female SR terrorists by railway from Moscow to the Nerchinsk penal complex in eastern Siberia. Spiridonova and four of her five companions on this journey into Siberian imprisonment had either killed or attempted to kill government officials whom the SR party accused of oppressive actions against helpless civilians; the sixth woman had made bombs for terrorist operations. Although Spiridonova and three of the other women had been sentenced to death by courts-martial, the tsarist government commuted their sentences to penal servitude for life. Only Spiridonova's name, however, was known across the Russian Empire, because two liberal newspapers had published her letter describing the physical abuse that she suffered from police and Cossacks during her arrest and initial detention; only Spiridonova had become a national martyr of the revolution.

By striking down the perpetrators of state violence against the people, Spiridonova and her SR terrorist peers in the revolution of 1905–07 were emulating an earlier generation of male and female populist terrorists in the 1870s and 1880s, the legends of whose heroic deeds pervaded the radical subculture of Russian society. In the tradition of its predecessor the People's Will, the populist organization that assassinated the tsar in 1881, the SR party justified the tactic of political terror as fulfilling three purposes: to awaken the revolutionary consciousness of the people; to threaten the tsarist state with retaliation for further repressive measures; and to force concessions from the state by disrupting the social order.

Sally A. Boniece is Professor of History at Frostburg State University, Maryland.

Slavonic and East European Review, 102, 1, 2024   doi:10.1353/see.00005

Moreover, SR propaganda reinforced the populist myth of terrorists as selfless avengers, portraying SR terrorists as heroes and heroines who willingly sacrificed their own lives to liberate Russia's peasants and workers from the immiseration, inequality and injustice of autocratic rule. SR terrorists set out to murder notorious representatives of tsarist authoritarianism fully expecting themselves to die on the gallows. 'From a moral-philosophical viewpoint', wrote a member of the SR party's central terrorist group, the Combat Organization, 'the act of killing must at the same time be an act of self-sacrifice'.[1]

Tuberculosis, the chronic illness that afflicted Spiridonova periodically throughout her life, was incorporated into the myth of her martyrdom when her liberal defence attorney publicly asserted it to have been caused by her police beating. Both at her court-martial and during her railway journey across the empire to Siberia, Spiridonova exhibited symptoms of an advanced stage of the disease. Behind the prison walls of the Nerchinsk complex, the female SR terrorists formed a 'commune' or collective of political prisoners that endeavoured to teach socialism to fellow inmates by personal example, a prison tradition established by earlier generations of convicted revolutionaries. Only Spiridonova among the women 'politicals' took no active part in upholding the prison commune, but rather was isolated by invalidism throughout her eleven years in the penal complex, according to memoirs written by her prison comrades.

Spiridonova, denied the martyr's death on the scaffold that she had anticipated for her terrorist act in 1906, seemingly succumbed to the martyrdom of chronic illness in Siberian imprisonment. Nevertheless, the fall of the tsarist autocracy in February 1917, in liberating Spiridonova from penal servitude, simultaneously restored her health, her energy and her drive to engage in radical politics. Over the next sixteen months, Spiridonova joined the Left SRs in fomenting and supporting a second revolution of 1917 that brought the Soviet government to power. Arrested by Soviet authorities after she turned against Bolshevik/Communist policy

[1]   Christopher Ely, *Underground Petersburg: Radical Populism, Urban Space and the Tactics of Subversion in Reform-Era Russia*, DeKalb, IL, 2016, pp. 231–64; Marina Mogil´ner, *Mifologiia 'podpol´nogo cheloveka': Radikal´nyi mikrokosm v Rossii nachala XX veka kak predmet semioticheskogo analiza*, Moscow, 1999, pp. 8–12, 27–30; Manfred Hildermeier, *The Russian Socialist Revolutionary Party before the First World War*, Münster, 2000, pp. 52–56; Susan Morrissey, 'Terrorism and *Ressentiment* in Revolutionary Russia', *Past and Present*, 246, 1, February 2020, pp. 191–226 (pp. 198–210); V. M. Chernov, 'Terroristicheskii element v nashei programme', in O. V. Budnitskii (ed.), *'Krov´ po sovesti': Terrorizm v Rossii. Dokumenty i biografiii*, Rostov, 1994, pp. 127–41; V. M. Zenzinov, *Perezhitoe*, New York, 1953, p. 108.

in the summer of 1918, Spiridonova spent the remaining two decades of her life in imprisonment and exile, racked by many more bouts of her disease. Spiridonova's pattern of revolutionary behaviour therefore alternated between active and passive self-sacrifice, the tuberculosis that enhanced her legend of martyrdom apparently waxing and waning according to the degree of her personal freedom.

The myth of Spiridonova's martyrdom
Mariia Aleksandrovna Spiridonova, the daughter of a non-hereditary noble, entered the pantheon of Russia's revolutionary martyrs in early 1906 after she fatally wounded a local district security chief with a revolver at the Borisoglebsk railway station in Tambov province. In her subsequent deposition to Tambov court authorities, Spiridonova declared that she had taken it upon herself to carry out the death sentence pronounced on her victim, Gavriil Nikolaevich Luzhenovskii, by the Tambov SR committee 'for his criminal flogging to death and excessive torturing of peasants' as a leader of punitive expeditions against rebellious villages in the Tambov countryside.[2] One of nearly two hundred acts of SR 'individual terror' committed in the Russian Empire during the revolution of 1905-07,[3] Spiridonova's assassination of Luzhenovskii in January 1906 was in fact preceded by the terrorist actions of the five women destined to become her comrades in Siberian imprisonment. Initially, as with the numerous earlier acts of political violence against tsarist officials, the fatal shooting of Luzhenovskii received no more than a mention in the national press. In the following month, however, the Spiridonova case gained notoriety across the country when two recently established liberal newspapers with national circulations published a letter that Spiridonova had written to her SR comrades from Tambov prison.

   Spiridonova's prison letter to the Tambov SRs described in dramatic detail not only her intentional stalking and killing of Luzhenovskii, but also the brutal circumstances of her arrest and initial detention in Borisoglebsk and Tambov, the provincial capital. While stating outright that police and Cossacks had stripped her, burnt her with cigarettes and beaten her until she was delirious, Spiridonova more obliquely insinuated that a Cossack officer had raped her as well.[4] Readers' responses published

[2] *Rus'*, no. 27, 12 February 1906.
[3] M. I. Leonov, *Esery v 1905–07 gg.*, Samara, 1992, p. 23.
[4] The letter in its entirety was published in *Rus'*, no. 27, 12 February 1906; excerpts were published in *Nasha zhizn'*, no. 368, 12 February 1906. For a full analysis of Spiridonova's letter and the public reaction to it, see Sally A. Boniece, 'The Spiridonova Case, 1906:

in one liberal newspaper over the next several weeks — whether from workers, peasants, university students, noblewomen or military officers — were united in decrying the abuse of Spiridonova's youth, gentility and gender by agents of the government.[5] Whereas a monarchist newspaper in Tambov labelled Spiridonova a 'human monster' and a conservative national newspaper judged her to be 'a sick soul, perhaps stunned by her own crime and the preparations for it', the liberal press extolled Spiridonova as 'a pure, virginal being, a flower of spiritual beauty that only the highest culture of Russia could produce', tragically fallen 'into the shaggy paws of brutally repulsive, brutally malicious, brutally salacious orangutans'.[6] V. E. Vladimirov, an investigative reporter sent by a liberal national newspaper to Tambov to ferret out additional information about the Spiridonova case, published a series of sensationalist articles that contrasted the courage and refinement of the terrorist Spiridonova with the callous cruelty of Russian officialdom.[7]

Thus Spiridonova, who had assassinated Luzhenovskii to save the Tambov peasants from his cruelty, gained national recognition as a martyr-heroine, but not always for the reasons that she and the SR party preferred. Breaking with the usual SR policy of concealing the identity of terrorists,[8] the Tambov SRs had forwarded Spiridonova's prison letter to a liberal newspaper one month after her arrest to propagandize her self-sacrifice on behalf of the revolution. 'Our personal feelings [about publicizing the case] had to be overcome, and however difficult it was to bring a comrade's sufferings and sores to light, we did this... and did this, as it turned out, not in vain', Tambov SR leader Stepan Nikolaevich Sletov wrote in a pamphlet later that year. 'The case of M. A. Spiridonova did not go unnoticed — it resounded as a loud slap in the face of despotism. The name of our comrade became a symbol of suffering Russia, a symbol of struggle to the end.' Yet Sletov's stated purpose in publishing his pamphlet was to refute publicly, at Spiridonova's request, the Vladimirov articles serialized in the liberal

Terror, Myth and Martyrdom', in Anthony Anemone (ed.), *Just Assassins: The Culture of Terrorism in Russia*, Evanston, IL, 2010, pp. 127–62.

    [5] See *Rus'*, nos. 28–46, 14 February–4 March 1906.

    [6] *Tambovskie gubernskie vedomosti*, no. 39, 19 February 1906; *Novoe vremia*, no. 10746, 13 February 1906; *Nasha zhizn'*, no. 388, 8 March 1906.

    [7] Vladimirov's seven articles were published in *Rus'* between 7 and 18 March 1906; shortly thereafter, they were collected and published, along with additional letters that Spiridonova wrote from prison to the Tambov SR committee, in V. Vladimirov, *Mariia Spiridonova*, Moscow, 1906.

    [8] This was a rule of the SR Combat Organization. See Boris Savinkov, *Vospominaniia terrorista*, Kharkov, 1926, p. 60.

press, which Sletov disparaged as 'pulp literature' because they omitted the socialist convictions that had inspired Spiridonova's act of terrorism.[9]

Defending Spiridonova before a Tambov court-martial in March, a prominent liberal attorney eloquently compared the 'oppressed, desecrated and sick Spiridonova' to 'sick and desecrated Russia' and warned the judges that should she receive the death sentence — 'the entire country will flinch from the anguish of state terror'.[10] After the court-martial sentenced Spiridonova to execution by hanging, her attorney informed the liberal press of a prison doctor's testimony that she had developed 'severe' tuberculosis 'as a result of her tortures' at the time of her arrest; the attorney also described his client as continually coughing into a blood-stained handkerchief during her trial.[11] Within a month, the tsarist government followed its standard practice in cases of female political crime and commuted Spiridonova's death sentence to penal servitude for life, making reference to 'her incurable illness — tuberculosis of the lungs'.[12] Spiridonova was then moved from Tambov prison to the Butyrka transit prison in Moscow, where five other female SR terrorists tried and sentenced in 1905–06 were already waiting to be dispatched to imprisonment in eastern Siberia. Throughout the women's three-week railway journey in the summer of 1906 to their final destination, the Nerchinsk penal complex, Spiridonova was feverish and coughing up blood.

Illness as Spiridonova's martyrdom
Frequently during her adult lifetime, Spiridonova was beset by resurgent episodes of pulmonary tuberculosis, the so-called white plague associated with rapid industrialization in the modern era.[13] One historian has suggested that the tubercle bacillus infected 'a near-totality of the population of many large European cities' around the turn of the twentieth century; however,

[9] S. Nechetnyi (S. N. Sletov), *Spekuliatsiia na chuzhikh ranakh*, n. pl., n.d., pp. 100–03. The time of composition and publication is clear from the contents of the pamphlet. Sletov, a Tambov native, was a member of the SR Central Committee.

[10] *Rus'*, no. 60, 18 March 1906.

[11] *Rech'*, no. 19, 13 March 1906.

[12] Gosudarstvennyi Arkhiv Rossiiskoi Federatsii (hereafter, GARF), f. 102, op. 203, d. 8, ch. 58, 2. 2, l. 32. After the public outcry against the state's execution of Sof 'ia Perovskaia of the People's Will in 1881, the government did not hang another woman for a political crime until Prime Minister P. A. Stolypin introduced a law on field courts-martial in August 1906. See A. Izmailovich, 'Iz proshlogo', in O. V. Budnitskii (ed.), *Zhenshchiny-terroristki v Rossii*, Rostov, 1996, pp. 325–423 (p. 367), and 'Primechaniia', in Budnitskii (ed.), *Zhenshchiny-terroristki v Rossii*, pp. 597–621 (p. 608, n. 13).

[13] René and Jean Dubos, *The White Plague: Tuberculosis, Man and Society*, Boston, MA, 1952, pp. 197–207.

then as now, 10 per cent or less of those exposed to the bacillus actually contracted the disease.[14] In Russia's industrial centres such as Moscow, St Petersburg and Odesa, the mortality rates for tuberculosis between 1900 and 1913 resembled the mortality rates for the disease in the major urban areas of Europe.[15]

Spiridonova's tuberculosis seems to have first manifested itself during her detention in Tambov prison in early 1906, prompting the allegation that her beating by police was the cause of her disease. She may nonetheless have suffered an earlier occurrence of it in 1902, when she withdrew from secondary school on the grounds of 'ill health'.[16] Indeed, Spiridonova's symptoms of fever, delirium, pain, emaciation and coughing up blood, as observed by her five terrorist companions on their train journey to Siberia in the summer of 1906, were indicative of an advanced state of tuberculosis.[17] Quite possibly the bacillus had been reactivated by her detention in Tambov, for the incidence of tuberculosis in tsarist prisons soared after the mass arrests of 1905–07 filled them beyond capacity.[18]

Her long history as a victim of chronic illness further illuminates Spiridonova's choices and behaviour while providing a fascinating dimension to her myth. In the nineteenth and early twentieth centuries, individuals diagnosed with tuberculosis or other such diseases 'became, in part, that diagnosis', a historian of medicine wrote; such persons began 'framing themselves and their behavior' in terms of their illness.[19] 'One

[14] David S. Barnes, *The Making of a Social Disease: Tuberculosis in Nineteenth-Century France*, Berkeley and Los Angeles, CA, 1995, p. 4. See also, Hans L. Rieder, *Epidemiologic Basis of Tuberculosis Control*, Paris and Berne, 1999, p. 44. Approximately one quarter of the world's population today is infected with tuberculosis; persons with latent tuberculosis have a 5–10 per cent lifetime risk of contracting the disease. 'Tuberculosis', World Health Organization, 7 November 2023 <https://www.who.int/news-room/fact-sheets/detail/tuberculosis> [accessed 25 January 2024].

[15] Peter K. Yablonskii, Aleksandr A. Vizel, Vladimir B. Galkin and Marina V. Shulgina, 'Tuberculosis in Russia: Its History and Its Status Today', *American Journal of Respiratory and Critical Care Medicine*, 191, 4, 15 February 2015, pp. 372–76 (p. 372).

[16] GARF, f. 102, op. 203, d. 8, ch. 58, t. 2, l. 77; S. V. Bezberezh'ev, 'Mariia Aleksandrovna Spiridonova: Istoricheskii portret', *Voprosy istorii*, 9, 1990, pp. 65–81 <https://rabkrin.org/mariya-aleksandrovna-spiridonova-istoricheskiy-portret-statya> [accessed 25 January 2024] (para 3).

[17] Izmailovich, 'Iz proshlogo', pp. 399–421. Spiridonova described herself as running a fever and expectorating blood in a letter that she wrote to Sletov during the journey. Rossiiskii Gosudarstvennyi Arkhiv Sotsial'no-Politicheskoi Istorii (hereafter, RGASPI), f. 564, op. 1, d. 34, l. 9.

[18] P. B. Kaganovich, *Iz istorii bor'by s tuberkulezom v dorevoliutsionnoi Rossii*, Moscow, 1952, pp. 213–19. See also, L. G. Averbukh, *Tuberkulez: Etapy bor'by, obreteniia i poteri*, Odesa, 2005, pp. 25–26.

[19] Charles E. Rosenberg, 'Framing Disease: Illness, Society and History', in Charles

died individually and rather slowly of tuberculosis', a sociological study of illness noted, 'so that the victim was in a position to perceive his condition, to form a self-image, and to discern the way in which others saw him'.[20] In Spiridonova's life story, a longing for martyrdom framed her illness, just as illness framed her longing for martyrdom. Her affliction with tuberculosis fulfilled her mission of self-sacrifice, at the same time that her self-sacrifice exacerbated her disease.

Like other radical women during the first Russian revolution, Spiridonova may have joined the SR party because the sacrificial component of SR terrorism held particular appeal for her. According to SR party tradition, terrorists who experienced moral anguish about committing murder, even in the name of the people's struggle against the tsarist autocracy, expected to give up their own lives as compensation for taking the lives of the tsar's representatives. Upper-class young women such as Spiridonova, frustrated with the educational and professional limitations imposed on them in strongly patriarchal Russia, found comradely acceptance from the men in the revolutionary underground, along with novel opportunities for service and self-sacrifice. As in Russian society as a whole, the feminization of virtue prevailed in Russia's radical subculture; male and female terrorists alike considered women to be natural candidates for revolutionary martyrdom, because women's inferior status in everyday life endowed them with spiritual authority.[21]

Though she justified her act of terrorism at her court-martial in March 1906 by claiming that Luzhenovskii 'was an oppressor of the people, and there was no means of restraint on him besides death to be found',[22] Spiridonova not only expected but actually desired to sacrifice her own life in restitution for taking his. 'If the authorities have me killed, I will die at peace with myself', she stated in her letter from Tambov prison published in February;[23] similarly, she concluded her speech at her court-martial with the assertion that she was 'happy to stand in defence of the Russian people

E. Rosenberg and Janet Golden (eds), *Framing Disease: Studies in Cultural History*, New Brunswick, NJ, 1992, p. xix.

[20] Claudine Herzlich and Janine Pierret, *Illness and Self in Society*, trans. Elborg Forster, Baltimore, MD, 1987, p. 30.

[21] Zenzinov, *Perezhitoe*, p. 108; Amy Knight, 'Female Terrorists in the Russian Socialist Revolutionary Party', *Russian Review*, 38, 2, April 1979, pp. 139–59 (pp. 143–44, 147–48); Barbara Alpern Engel, *Mothers and Daughters: Women of the Intelligentsia in Nineteenth-Century Russia*, Cambridge, 1983, pp. 4–5, 173; Barbara Heldt, *Terrible Perfection: Women and Russian Literature*, Bloomington, IN, 1987, p. 12.

[22] *Dvadtsatyi vek*, no. 3, 27 March 1906.

[23] *Rus'*, no. 27.

and to die for them'.[24] After being sentenced to execution, Spiridonova wrote to the Tambov SRs of her intense yearning for her own death because of its 'value to society' in the cause of revolution; commutation she would therefore regard 'as vengeance, as a fresh insult' from the tsarist government.[25] When she learned at the end of March that the government had commuted her sentence to life imprisonment, she begged her SR comrades in another letter to agree with her resolve to kill herself, arguing that 'staying alive is sometimes an incomparably greater sacrifice to the cause than dying for its success'.[26] Her farewell letter sent to her friends on the eve of her transfer in May from Tambov to Moscow, and thence to Siberia, conveyed that Spiridonova was still struggling to resign herself to what she anticipated to be 'the unavoidable abuses of a life in penal servitude'.[27]

The 'triumphal procession' into Siberian imprisonment

Held for a month in solitary confinement in the Butyrka transit prison in Moscow, Spiridonova did not meet the five women SR terrorists with whom she would share imprisonment at the distant eastern outskirts of the empire — Anastasiia Alekseevna Bitsenko, Lidiia Pavlovna Ezerskaia, Revekka Moiseevich Fialka, Aleksandra Adol'fevna Izmailovich and Mariia Markovna Shkol'nik — until the night of their departure from the Butyrka.[28] Her dread and despair concerning her fate surely lifted somewhat when the public response to the six terrorists' three-week railway journey across Siberia proved to be nothing short of phenomenal. In the summer of 1906, with relations between the reform-minded new Russian parliament and the tsar's resistant government at the point of political paralysis, an outbreak of rural disorders and industrial strikes was sweeping the country.[29] The train transporting Spiridonova and her future prison comrades to the Nerchinsk penal complex in the Transbaikal region (Zabaikal'e) set off from Moscow in late June, at the height of the disturbances.

[24] *Dvadtsatyi vek*, no. 3.
[25] Vladimirov, *Mariia Spiridonova*, p. 117.
[26] Ibid., p. 119.
[27] Ibid., p. 120.
[28] Izmailovich, 'Iz proshlogo', pp. 395–96. According to the liberal press, the other political prisoners in the Butyrka as of 23 May were planning a hunger strike to protest Spiridonova's 'complete isolation' in the Pugachev tower and the lack of medical attention for her severe headaches and heavy expectoration of blood. *Nasha zhizn'*, no. 453, 24 May 1906.
[29] Abraham Ascher, *The Revolution of 1905*, 2 vols, vol. 2: *Authority Restored*, Stanford, CA, 1992, pp. 111, 117–18, 132–37, 162–63.

Ever-increasing numbers of demonstrators gathered to greet the women's train as it travelled eastward, because they had heard in advance of its arrival — either from telegrams sent ahead by disembarking passengers,[30] or through an underground communications network of railroad employees and city workers[31] — that it was carrying the revolutionary heroine Spiridonova away to remote imprisonment. The crowds that met the train at station stops across Siberia during that summer of urban and rural unrest knew Spiridonova's name, but not the name of her victim, Tambov security chief Luzhenovskii. Conversely, people knew the name of Anastasiia Bitsenko's victim, General-Adjutant Viktor Viktorovich Sakharov, the leader of punitive expeditions against the rebellious peasants of Saratov province — but not the name of the assassin herself, who had refused to disclose it to authorities until after her trial and sentencing. Some excited Siberian demonstrators even identified Spiridonova, the terrorist revered across the empire, as the killer of General Sakharov.[32]

Addressing the crowds from the platform of their coach, the six women would introduce themselves by name, state their allegiance to the SR party and tell about the individual acts of terrorism that had resulted in their sentences of Siberian imprisonment.[33] Like Spiridonova, three of the other five terrorists had originally been sentenced by courts-martial to hang for their crimes: thirty-one-year-old Anastasiia Bitsenko, for her assassination of General Sakharov in November 1905; twenty-eight-year-old Aleksandra Izmailovich, for her January 1906 attempt to assassinate the Minsk police chief complicit in local anti-Jewish violence; and twenty-four-year-old Mariia (Mania) Shkol'nik, for her attempted assassination of the governor of Chernigov province, another harsh suppressor of peasant uprisings, in January 1906. After weeks of awaiting execution, each of the other three women learned, as did Spiridonova, that her death sentence had been commuted to penal servitude for life. Forty-year-old Lidiia Ezerskaia, who in October 1905 attempted to assassinate the governor of Mogilev province, another leader of anti-Jewish pogroms, received the comparatively lighter

---

[30] Izmailovich, 'Iz proshlogo', p. 399.

[31] M. M. Shkol'nik, 'Zhizn' byvshei terroristki', in Budnitskii (ed.), *Zhenshchiny-terroristki v Rossii*, pp. 237–324 (p. 303). This is a reprint of the first edition (1927) of Shkol'nik's memoir.

[32] Izmailovich, 'Iz proshlogo', pp. 399, 409. In withholding her identity (GARF, f. 102, op. 203, d. 8, ch. 52, t. 1, l. 44), Bitsenko was complying with the policy of the SR Combat Organization.

[33] Izmailovich, 'Iz proshlogo', pp. 399–402.

sentence of thirteen years and six months from a civil court, and nineteen-year-old Revekka (Riva) Fialka, arrested in Odessa in June 1905 for constructing bombs in an SR 'laboratory', was given the shortest sentence, ten years, by a court-martial.[34] Together with Spiridonova, these five terrorists would become known among the revolutionary prisoners as the *shesterka* or 'the six', the first group of female political convicts to enter Akatui and Mal'tsev prisons in the Nerchinsk complex.

Alexandra Izmailovich later described the six terrorists' journey across Siberia as a 'triumphal procession', remarking that it seemed not as though the women were being transported under guard to serve lengthy periods of imprisonment, but rather as though they travelling of their own volition, 'to convoke a series of mass meetings and thus conduct a review of revolutionary forces'.[35] In their memoirs, she and Shkol'nik recalled the countless gifts of flowers, candy, oranges, money and jewellery that the crowds threw into the women's coach, and the cheers, applause and even weeping with which workers, townspeople and peasants responded to Spiridonova when she spoke to them from the windows.[36] Spiridonova wrote to the SR leader Sletov during the journey that 'even the humble stations yield bouquets, speeches and tears. Everyone considers it his duty to greet us affectionately, assuring us: You will soon return!'[37]

Watching Spiridonova as she stood at the windows of their coach day and night to speak with the people who thronged it whenever the train stopped, her fellow terrorists began to speculate that the adulation of the crowds meant too much to her, according to Izmailovich. Spiridonova would greet her audience with smiles, patiently answer their numerous questions and discuss the SR party programme with them in clear and simple language. Between stations, however, she lay motionless and feverish, coughing up blood, her face twitching with nerves, only to return to the windows at the next stop, hiding her facial tics with her shawl and coughing discreetly into a handkerchief. When her travel companions, alarmed by her symptoms, attempted to talk her out of holding such meetings at night stops, she got angry. Yet after a longer acquaintance with Spiridonova, Izmailovich wrote, the other women came to realize that she

---

[34] The six women's terrorist activities, arrests, detention and sentencing have been recounted more fully in Boniece, 'The Spiridonova Case', and in Sally A. Boniece, 'The 'Shesterka' of 1905–06: Terrorist Heroines of Revolutionary Russia', *Jahrbücher für Geschichte Osteuropas*, 58, 2, 2010, pp. 172–91.

[35] Izmailovich, 'Iz proshlogo', p. 390.

[36] Ibid., pp. 399–402, 409–10; Shkol'nik, 'Zhizn' byvshei terroristki', p. 303.

[37] RGASPI, f. 564, op. 1, d. 34, l. 8.

had endangered her fragile health to speak to the crowds not out of egoism, but out of 'a love approaching ecstasy, like that of the early Christian martyrs who burned at the stake [...], a radiant love for every person, for all people [...] And now this love demanded that [...] she neither hide her face from the stares of strangers, nor brush aside their impertinent questions'.[38]

In the portrayal of Izmailovich, who would become her closest companion in tsarist imprisonment, Spiridonova throughout their journey to Siberia was imbued with a sense of her sacred duty as a symbol of the revolution surging across the empire that summer. For Spiridonova, to ignore the crowds who clamoured for her attention at every station would have been to betray the very ideals that she served; she considered her own welfare to be insignificant in comparison to the welfare of Russian society, whose anguish she shared. 'She stood in the first rank of terrorists', Izmailovich stated, 'but she was not only a proud avenger for the suffering of the Russian people. Like them, oppressed and tormented for centuries, she had drunk to the dregs the bitter cup of humiliation'. From the perspective of Izmailovich, Spiridonova's abuse at the hands of tsarist officialdom and her physical frailty awakened a compassion bordering on love in the empire's citizens; her 'strong and powerful spiritual beauty' elevated her to a figure of worship. 'The crowds did not know the rest of us', wrote Izmailovich:

> But who did not know her name? [...] It had become a banner uniting all who seethed with holy indignation — Socialist Revolutionaries, Social Democrats, Constitutional Democrats, ordinary people unaffiliated with parties. She belonged not only to the SR party. She belonged to all who carried her in their hearts as a banner of their protest.[39]

The SR men and women of the Akatui prison commune, 1906–07
On their arrival at Akatui prison in the Nerchinsk penal complex in July 1906, the six female terrorists were greeted joyfully by several leading male SR terrorists who had been transferred to Akatui from the Butyrka prison in the spring, as well as by a multitude of sympathetic 'non-party' workers, soldiers, sailors and civil servants serving time at Akatui for their participation in the social and political disorders of the Transbaikal region in 1905. In a letter sent from the Butyrka in March before their departure for Siberia, the SRs Petr Vladimirovich Karpovich, Egor Sergeevich

---

[38] Izmailovich, 'Iz proshlogo', pp. 414–16.
[39] Ibid., pp. 409, 416.

Sozonov, Leiba Vul'fovich Sikorskii and Grigorii Andreevich Gershuni had hailed Spiridonova, then imprisoned in Tambov, as 'a symbol not only of our tortured country, bleeding under the heel of the drunken, unruly Cossack — but also of young, struggling, determined and self-sacrificing Russia'. When she reached Akatui to serve her sentence with them, the men assured Spiridonova, 'you will join our family' of SR prisoners, among whom 'you will meet with so much brotherly love and warm concern that your wounds will be healed'.[40] All of the male political prisoners at Akatui were 'tremendously excited' to live under the same roof as Spiridonova, Sozonov wrote to his mother, and as they welcomed her and her companions in the prison courtyard, 'Each of us sought to express all of our love and reverence for this glorious young woman'. Although Spiridonova was still experiencing fever and delirium and coughing up blood on the day that she entered Akatui, Sozonov reported to his family one month later that her health was improving 'not daily but hourly'; two months later, he wrote that Spiridonova had recovered and become 'the same comrade as the others', comfortable in her interactions with fellow prisoners instead of easily unnerved by a word or gesture.[41]

That Spiridonova's health was restored — albeit temporarily — after she passed beyond the prison gate at Akatui may have been due to the 'clublike' atmosphere of the prison in 1906. Here radical men and women, many of their names or faces familiar to each other from the socialist underground, resided and mingled with the expectation that they would soon be liberated by the ongoing revolution. The first of several prisons within the Nerchinsk complex to house political convicts between 1905 and 1917, Akatui was built to accommodate eighty-four inmates, but it held over one hundred in the summer of 1906 and 120 by early 1907. As waves of agrarian and industrial disturbances challenged tsarist authority across the empire, the administration of this penal complex in the remote Transbaikal had grown lax; the political prisoners at Akatui therefore enjoyed a considerable degree of autonomy. With their cells unlocked and their guards appearing only once a day for roll call, the 'politicals' could drink tea, take walks and discuss current events in European Russia together, keeping well informed by the newspapers and books that they were allowed to receive in the mail.[42]

[40] *Mysl'*, no. 14, 5 July 1906; excerpt reprinted in *Dvadtsati vek*, no. 98, 6 July 1906.
[41] *Pis'mo Egora Sozonova k rodnym, 1895–1910 gg.*, Moscow, 1925, pp. 95–96, 99, 102.
[42] G. M. Kramarov, 'Nerchinskaia katorga (1907–1910 gg.)', *Katorga i ssylka*, 3, 1922, pp. 57–70 (pp. 59–60); M. Spiridonova, 'Iz zhizni na Nerchinskoi katorge', in Budnitskii (ed.), *Zhenshchiny-terroristki v Rossii*, pp. 427–99 (pp. 427, 436–37, 451); Shkol'nik, 'Zhizn'

More important, there was the tradition handed down by earlier cohorts of imprisoned revolutionaries to follow: the SRs, at twenty-five to thirty outnumbering the few anarchists and Social Democrats (SDs) among the socialist convicts at Akatui, organized courses, lectures and study circles that were particularly intended to educate the much larger contingent of 'non-party' political prisoners. Gershuni lectured on the history of the Russian revolutionary movement to the entire prison population; Izmailovich taught general education to a class of soldier, sailor and worker inmates; Ezerskaia and Sozonov led study circles. On the porch in the evening, a choir of prisoners would sing revolutionary songs, and when the mail came, Gershuni would immediately read the newspapers aloud to all of the prisoners. In her later account eulogizing the male SR leaders with whom she had been incarcerated at Akatui in 1906, Spiridonova wrote that the SR prisoners felt a responsibility as 'professional revolutionaries' to exemplify the 'directive' for communal behaviour inherited from 'the older generations of freedom fighters', thus inculcating a sense of socialist 'moralism' among the unaffiliated majority of Akatui's inmates.[43]

The 'socialist collective' or communal lifestyle that the male SR prisoners established at Akatui in 1906 was a code of conduct that originated with the Decembrists, the first political convicts sent into penal servitude in the Nerchinsk district in 1826. An unwritten set of revolutionary ethics for prison life, this code was carried forward over the decades by successive groups of radical convicts incarcerated in Nerchinsk, who taught it to newly arriving comrades. The SD and former populist Lev Grigor'evich Deich, an inmate of the penal complex in the 1880s, defined the prison collective as 'an entirely harmonious and well-functioning organization that had been developed over the course of many years, through the communal efforts of the prisoners themselves to manage their shared existence. The fundamental principle of the organization was equality of rights and responsibilities'. In 1906, Spiridonova and her female terrorist comrades joined the socialist commune created by the SR men at Akatui, participating in its shared economy and adhering to its rules on personal conduct, interaction with prison authorities, cooperative living arrangements and daily tasks.[44]

byvshei terroristki', p. 304.

[43] Spiridonova, 'Iz zhizni na Nerchinskoi katorge', pp. 429–30, 451.

[44] M. N. Gernet, *Istoriia tsarskoi tiur'my*, 3rd edn, 5 vols, vol. 2: *1825–1870*, Moscow, 1961, pp. 188–89; Daniel Beer, *The House of the Dead: Siberian Exile under the Tsars*, New York, 2017, pp. 116–19; L. G. Deich, *16 let v Sibiri*, 2nd edn, St Petersburg, 1906–08, p. 215; Kramarov, 'Nerchinskaia katorga', pp. 57–59; L. A. Kolesnikova, *Narodnicheskaia*

Despite recovering her health in the autumn of 1906, however, Spiridonova suffered a decline in January 1907, when the new chief of the Nerchinsk penal complex ordered the six female political prisoners at Akatui to be transferred to a separate facility for women only. The tsarist government's reassertion of authority in the latter half of 1906, through martial law, mass arrests and an accelerated judicial process, mandated the return to a stringent prison regimen. Since Akatui had been filled well beyond capacity by a continuous influx of convicted revolutionaries, the Nerchinsk administration began to redistribute portions of Akatui's inmates, male as well as female, among neighbouring prisons in the penal complex. In February 1907, both Spiridonova and Shkol'nik lay ill in bed at Akatui, Spiridonova with reactivated tuberculosis and Shkol'nik with pneumonia; nevertheless, all six SR women were removed from Akatui and transported by sleigh to Mal'tsev, which would serve until 1911 as the designated prison for female political convicts. More than a month after the women's transfer, Sozonov and his comrades who had been moved to Algachi men's prison heard rumours that Spiridonova was still bedridden and coughing up blood at Mal'tsev.[45]

Spiridonova's martyrdom in the Mal'tsev prison commune, 1907–11
As the first political convicts to enter Mal'tsev women's prison, Spiridonova and her five SR terrorist comrades formed a collective there that embraced all incoming 'politicals' and followed the principles of communal living practised by the SR men at Akatui and their revolutionary predecessors in Siberian imprisonment. Over the next four years, sixty-two female political convicts were confined at Mal'tsev, more than half of whom were SRs, the others primarily SDs and anarchist-communists; the prison also housed around 100 female criminal convicts, but separately from the 'politicals'. Required by the prison administration to perform only the basic chores of housekeeping in the three common cells where they lived, the political

memuaristika (Po materialam istochnikovogo kompleksa zhurnala 'Katorga i ssylka'), Nizhnii Novgorod, 1999, pp. 68–72.
    [45] A. A. Fomin, 'Nerchinskaia katorga poslednikh desiatiletii (1888–1917)', in A. Dikovskaia-Iakimova and V. Pleskov (eds), *Kara i drugie tiur'my Nerchinskoi katorgi: Sbornik vospominanii, dokumentov i materialov*, Moscow, 1927, pp. 15–54 (pp. 25–26); N. N. Zhukov, '"Rezhim kluba ili vozmutitel'noe izdevatel'stvo nad zakonom"', in M. A. Braginskii (ed.), *Nerchinskaia katorga: Sbornik Nerchinskogo zemliachestva*, Moscow, 1933, pp. 120–29 (pp. 120–22); Ascher, *The Revolution of 1905*, vol. 2, *Authority Restored*, pp. 245–50; Beer, *The House of the Dead*, pp. 357, 359; Spiridonova, 'Iz zhizni na Nerchinskoi katorge', pp. 471–72, 474–75; Shkol'nik, 'Zhizn' byvshei terroristki', pp. 306–09; *Pis'mo Egora Sozonova k rodnym*, pp. 121–23, 129.

inmates at Mal'tsev made a compact to occupy their days fully with studying, both individually and in groups, a variety of subjects ranging from foreign languages to literature and philosophy, and/or with teaching those among them who had less education. For reading materials, the women relied on their communal 'library' of books that the original six prisoners brought from Akatui, more books contributed by later arriving prisoners, and still more books mailed by friends and relatives. Eventually the 'library' at Mal'tsev held up to eight hundred volumes covering all subjects from history to mathematics, almost three hundred of them in French, German or English, but no books on political science and economics, which were forbidden by the prison administration.[46]

What motivated the female political convicts incarcerated at Mal'tsev to fill their empty hours with intensive learning, according to the memoirs that they later wrote, was their youth and their relatively short experience of the revolutionary movement. Most of the women were under thirty years old — and a quarter of them were under twenty-one — when they were arrested for the political crimes that sent them to Mal'tsev; more than half of them had worked in the radical underground for three years or less. Although a majority of the women had received a secondary or higher education, all of them were 'deeply conscious' of being insufficiently prepared to become professional revolutionaries, much less state prisoners stripped of their civil rights and identities. Consequently, they found it necessary to 'rethink everything from the very beginning' and to build firm and rational foundations for their political philosophies. Like many of Russia's intellectuals outside the prison walls, the women of the Mal'tsev commune were reevaluating their goals and ideals in the aftermath of the failed revolution of 1905–07.[47]

[46] F. Radzilovskaia and L. Orestova, 'Mal'tsevskaia zhenskaia katorga, 1907–11', in Budnitskii (ed.), *Zhenshchiny-terroristki v Rossii*, pp. 500–42 (pp. 502, 508, 511–16, 522–24); F. N. Radzilovskaia and L. P. Orestova, 'Statisticheskie svedeniia o sostave zhenskoi politicheskoi Nerchinskoi katorgi (Mal'tsevskaia i Akatuiskaia tiur'my), 1906–1917 gg.', in M. M. Konstantinov (ed.), *Na zhenskoi katorge: Sbornik vospominanii*, 2nd edn, Moscow, 1932, pp. 257–64 (p. 260); A. Bitsenko, 'V Mal'tsevskoi zhenskoi katorzhnoi tiur'me, 1907–10 gg. (K kharakteristike nastroenii)', in Budnitskii (ed.), *Zhenshchiny-terroristki v Rossii*, pp. 543–63 (p. 543); I. Kakhovskaia, 'Iz vospominanii o zhenskoi katorge', in Konstantinov (ed.), *Na zhenskoi katorge*, pp. 55–94 (pp. 77, 80–83), and A. Pirogova, 'Na zhenskoi katorge', in Konstantinov (ed.), *Na zhenskoi katorge*, pp. 175–204 (p. 180).
[47] Radzilovskaia and Orestova, 'Mal'tsevskaia zhenskaia katorga', pp. 519–20; Razilovskaia and Orestova, 'Statisticheskie svedeniia o sostave zhenskoi politicheskoi Nerchinskoi katorgi', pp. 259–60; Kakhovskaia, 'Iz vospominanii o zhenskoi katorge', p. 83; Bitsenko, 'V Mal'tsevskoi zhenskoi katorzhnoi tiur'me', p. 543; Spiridonova, 'Iz zhizni na Nerchinskoi katorge', p. 485; Aileen Kelly, 'Self-Censorship and the Russian

However, Spiridonova, isolated by chronic invalidism for the remainder of her imprisonment, undertook no substantive role in the socialist collective at Mal'tsev. Rather than living in one of the common cells for 'politicals' in the main prison building, Spiridonova and her devoted nurse Aleksandra Izmailovich shared one of the few solitary cells designated for sick prisoners in a smaller separate structure.[48] The memoirs of her fellow prisoners depicted Spiridonova as 'very seriously ill' and occasionally delirious or unconscious for long periods; in December 1907, her condition became so grave that Egor Sozonov, now corresponding with Mal'tsev 'politicals' from Zerentui men's prison three miles away, relayed in alarm to his family that Spiridonova was 'going out like a candle'.[49] Paulina (Pavla) Frantsevna Metter, a former hospital nurse dedicated to tending her sick Mal'tsev comrades, characterized Spiridonova's malady as 'attacks of nerves', and Irina Konstantinovna Kakhovskaia, who began a lifelong friendship with Spiridonova at Mal'tsev, wrote that Spiridonova was prostrated by 'nervous shock' as well as tuberculosis throughout her incarceration.[50] In May 1909, the physician for the Nerchinsk penal complex, Nikolai Vasil'evich Rogalev, described the bedridden Spiridonova as 'poor in build and nourishment' and 'suffer[ing] from greatly pronounced anaemia and tuberculosis'.[51]

In contrast to Spiridonova, the other five female political convicts with whom she arrived at Mal'tsev were active and committed participants in the socialist collective that they founded. Elected the 'political leader' of the commune, Anastasiia Bitsenko conducted all necessary conversations and negotiations with the prison administration on behalf of her fellow inmates. Riva Fialka served for a time as 'economic leader' or manager of the communal funds and purchaser of extra provisions to supplement the dreary prison diet. At the initiative of Spiridonova's nurse Izmailovich, the women 'politicals' started a kindergarten and school for the children of criminal convicts and planted flower gardens in the prison courtyard during the short Siberian summers. Evidently spending much of her time

Intelligentsia, 1905–14', *Slavic Review*, 46, 2, Summer 1987, pp. 193–213 (pp. 198–200).

[48] 'Kreml' za reshetkoi (Pis'mo iz kremlevoi tiur'my M. A. Spiridonovoi i A. A. Izmailovich): Pervyi arrest (pis'mo A. A. Izmailovich)', in *Kreml' za reshetkoi (Podpol'naia Rossia)*, Berlin, 1922, pp. 7–14 (p. 11); Radzilovskaia and Orestova, 'Mal'tsevskaia zhenskaia katorga', p. 503.

[49] Ibid., p. 510; *Pis'mo Egora Sozonova k rodnym*, pp. 155, 158.

[50] P. F. Metter, 'Stranichka proshlogo', in Konstantinov (ed.), *Na zhenskoi katorge*, pp. 117–36 (p. 125); I. K. Kakhovskaia, 'V TsK KPSS', in *Politicheskii dnevnik, 1964–70* (Amsterdam: Fond imeni Gertsena, 1972), pp. 707–40 (p. 731).

[51] GARF, f. 29, op. 1, d. 1350, l. 223.

with her comrades who lived in the main building, Izmailovich, one of the
better educated prisoners, also led what were remembered as 'stimulating'
discussions of Russian literature during the commune's daily classes.[52]

Moreover, two of the original six women 'politicals' to enter Mal'tsev,
Mania Shkol'nik and Lidiia Ezerskaia, contributed regularly to the
prison collective in spite of their poor health. Though she was extremely
emaciated and often weak from anaemia, Shkol'nik always did her share of
the laundry and heavy cleaning, refusing to acknowledge the debility that
would excuse her from communal duties.[53] Ezerskaia, like Spiridonova
one of the rare inmates whom the prison administration considered to
be chronically ill, was moved to a solitary cell when her bronchial asthma
worsened and sent to Nerchinsk's only hospital facility at Zerentui on
at least one occasion. Yet in the recollections of her prison companions,
Ezerskaia was a cheerful, vivacious and sympathetic friend who enjoyed
giving lessons in French and German and practising her professional
skills as a dentist on anyone in need, political and criminal convicts
alike. Spiridonova herself wrote, without reference to her own history as
an invalid prisoner, that most of the other 'politicals' at Mal'tsev did not
realize how dangerously ill Ezerskaia was, because their lively comrade
made so little of her recurrent symptoms.[54]

During her years of illness and isolation from her comrades in
the Mal'tsev commune, Spiridonova nevertheless conducted an intense
correspondence with Egor Sozonov, who was incarcerated at nearby
Zerentui from the summer of 1907 until his death in the autumn of 1910.
A clandestine mail service ensured the regular passage of letters between
the men's and women's prisons in that period, delivered either by criminal
convicts traveling back and forth to work or by the kindly doctor Rogalev,
acclaimed in prison memoirs as 'the prisoners' greatest friend'. Not only
had the original six Mal'tsev 'politicals' become acquainted with some of
Zerentui's inmates when they were imprisoned together at Akatui in 1906,
but other members of the Mal'tsev commune likewise knew comrades
from the revolutionary underground that were serving sentences at

[52] Radzilovskaia and Orestova, 'Mal'tsevskaia zhenskaia katorga', pp. 506–07, 513–14,
527–28, 532, 535–36; Kakhovskaia, 'Iz vospominanii o zhenskoi katorge', pp. 91–92.
[53] Metter, 'Stranichka proshlogo', pp. 125, 128; GARF, f. 29, op. 1, d. 1350, l. 224.
[54] Radzilovskaia and Orestova, 'Mal'tsevskaia zhenskaia katorga', pp. 508, 514; L. P.
Orestova, 'Lidiia Pavlovna Ezerskaia', in Konstantinov (ed.), *Na zhenskoi katorge*, pp.
225–33 (pp. 225–26); Metter, 'Stranichka proshlogo', pp. 121, 125; *Pis'mo Egora Sozonova k
rodnym*, pp. 155, 158; Spiridonova, 'Iz zhizni na Nerchinskoi katorge', pp. 472–73. Ezerskaia
died of bronchial asthma in exile in 1915; Spiridonova discussed only deceased prison
comrades in her memoir of 1920 and had far more to say about the SR men.

Zerentui. The male and female socialist prisoners wrote to each other about political events in Russia, about the books they were reading and their developing philosophies, and about prison news and prison tactics; many times, individual women shared their letters from Zerentui with the Mal'tsev commune. Thus the women 'politicals' imprisoned at Mal'tsev came to recognize that by virtue of their gender, they were spared the indignities to which male prisoners in the Nerchinsk complex might be subjected, depending on a warden's disposition: familiar address from administrators, commands to 'stand at attention' and threats of corporal punishment.[55]

When recounting in her memoir how her friendship with Sozonov deepened through their prison correspondence, Spiridonova implied that she herself read and wrote extensively during her time at Mal'tsev. An invalid not engaged in communal classes and activities in the main building, she may have pursued her studies alone in her cell or in the company of her close friend and attendant Izmailovich; certainly, Spiridonova was stimulated by her written exchange of impressions and ideas with Sozonov. In her memoir, she praised him as a compassionate mentor who 'helped me more than once to extricate myself from a number of theoretical doubts of both an objective and a subjective nature'. She disagreed, however, with Sozonov's stance on prison tactics: that professional revolutionaries must protest administrative insults to the human dignity of their fellow political prisoners, by suicide if necessary.[56] Sozonov took his own life after a new warden at Zerentui ordered political convicts to be subjected to corporal punishment in November 1910, an event that devastated not just Spiridonova but every woman in the Mal'tsev commune.[57]

Written to memorialize Sozonov and other male SR leaders with whom she had been imprisoned in 1906, Spiridonova's account of life in the Nerchinsk complex revealed little directly about her personal experiences. Most telling, perhaps, was her remark that it was 'impossible to be healthy in prison', because 'prison is torture', an environment in which all human weaknesses and tensions 'are revealed, accentuated, intensified'. The adjustment to prison was the most excruciating, she said, for the SR

[55] Spiridonova, 'Iz zhizni na Nerchinskoi katorge', pp. 487, 491; Radzilovskaia and Orestova, 'Mal'tsevskaia zhenskaia katorga', pp. 530–31, 533–34; Izmailovich, 'Iz proshlogo', p. 422; Kakhovskaia, 'Iz vospominanii o zhenskoi katorge', pp. 80–81, 90.
[56] Spiridonova, 'Iz zhizni na Nerchinskoi katorge', pp. 484–85, 496–97.
[57] V. Pirogov, 'Smert' E. S. Sozonova', *Katorga i ssylka*, 3, 1922, pp. 71–74; Pirogova, 'Na zhenskoi katorge', p. 182; Kakhovskaia, 'Iz vospominanii o zhenskoi katorge', pp. 93–94; Bitsenko, 'V Mal'tsevskoi zhenskoi katorzhnoi tiur'me', pp. 562–63.

terrorists whose death sentences had recently been commuted to penal servitude for life.[58] Here Spiridonova was undoubtedly referring to herself, Bitsenko, Izmailovich and Shkol'nik, all of whom had been sentenced to the gallows between January and March 1906 for their crimes against the state, though she used neither names nor first-person pronouns in her discussion.

Like Shkol'nik and Izmailovich, whose memoirs described their being overwhelmed with a love for all humankind while they awaited execution,[59] Spiridonova wrote that political prisoners under the death sentence entered a state of 'unearthly fascination, which they always remember as the brightest and happiest period of their lives, a period when *time was not*, when they experienced a deep solitude yet simultaneously an unprecedented, heretofore inconceivable loving unity with every human being and with the entire world'. To exchange this exalted 'existence between life and the grave' for perpetual imprisonment was 'a shock to the entire nervous system'.[60] Spiridonova's letters to the Tambov SRs in the spring of 1906 testified that she did in fact undergo the traumatic 'shock' of relinquishing her vision of a martyr's death for the reality of penal servitude for life.[61] Bitsenko, Izmailovich and Shkol'nik were forced to adjust to the same reality,[62] but those three convicted SR terrorists all committed themselves to the duties and lifestyle of the Mal'tsev commune, whereas Spiridonova spent her days sequestered in a solitary cell by chronic illness.

Spiridonova's invalidism in the Nerchinsk prison complex was consistent with the mythology of her extreme suffering, a legacy, even as her scars began to fade, of the tortures she had endured for the cause. Shortly before she was transported from Tambov to Moscow in May 1906, prison personnel recorded that Spiridonova's face, shoulder and knees showed 'traces of skin abrasions and scabs', presumably from her beating by police and Cossacks in January. Upon meeting the feverish and coughing Spiridonova at Akatui prison in July 1906, Sozonov explained in a letter

[58] Spiridonova, 'Iz zhizni na Nerchinskoi katorge', p. 433. Her memoir eulogized Petro Kornil'evich Sidorchuk, Petr Karpovich, Grigori Gershuni and Prosh Perchevich Prosh'ian as well as Egor Sozonov.

[59] Shkol'nik, 'Zhizn' byvshei terroristki', pp. 298–99; Izmailovich, 'Iz proshlogo', pp. 365–66.

[60] Spiridonova, 'Iz zhizni na Nerchinskoi katorge', p. 433.

[61] See pp. 104–05 above.

[62] Both Shkol'nik and Izmailovich wrote of the anguish they experienced when their death sentences were commuted to life imprisonment (Shkol'nik, 'Zhizn' byvshei terroristki', p. 300; Izmailovich, 'Iz proshlogo', p. 368).

to his mother why he was unable to describe her appearance: 'When you look at her, your heart cowers from the grievous memories of what she has had to bear; the past suppresses the present.' Five years later, according to the permit issued for Spiridonova's transfer from Mal'tsev prison back to Akatui in April 1911, 'a trace of a past abrasion' could be found only on her forehead.[63] Her invalidism and tubercular episodes, however, would persist until the prisons opened in 1917.

SR plots for escape from Akatui and Mal'tsev prisons, 1906–11
The prison commune, with its code of conduct developed by generations of incarcerated revolutionaries, provided both guidance and solace for many disoriented and dejected political convicts, but it resigned none of them to life behind bars. 'The thought of escape never leaves the prisoner', wrote Mania Shkol'nik, while a former male political inmate of the Nerchinsk complex declared, 'I don't know of a single prisoner who wouldn't start thinking about escape on the day he was arrested'.[64] Even in the summer of 1906 — when the revolution against the autocracy had yet to be suppressed, and the regime at Akatui was so unrestrictive that the prisoners themselves called it a 'republic' — the socialist men imprisoned at Akatui were occupied with planning a mass escape and digging underground passages to facilitate it. After the criminal convicts betrayed these preparations for a communal escape to the prison administration, the male SR leaders decided that an individual escape had a better chance of success.[65]

Selecting Grigorii Gershuni, the revered founder of the SR Combat Organization, as the first candidate for an escape from Akatui, the prison leaders agreed that Spiridonova would be next, followed by others among the better-known SRs. Shkol'nik took note of the hierarchical nature of their strategy, which 'pushed us, the party workers, into the background', and continued to 'dream constantly' of herself escaping. When Spiridonova described Gershuni's audacious escape from Akatui inside a barrel of pickled cabbage in October 1906, aided by Sozonov's visiting fiancée and other SR sympathizers outside the prison walls, she made no allusion to her own desire to break out of prison. Still Shkol'nik, who managed to escape from the Irkutsk prison hospital in 1911 after an emergency appendectomy,

[63] *Pis'mo Egora Sozonova k rodnym*, p. 97; GARF, f. 29, op. 2, d. 3790.
[64] Shkol'nik, 'Zhizn' byvshei terroristki', p. 304; Kramarov, 'Nerchinskaia katorga', p. 67.
[65] Fomin, 'Nerchinskaia katorga poslednikh desiatiletii', p. 25; Shkol'nik, 'Zhizn' byvshei terroristki', p. 304; Spiridonova, 'Iz zhizni na Nerchinskoi katorge', pp. 464–66.

wrote that Spiridonova 'constantly shared with me her plans [for escaping]' during their time at Akatui and Mal´tsev.[66]

Some of the SR plots to liberate Spiridonova from Siberian imprisonment between 1906 and 1911, if not all of them, were discovered by the security police. Either futile or foiled, these conspiracies nonetheless indicated that Spiridonova wished to flee from her martyrdom of illness behind the prison walls and that SR comrades and supporters were determined to rescue her. In the summers of 1908 and 1910, the police heard rumours of plots to free Spiridonova, Shkol´nik and Fialka from Mal´tsev;[67] in the autumn of 1910, more complicated and better-funded schemes to free Sozonov, Shkol´nik and Spiridonova from Zerentui and Mal´tsev were aborted by prison officials and police.[68] Former Mal´tsev prisoners recalled yet another failed SR plan for Spiridonova to escape in April 1911, during the four-day journey on which the female political convicts were transferred from the relatively lenient environment of Mal´tsev to a harsher prison regimen at Akatui. When the promised assistance from outside did not arrive by their third day of travel, Spiridonova threw away the revolver that she had been carrying at the final rest stop before Akatui.[69]

Spiridonova's martyrdom in the Akatui prison commune, 1911–17
Of the original six 'politicals' at Mal´tsev, only Mariia Spiridonova, Anastasiia Bitsenko and Aleksandra Izmailovich were among the twenty-eight women moved to Akatui in 1911, targets of the central prison administration's drive to establish stricter control throughout the system.[70] Their other three SR terrorist comrades, Riva Fialka, Lidiia Ezerskaia and Mania Shkol´nik, had all left Mal´tsev prison in 1910. A minor at the time of her conviction, Fialka received a reduction of her sentence and was

[66] Shkol´nik, 'Zhizn´ byvshei terroristki', p. 305; Mariia Shkol´nik, *Zhizn´ byvshei terroristki*, 2nd edn, Moscow, 1930, pp. 103–04. Some information given in the second edition of Shkol´nik's memoir (1930) was not included in the first edition (1927) reprinted in the Budnitskii collection, hence the separate citations.

[67] GARF, f. 102, op. 238, d. 9, ch. 86, litera A, ch. 2, l. 113; GARF, f. 102, op. 240, d. 9, ch. 27, litera B, ll. 207, 256.

[68] GARF, f. 102, op. 241, d. 270, ll. 25, 36; Radzilovskaia and Orestova, 'Mal´tsevskaia zhenskaia katorga', p. 530; V. N. Figner, '"Tiuremnoe zveno"', in Konstantinov (ed.), *Na zhenskoi katorge*, pp. 5–12 (pp. 11–12).

[69] Radzilovskaia and Orestova, 'Mal´tsevskaia zhenskaia katorga', p. 541. The police had become aware two months earlier of an SR plot to free the Mal´tsev prisoners during their transfer to Akatui (GARF, f. 102, op. 241, d. 9, ch. 27, litera B, l. 38); this probably explains why the exact date of their transfer was withheld from the women until shortly before they departed (Pirogova, 'Na zhenskoi katorge', pp. 183–84).

[70] Radzilovskaia and Orestova, p. 540; Pirogova, 'Na zhenskoi katorge', pp. 181–82.

released into compulsory settlement elsewhere in eastern Siberia. Because of her advanced chronic illness, Ezerskaia also received a reduction of her sentence and was released into settlement. Shkol'nik, sentenced to life imprisonment, developed appendicitis in the autumn of 1910 and was transferred first to the hospital at Zerentui prison, then to the prison hospital in Irkutsk, from which she escaped after her operation in 1911.[71]

Although female political convicts were confined for four years at Mal'tsev prison and for six years at Akatui prison, far less is documented about the bleaker years spent at Akatui by fewer and fewer prisoners. Izmailovich and Bitsenko wrote little about their final years in tsarist imprisonment, and Spiridonova wrote nothing; the single detailed account of the women's commune at Akatui came from the SR Antonina Iakovlevna Pirogova. According to Pirogova, the socialist prisoners who were transferred to Akatui kept their compact to occupy their free time with intellectual pursuits, but the labour duties imposed on them by the prison administration limited their hours of study to the evenings, after they were locked into their common cell. During the day, the women 'politicals' were required to work in the prison bookbindery. Bitsenko recalled, however, that since the women were not supervised while they were bookbinding, they could slip in some studying then if they wished.[72]

Mariia Spiridonova, afflicted with chronic illness, was excused from forced labour in the bookbindery.[73] As she had done at Mal'tsev prison, Spiridonova stayed in her solitary cell at Akatui by day and by night, under the care of her nurse and cellmate Izmailovich.[74] In May 1912, when her oldest sister Evgeniia Spiridonova travelled to Akatui village in the hope of seeing Mariia face-to-face for the first time in six years, the prison administration informed Evgeniia that Mariia was 'gravely ill', and regional authorities denied Evgeniia's request to visit her.[75]

[71] 'Fialka-Rachinskaia, Revekka Moiseevna', in Politicheskaia katorga i ssylka: Biograficheskii spravochnik chlenov o-va politkatorzhan i ssyl'no-poselentsev, Moscow, 1934, p. 663; 'Primechanie', in G. N. Chemodanov, Nerchinskaia katorga: Vospominaniia byvshego nachal'nika konvoinoi komandy, 2nd edn, Moscow, 1930, p. 186, ff. 22, 23, 24; Orestova, 'Lidiia Pavlovna Ezerskaia', p. 228; Shkol'nik, 'Zhizn' byvshei terroristki', pp. 312–24.

[72] Pirogova, 'Na zhenskoi katorge', pp. 190–91; Bitsenko, 'V Mal'tsevskoi zhenskoi katorzhnoi tiur'me', p. 558.

[73] Pirogova, 'Na zhenskoi katorge', p. 190.

[74] 'Kreml'' za reshetkoi: Pervyi arrest (pis'mo A. A. Izmailovich)', p. 11; Pirogova, 'Na zhenskoi katorge', p. 192.

[75] GARF, f. 29, op. 2, d. 3790.

The outbreak of the Great War in 1914, and the nationalist fervour with which many European as well as Russian socialists supported their countries' participation in the conflict, further disheartened the women's commune at Akatui. For political convicts confined in remote prisons and deprived of communication with the world outside, Izmailovich wrote, the 'compromising' wartime patriotism of these so-called socialists seemed to mark 'the deepest crisis of socialism, sinking the perspectives and the path of socialism into despairing pitch darkness'.[76] The melancholy of the women who remained at Akatui was also enhanced by their dwindling numbers over the years: in 1914, there were only ten 'politicals' living inside the prison, and by 1917, there were only seven, among them Spiridonova, Izmailovich, Bitsenko and the memorist Pirogova. All were serving life sentences but Pirogova, sentenced to fifteen years; without the prospect of revolution or release, she said, 'We had no reason to wait for tomorrow or to prepare for it'. Yet the women continued their self-directed studies, now intent on 'acquiring knowledge for its own sake' rather than on fortifying themselves for a future struggle against the autocracy.[77]

Revolution and liberation, 1917
Unchanging as life may have seemed to political convicts in Siberia during the years of the Great War, Russia's disastrous losses to Germany, high casualties and shortages of food and fuel led to an uprising of striking workers and mutinous soldiers in Petrograd and the collapse of the tsarist regime in the last week of February 1917; in the first weeks of March, the revolution spread to major cities across the empire.[78] The women 'politicals' imprisoned at Akatui were officially informed of the February Revolution on a night in early March, when the warden summoned them from their cells to receive his formal congratulations on their amnesty by the new Provisional Government. Because the government's telegrammed list of political prisoners to be released did not include two anarchists among the ten female convicts who were then living under the prison's jurisdiction (seven inside the prison walls and three in a nearby courtyard), the other eight women refused to accept their freedom until it was granted to all of

---

[76] Izmailovich, 'Iz proshlogo', p. 423.

[77] Pirogova, 'Na zhenskoi katorge', pp. 197–200.

[78] Peter Gatrell, *Russia's First World War: A Social and Economic History*, Harlow, 2005, pp. 19–21, 29, 199–200, 246; Rex Wade, *The Russian Revolution, 1917*, 3rd edn, Cambridge and New York, 2017, pp. 16–51. The empire's capital, christened St Petersburg ('Peter's city' in German) by its Germanophile founder Peter the Great, was rechristened Petrograd ('Peter's city' in Russian) at the start of the Great War.

them: the ultimate act of unity by the women's prison commune. Two days later, a second official telegram permitted all ten female convicts to depart Akatui together, riding in sleighs filled with hay and sheepskins toward a train specially designated to transport the liberated political inmates of the Nerchinsk complex to Chita, the industrial centre of the Transbaikal region.[79]

With Bitsenko and Izmailovich, Spiridonova had travelled to eastern Siberia during the revolutionary year of 1906 in a 'triumphal procession' of terrorist-heroines that remained in public memory eleven years later. Local citizens exhibiting 'some kind of bestial curiosity' about the former prisoners surrounded their train before it set off for Chita, Pirogova wrote; several 'garishly dressed ladies' even burst into the women's coach, avidly looked over the passengers in their drab prison attire and demanded, 'But where is Spiridonova?' The response of Spiridonova, 'the celebrity among us', Pirogova did not note beyond recording that the Akatui comrades found the experience 'annoying and disagreeable' and 'breathed a sigh of relief' once the train began to move. On their early morning arrival at Chita, the freed 'politicals' were welcomed by crowds of enthusiastic city residents who had spent the night at the station waiting for them. It seemed to Pirogova that all of Chita 'was intoxicated with happiness and had never greeted dearer guests'.[80]

As the next several months would demonstrate, the demise of the Russian autocracy not only freed Mariia Spiridonova from penal servitude in Siberia but also restored her health and her vigour for radical activism. If imprisonment had triggered her tuberculosis, freedom apparently induced its remission. Moreover, instead of erasing her from public memory, Spiridonova's decade of incarceration and illness under the tsarist regime enhanced her political cachet in the new revolutionary era. She stood foremost in the pantheon of revolutionary martyrs, both living and dead, who could now be celebrated openly in Russia's first experience of civil and political liberties.[81]

---

[79] Pirogova, 'Na zhenskoi katorge', pp. 200–04.

[80] Ibid., p. 204.

[81] On the cult of the 'freedom fighter' in 1917, see Orlando Figes and Boris Kolonitskii, *Interpreting the Russian Revolution: The Language and Symbols of 1917*, New Haven, CT, 1999, pp. 74–75. On February as a religious revolution, see Boris Kolonitskii, 'The "Russian Idea" and the Ideology of the February Revolution', in Teruyuki Hara and Kimitaka Matsuzato (eds), *Empire and Society: New Approaches to Russian History*, Sapporo, 1997, pp. 41–71 (pp. 44–55).

When they returned to European Russia from Siberian imprisonment in the spring of 1917, Spiridonova and her SR terrorist comrades joined the internationalist Left SRs, opponents of the liberal-moderate socialist Provisional Government and its continued prosecution of the war. Renowned as the 'Mal'tsev circle' among the Left SRs in Petrograd and Moscow, these terrorist-heroines — Spiridonova, Anastasiia Bitsenko, Aleksandra Izmailovich and Irina Kakhovskaia — 'formed the core of our party's elite', in the words of a male Left SR activist.[82] Spiridonova, who had spent her years at Mal'tsev and Akatui secluded by chronic illness from the daily give-and-take of the women's prison commune, nonetheless soon emerged as the dominant figure of the Mal'tsev circle.

Though she had last given speeches to the crowds greeting her Siberian-bound train in 1906, Spiridonova reclaimed her oratorical skills when she entered politics at the national level in 1917. At public rallies and assemblies in Petrograd throughout the summer, she campaigned with her fellow Left SRs for a genuine socialist revolution to follow the overthrow of the tsarist regime. Worsening war news and insufficiencies of wages and provisions turned the labouring population away from the Provisional Government and toward the Bolsheviks and Left SRs, vigorous proponents of an immediate peace and the transfer of power to the workers', soldiers' and peasants' councils, or soviets.[83] Spiridonova's forthright advocacy on behalf of the lower classes, enhanced by her legend of revolutionary martyrdom, made her an influential spokesperson for the ascendent anti-war and anti-government left.

By the autumn of 1917, Spiridonova had become the Left SR leader most visibly and popularly identified as the champion of the Russian peasants. An American female journalist who met Spiridonova at the Democratic Conference in September observed: 'All day long, in and out of convention, the peasants came flocking to see her, and would talk to no one else.'[84] After

---

[82] On 'the core of our party's elite', see G. Smolianskii, *Obrechennye: Byl'*, Moscow, 1927, p. 11. On the 'Mal'tsev circle', see Oliver H. Radkey, *The Agrarian Foes of Bolshevism: Promise and Default of the Russian Socialist Revolutionaries, February to October 1917*, New York, 1958, p. 192. Irina Kakhovskaia had been released from Akatui prison into compulsory settlement in 1914 and was living in Chita at the time of the February Revolution. 'Kakhovskaia Irina Konstantinovna', in *Politicheskie partii Rossii, Konets XIX–pervaia tret' XX veka: Entsiklopediia*, Moscow, 1996, pp. 245–46.

[83] Wade, *The Russian Revolution, 1917*, pp. 185–88; Michael Melancon, 'The Left Socialist Revolutionaries and the Bolshevik Uprising', in Vladimir N. Brovkin (ed.), *The Bolsheviks in Russian Society: The Revolution and the Civil Wars*, New Haven, CT and London, 1997, pp. 59–80 (pp. 61–68).

[84] Bessie Beatty, *The Red Heart of Russia*, New York, 1918, pp. 375–76.

the Bolshevik party forced the dissolution of the Provisional Government by seizing power through the Petrograd Soviet in late October, the Left SRs joined the Bolsheviks in a left-socialist coalition government. Spiridonova, one of the closer Left SR allies of the Bolsheviks in the autumn of 1917, was elected head of the Peasants' Section of the All-Russia Soviet Executive Committee, the acting Soviet parliament.

In January 1918, during the two parties' collaboration on a land socialization law, the entire Third Soviet Congress of workers', soldiers' and peasants' deputies rose at the urging of their Bolshevik chairperson to greet Spiridonova with a 'stormy ovation' on the twelfth anniversary of her assassination of Luzhenovskii, the oppressor of Tambov peasants.[85] Her own party marked the anniversary with an article acclaiming Spiridonova, who had wielded her 'sword of righteousness' and suffered 'long years of martyrdom' for the people's sake, as 'the pure reflection of our revolution'.[86] However, the Bolshevik-Left SR coalition lasted only until March 1918, when the Left SRs resigned from the Soviet executive organ, the Council of People's Commissars, to protest the punitive peace treaty that the Bolsheviks had signed with the German Empire. Arrested by the Bolshevik government in July 1918 for participating in the Left SRs' plot to assassinate the German envoy in Moscow, Spiridonova was never again to have either her freedom or her health fully restored.

Spiridonova's pattern of active and passive self-sacrifice
A martyr-heroine of the tsarist era resurrected by the February Revolution, Spiridonova resumed her life as a political prisoner under the Soviet government. She had enjoyed just sixteen months of complete liberty, which she dedicated to pursuing her vision of socialist equality and justice for Russia's labouring classes. As her Left SR comrades declared, Spiridonova's 'second martyrdom' began with her arrest in July 1918.[87] From that time on, she lived in detention, in prison or in exile, sometimes enduring lengthy episodes of illness, until her execution on the orders of Josef Stalin in 1941.[88]

---

[85] *Golos trudovogo krest'ianstva*, no. 47, 19 January 1918.

[86] I. Z. Steinberg, 'Mukam revoliutsii (12-ia godovshchina vystrela)', *Znamia truda*, no. 121, 18 January 1918.

[87] Isaac Steinberg, *Spiridonova: Revolutionary Terrorist*, trans Gwenda David and Eric Mosbacher, London, 1935, p. 217.

[88] The tale of Spiridonova's second martyrdom is told in Sally A. Boniece, '"You Can Kill Me ... But I Shall Die Standing": Mariia Spiridonova's Letter to the NKVD, 1937', in Michael S. Melancon and Donald J. Raleigh (eds), *Russia's Century of Revolutions: Parties, People, Places; Studies Presented in Honor of Alexander Rabinowitch*, Bloomington, IN,

The contrast between Spiridonova's decade of invalidism in the Nerchinsk penal complex and her energetic plunge into national politics on regaining her freedom in 1917 would seem to be a striking one. Yet periods of hyperactivity alternating with bouts of illness are characteristic of tuberculosis,[89] and this was the pattern that dominated Spiridonova's life. Invariably, she suffered the worst episodes of her tuberculosis when her ability to take action was most curtailed: during her terms of imprisonment, whether under the tsarist or the Soviet system.

In 1906, Spiridonova and the Tambov SRs deliberately put in the public eye her act of political violence against the autocratic state and the state's retaliatory violence against her, thus creating a lasting legend of her extraordinary self-sacrifice. When she was removed from the political arena by arrest and imprisonment, Spiridonova succumbed to extended, often severe bouts of illness from which she appeared to recover once a measure of her freedom was restored. Nevertheless, as much as her image and audience may have mattered to her, Spiridonova was most powerfully motivated by her empathy for Russia's less fortunate classes and her conviction that socialist revolution would eradicate inequities from their lives. On behalf of the labouring people of her country, she chose to immerse herself in political activism that endangered her own freedom and, in consequence, her health.

For Spiridonova, maintaining her aura of exceptional martyrdom may have been particularly important during her imprisonment at Mal'tsev and Akatui with her SR terrorist comrades, all of whom had similarly experienced arrest, trial and sentencing by the tsarist state. Tuberculosis in Spiridonova's life and myth indeed ensured unending opportunity for martyrdom, for it encompassed both the romantic concept of the disease typical of the earlier half of the nineteenth century — its association with wealth, youth, womanhood and fragility — and its later association, after the discovery of the tubercle bacillus in 1882, with the miserably unsanitary living conditions of the lower classes.[90] Her disease imbued Spiridonova, the daughter of a non-hereditary noble, with an ethereal quality of saintly suffering when she was only twenty-one, but the bacillus was activated (or reactivated) when she entered the grim and unhygienic environment of prison, where impoverished and criminal elements of Russia's society lived alongside revolutionaries. Just as incarceration intensified Spiridonova's

2012, pp. 111–32.

[89] Dubos, *The White Plague*, pp. 64, 127–28.

[90] On the romantic and proletarian aspects of tuberculosis, see Herzlich and Pierret, *Illness and Self in Society*, pp. 24–29.

illness, her illness and isolation during her incarceration intensified Spiridonova's aura as a martyr-heroine.[91]

[91] An analogous, though apolitical, martyrdom of illness crowns Thérèse Martin of Lisieux, a French nun of the cloistered Carmelite order who died of tuberculosis at age 24 in 1897. Sister Thérèse, who had never experienced life beyond her middle-class family's home or the convent, created her own aura of self-sacrificing piety by penning an autobiography that exalted her physical suffering as spiritual redemption. Canonized in 1925, Thérèse remains one of the most popular Catholic cult figures to this day. For an analysis of the 'consumptive career' and mythology of St Thérèse, see Barnes, *The Making of a Social Disease*, pp. 63–73. Additionally, an enclosed convent resembles a prison in many respects. In nineteenth-century Europe, the sites of 'the most extreme cases of overcrowding' became the sites of the most endemic tuberculosis. Prisons ranked first and convents second for most overcrowded conditions and most endemic tuberculosis. Thomas Dormandy, *The White Death: A History of Tuberculosis*, New York, 2000, pp. 79–81.

The Sozonov Case, 1910:
The Making of a Russian
Revolutionary Martyrology

BEN PHILLIPS

'I owe my life to the awakening of society and the people;
hence they have won the right to my life a second time.'
Egor Sozonov, 1905[1]

'Безумству храбрых поем мы песню.'
(We sing our song to the madness of the brave.)
Maksim Gor´kii[2]

CAN a victim of suicide be venerated as a martyr? From St Augustine onwards, Christian thinkers have answered this question in the negative: if martyrdom is a virtuous death, suicide is contrary to moral law.[3] Russia, however, appears to present an exception to this rule. One of the most distinctive characteristics of the Russian tradition of martyrdom, both religious and secular, is the prevalence of suicide-martyrs. This tendency first took shape during the Church Schism (*raskol*) of the seventeenth century, when the mass self-immolations of Old Believers and other religious dissenters opposed to the reforms of the Patriarch Nikon created a lasting link between martyrdom and suicide in Russian cultural

Ben Phillips is Lecturer in Modern Russian History at the University of Exeter.
The author wishes to thank Elizabeth Harrison, Matt Rendle, Anna Maslenova and the two anonymous readers for *SEER* for their generous feedback on this article.

[1] S. P. Mel´gunov (ed.), *E. S. Sozonov: materialy dlia biografii. Vospominaniia, pis´ma, dokumenty, portrety*, Moscow, 1919, p. 18.
[2] 'Pesnia o sokole', in M. Gor´kii, *Polnoe sobranie sochinenii v 25 tomakh*, tom 2: *Rasskazy, ocherki, nabroski, stikhi. 1894–1896*, Moscow, 1969, pp. 42–47 (p. 47).
[3] On the historical and theological roots of this distinction, see Arthur J. Droge and James D. Tabor, *A Noble Death: Suicide and Martyrdom among Jews and Christians in Antiquity*, San Francisco, CA, 1991, and Alexander Murray, *Suicide in the Middle Ages*, 2 vols, vol. 2: *The Curse on Self-Murder*, Oxford, 2000 (esp. pp. 86–121).

doi:10.1353/see.00006

memory.[4] Some two centuries later, in the context of the revolutionary struggle against tsarism (*c.*1881–1917), the figure of the suicide-martyr once more achieved political and cultural salience: socialists who took their own lives for the cause were venerated no less than those who died at the barricades or on the scaffold. This article examines one ostensibly famous, yet (to date) conspicuously under-researched, case in point.

On the morning of 15 July 1904, on the street outside St Petersburg's Varshavskii railway station, Egor Sozonov,[5] a member of the Socialist-Revolutionary (SR) Party's Combat Organization (*boevaia organizatsiia*, i.e. terrorist wing), threw a bomb that killed the Minister of the Interior, V. K. Pleve. Arrested at the scene, Sozonov evaded the death penalty and was instead sentenced to hard labour (*katorga*) and exile for life. Some six years later, on 27 November 1910 (O.S.), he committed suicide in his Siberian prison cell in protest at the use of corporal punishment against his fellow political prisoners. In a note, Sozonov explained that he believed his death — which in effect represented the denouement of several years' bitter conflict with the prison authorities — could prevent the deaths of others, writing that 'if not for the vanishing hope that my death might lower the price demanded by Moloch, I would stay to fight alongside you'.[6]

Sozonov's death provoked a nationwide scandal. The weeks that followed saw questions asked in the Duma, blanket coverage in the liberal and revolutionary press, street demonstrations in major cities and, conversely, barely-concealed jubilation from the forces of the right. In later years, Sozonov was celebrated as a martyr and hero of the anti-tsarist struggle. When his remains were formally repatriated to his hometown of Ufa in May 1917, his funeral train was met at every station along the Trans-Siberian railway by delegations from local soviets, military honour guards and crowds of spectators. 'Thus liberated Russia honours her fallen sons', one SR pamphleteer wrote, 'martyrs in the cause of freedom'.[7]

As a whole, the Sozonov case — his decision to die, the morphine overdose by which he did so, the suicide note in which he explained his

---

[4] On Old Believer suicides, see D. I. Sapozhnikov, *Samosozhzhenie v russkom raskole s vtoroi poloviny XVII veka do kontsa XVIII: istoricheskii ocherk po arkhivnym dokumentam*, Moscow, 1891, and Robert O. Crummey, *The Old Believers and the World of Antichrist: The Vyg Community and the Russian State, 1694–1855*, Madison, WI, 1970, pp. 39–57. On suicide in Russian culture generally, see Susan K. Morrissey, *Suicide and the Body Politic in Imperial Russia*, Cambridge, 2006.

[5] The alternate spelling Sazonov appears in many sources.

[6] V. Chernov, 'Pamiati Egora Sozonova', *Znamia truda*, 33, January 1911, p. 6.

[7] *Egor Sergeevich Sazonov. Izdanie Pskovskoi gruppy partii sotsialistov-revoliutsionerov*, Pskov, 1917, p. 15.

actions, and the reactions his death elicited — conformed to a series of inter-related 'behavioural models' that had taken shape within the Russian radical subculture decades earlier.[8] The first revolutionary prison suicides took place in the late 1880s. As a political act and means of resistance, the prison suicide drew on various sources: the deep roots of Russian martyr culture, radical imaginings of tsarist prisons and exile as sites of heroic resistance to tyranny, and the asceticism that characterized the revolutionary underground before 1917. Just as importantly, however, prison suicides were linked both chronologically and discursively to the terror campaigns waged against the tsarist regime by the People's Will organization (Narodnaia volia, 1878–81) and, later, by the SRs (1901–11). Much as terrorist attacks were seen by most revolutionaries as legitimate acts of reprisal against the violence and capriciousness of the autocratic state, so too, on a microcosmic level, was the prison suicide, which became, in the words of one historian, a 'symbol of revolutionary transcendence' in the face of state repression.[9] In Sozonov's case, this connection between suicide and the legitimating narratives of terror was especially explicit.

Sozonov's death is mentioned in virtually every study of revolutionary terrorism and the SR Party, and in many general histories of the period. Up to now, however, it has evaded detailed analysis.[10] This article therefore

[8]   The idea of 'behavioural models' in Russian radical culture originates in Ju. M. Lotman, 'The Decembrist in Everyday Life' in Lotman and B. A. Uspenskij, *The Semiotics of Russian Culture*, ed. Ann Shukman, Ann Arbor, MI, 1984, pp. 71–123. Lotman's approach has been adopted by several historians, including Marina Mogil´ner, *Mifologiia podpol´nogo cheloveka: radikal´nyi mikrokosm v Rossii nachala XX veka kak predmet semioticheskogo analiza*, Moscow, 1999; Claudia Verhoeven, *The Odd Man Karakozov: Imperial Russia, Modernity, and the Birth of Terrorism*, Ithaca, NY, 2009, and Sally A. Boniece, 'The Spiridonova Case, 1906: Terror, Myth, and Martyrdom', *Kritika: Explorations in Russian and Eurasian History*, 4, 3, 2003, pp. 571–606.
[9]   Morrissey, *Suicide and the Body Politic*, p. 275. There were of course divergent understandings of terrorism within the revolutionary left. For recent studies, see Anna Geifman, *Thou Shalt Kill: Revolutionary Terrorism in Russia, 1894–1917*, Princeton, NJ, 1993; O. V. Budnitskii (ed.), *Krov´ po sovesti: terrorizm v Rossii. Dokumenty i biografii*, Rostov-on-Don, 1994, and idem, *Terrorizm v rossiiskom osvoboditel´nom dvizhenii: ideologiia, etika, psikhologiia (vtoraia polovina XIX–nachalo XX vekov)*, 2nd edn, Moscow, 2016; R. A. Gorodnitskii, *Boevaia organizatsiia partii sotsialistov-revoliutsionerov v 1901– 1911 gg*, Moscow, 2000; Antony Anemone (ed.), *Just Assassins: The Culture of Terrorism in Russia*, Evanston, IL, 2010, and Lynn Ellen Patyk, *Written in Blood: Revolutionary Terrorism and Russian Literary Culture, 1861–1881*, Madison, WI, 2017.
[10]   The most detailed study of Sozonov's case to date can be found in my recent monograph: *Siberian Exile and the Invention of Revolutionary Russia, 1825–1917: Exiles, Émigrés and the International Reception of Russian Radicalism*, Abingdon, 2022, pp. 137–49. Here I revisit the case, drawing on sources that (due to the Covid-19 pandemic) were hitherto unavailable to me. There are two article-length studies in Russian, neither of which explores Sozonov's death in any detail: R. A. Gorodnitskii, 'Egor Sozonov:

has two objectives. First, it reconstructs, in as much detail as possible, the events surrounding the 'Zerentui tragedy' of 1910 and the various reactions it elicited: from the revolutionary left and the radical right, from educated society more broadly, and from the state. Secondly, it examines how Sozonov's death was understood in relation to the dominant political and socio-cultural discourses of the time, and how these discourses collectively shaped his later martyr-myth: a 'just assassin', altruistic and morally pure, who had 'sacrificed his life twice over'[11] — once to free the Russian people from tyranny, a second time to spare the lives of his comrades.

E. S. Sozonov (1879–1910): Revolutionary and terrorist

Egor Sergeevich Sozonov was born in May 1879 in Viatka province, the youngest of three brothers. He was a shy, withdrawn child, due in part to frequent bouts of ill health.[12] At the age of ten, his family moved to the regional capital, Ufa, and thence into the Ural timber trade, where they made their fortune. Sozonov's family background was, at first glance, an inauspicious one for a budding revolutionary: not only did his parents belong to Russia's nascent capitalist class, they were — as he later acknowledged in an autobiographical note written for his defence lawyer in 1904 — 'upstanding [blagomysliashchie], religious and monarchist by disposition'.[13] Yet although Sozonov would later reject his parents' political conservatism, his strict Old Believer upbringing — as several who knew him later observed — did much to shape his moral and psychological makeup.[14] His religious faith remained undimmed throughout his life: in a letter to his family from prison in 1906, he wrote that 'we, the socialists, are carrying on the work of Christ, who preached fraternal love among men, carried along with him the wretched of the earth and died, as a political criminal, for his fellow man'.[15]

mirovozzrenie i psikhologiia esera-terrorista', Otechestvennaia istoriia, 5, 1995, pp. 168–74, and N. A. Troitskii, 'Delo Egora Sozonova', Otechestvennaia istoriia, 2, 2014, pp. 50–54.

[11] 'Rech' na vechere pamiati E. Sozonova (26 noiabria 1921 goda)', in V. N. Figner, Polnoe sobranie sochinenii v semi tomakh, tom 5: Ocherki, stat'i, rechi, Moscow, 1932, pp. 447–56 (p. 455).

[12] A. L. Sozonova, 'E. S. Sozonov po vospominaniiam ego materi', in B. P. Koz'min and N. I. Rakitnikov (eds), Pis'ma Egora Sozonova k rodnym, 1895–1910, Moscow, 1925, pp. 47–50 (p. 47).

[13] E. S. Sozonov, Ispoved' (dlia moego zashchitnika), St Petersburg, 1906, p. 42.

[14] See, for instance, M. A. Spiridonova, 'Iz zhizni na Nerchinskoi katorge', Katorga i ssylka, 16, 1925, pp. 115–33 (pp. 117–18), and P. S. Ivanovskaia, V boevoi organizatsii: vospominaniia, 2nd edn, Moscow, 1929, p. 45.

[15] Pis'ma Egora Sozonova k rodnym, p. 84.

In 1898, Sozonov left home to enrol in the medical faculty of Moscow University. He initially had little interest in politics, and his first (brief) arrest in 1900 was apparently a case of mistaken identity. He was nonetheless drawn into the radical student movement of the time and, the following year, was expelled from university for his part in unsanctioned demonstrations (*skhodki*).[16] The harsh treatment Sozonov received at the hands of the authorities marked the beginning of his political radicalization, and when he returned to Ufa, his mother later recalled, he had changed beyond recognition, becoming 'extremely interested in revolutionary literature, associating with socialists and political exiles, and, before long, devoting himself entirely to his new cause'.[17] Shortly after his return, he joined the SR Party and quickly became one of the leaders of its Ufa committee. He was arrested for a second time in 1902: following a lengthy spell in pre-trial detention, he was exiled to Siberia, but absconded and escaped overseas to Switzerland.[18]

Like others of his generation, Sozonov's decision to take up arms against tsarism was motivated by the deep revulsion he felt at the bloody means by which the state, in the years immediately preceding 1905, sought to contain growing popular unrest across Russia. Once overseas, he enlisted in the Combat Organization: just over a year later, on 15 July 1904, he threw the bomb that killed Minister of the Interior V. K. Pleve, the state official who, to quote one historian, symbolized more than any other 'the capriciousness and intransigence of the autocratic regime' at the time.[19] In a statement written afterwards in prison for his defence lawyer, Sozonov accused the deceased of crimes greater than his own. Pleve, he argued, had 'declared war on Russia itself, coating her soil with the blood of her citizens'.[20] Although a standard part of political trials in imperial Russia, such rhetoric resonated with the public mood on the eve of 1905, the moment at which popular support for terrorist attacks against the regime was, insofar as measurable, at its highest: almost overnight, the young revolutionary became a hero to liberal and educated society. He was toasted at opposition banquets and meetings, while members of his family who came to Petersburg to visit him in prison were mobbed by crowds of

---

[16] On the student movement of the early twentieth century, see Susan K. Morrissey, *Heralds of Revolution: Russian Students and the Mythologies of Radicalism*, Oxford, 1998.

[17] Sozonova, 'Po vospominaniiam', p. 49.

[18] *E. S. Sozonov: materialy dlia biografii*, pp. 27–29.

[19] Abraham Ascher, *The Revolution of 1905*, 2 vols, vol. 1: *Russia in Disarray*, Stanford, CA, 1988, p. 54.

[20] Sozonov, *Ispoved'*, pp. 31–33.

supporters.[21] When Sozonov was brought to trial in November, his defence lawyer caused a commotion in the courtroom by claiming that the bomb that killed Pleve had been filled 'not so much with dynamite as with the tears, grief and sorrows of the Russian people'.[22]

It is testament to the strength of public feeling (and to the more liberal climate that briefly prevailed under P. D. Sviatopolk-Mirskii, Pleve's successor at the Ministry of Internal Affairs) that the court declined to confer the expected death sentence: Sozonov was sentenced to *katorga* and exile for life. He served the first year of his sentence in the Shlissel'burg fortress, home since the 1880s to the terrorists of the previous generation. When the fortress was closed in early 1906, he and his fellow inmates were transferred to the Nerchinsk *katorga* complex in Eastern Siberia, a sprawling network of prisons situated some 500 miles southeast of Lake Baikal to which, for nearly a century, most high-profile political prisoners in Russia had been sent. By this point, Sozonov's sentence had been significantly curtailed, by a series of amnesties granted to political prisoners in 1905, from life to just seven years: he was due for release in January 1911.

The 'prison struggle'

From around 1907 onwards, the conditions confronting Russian political prisoners began to deteriorate drastically. Prompted in part by an unprecedented wave of violent disorders that swept prison and exile at the height of the 1905 revolution,[23] the prison authorities — acting in the spirit of Stolypinite reaction — sought to restore order by all available means. During this period, many Russian prisons became synonymous with extreme brutality and human rights abuses, the most egregious instances of which (in a paradox characteristic of Russia's 'constitutional era') were reported in the newly-uncensored press and even, in some cases, investigated by the State Duma.[24] Revolutionary memoirs often refer to this period as the 'prison struggle' (*tiuremnaia bor'ba*), a time when

[21] A. V. Bogdanovich, *Tri poslednikh samoderzhtsa*, Moscow, 1990, p. 314; 'Tri silueta: Breshkovskaia, Gershuni, Sazonov', in N. P. Karabchevskii, *Okolo pravosudiia: stat'i, soobshcheniia, sudebnye ocherki*, 2nd edn, St Petersburg, 1908, pp. 196–206 (pp. 205–06).

[22] N. P. Karabchevskii, *Rechi: 1882–1914*, 3rd edn, Petrograd, 1916, p. 498.

[23] Official statistics reveal 5,961 prison breaks and 278 riots during 1906–07 alone, with forty–four prison officers murdered by inmates during the same period. See 'Iz otcheta po glavnomu tiuremnomu upravleniiu za 1908 god', *Tiuremnyi vestnik*, 2, 1910, pp. 62–67.

[24] On the most notorious prison scandal of the time (involving the Orel *katorga* 'central'), see M. N. Gernet, *Istoriia tsarskoi tiur'my*, 3rd edn, 5 vols, vol. 5, Moscow, 1960–63, pp. 289–304.

political prisoners were forced to resort to extreme means of protest in defence of their rights and, as one put it, 'unite in common cause against an administration that wielded the sword of Damocles over our heads'.[25]

Confrontations between Russian political prisoners and their guards were not without precedent: by the late nineteenth century, the former had a well-established tradition of resistance to the prison authorities and, more broadly, of treating prison and exile as an extension of the wider struggle against tsarism. Prison protests were often provoked by officials exceeding their powers and engaging in various kinds of demeaning behaviour, including the arbitrary withdrawal of political prisoners' traditional privileges and address with the informal pronoun (*ty*). Before 1907 such incidents were the exception rather than the rule,[26] but were much more common in periods of 'reaction', including the late 1860s and the reign of Alexander III (1881–94).

Protest tactics employed by political prisoners ranged from minor acts of insubordination (refusing to doff caps or obey orders from prison officials) to hunger strikes and, in the most extreme cases, suicide.[27] The 1880s saw several such cases. In 1884–85, two terrorists incarcerated at the Shlissel´burg fortress, Egor Minakov and Ippolit Myshkin, were executed by firing squad for deliberate assaults on prison officials — actions that they undertook in protest at the indignities to which they and their fellow prisoners were subjected, and which both knew would lead directly to their deaths. Two years later, another inmate of the fortress, Mikhail Grachevskii, died through self-immolation, apparently after suffering a mental breakdown in similar circumstances.[28] Finally, in 1889, six inmates of the Kara *katorga* prison — four of them women — took fatal overdoses of morphine after one of their number, Nadezhda Sigida, was subjected to one hundred blows of the lash for striking a prison officer in the face.[29] This latter incident, which quickly became known as the

---

[25] G. M. Kramarov, 'Nerchinskaia katorga 1907–1910 gg', *Katorga i ssylka*, 3, 1922, pp. 57–70 (p. 65).

[26] With some notable exceptions, most political prisoners in the nineteenth century were not treated badly. See Jonathan Daly, 'Political Crime in Late Imperial Russia', *Journal of Modern History*, 74, 1, 2002, pp. 62–100.

[27] For a transnational study of prison hunger strikes that focuses on the Russian origins of the tactic, see Kevin Grant, 'British Suffragettes and the Russian Method of Hunger Strike', *Comparative Studies in History and Society*, 53, 1, 2011, pp. 113–43.

[28] On the deaths of Minakov, Myshkin and Grachevskii, see L. A. Volkenshtein, *13 let v Shlissel´burgskoi kreposti: zapiski*, ed. V. L. Burtsev, Purleigh, 1900.

[29] For first-hand accounts see G. F. Osmolovskii, 'Kariiskaia tragediia: iz vospominanii', *Byloe*, 6, 1906, pp. 59–80, and E. N. Koval´skaia and G. F. Osmolovskii (eds), *Kariiskaia tragediia 1889 goda: vospominaniia i materialy*, Petrograd, 1920.

'Kara tragedy' (*Kariiskaia tragediia*), received considerable publicity both within Russia and overseas, prompting an international protest campaign against the Siberian exile system.[30] Sigida and other prison suicides were glorified as martyrs, and their actions inscribed in the cultural codes of the revolutionary underground: in later years, many more would follow their example.

Any explanation for the genesis of the prison suicide as a political tactic must take account of several cultural factors. Firstly, the 'prison struggle' resonated with the radical cultural imagination, which, since the time of Radishchev and the Decembrists, had romanticized prison and exile as sites of 'triumph and suffering'.[31] Secondly, the Russian revolutionary movement of the late nineteenth century (and the terrorist subculture that emerged from the late 1870s especially) was characterized by a spirit of asceticism, and a desire to suffer in the name of higher ideals, that lent itself to the pursuit of martyrdom. Since many *narodniki* also displayed a particular reverence for the Old Believers (whom they regarded as, in a sense, their spiritual ancestors and champions of the common people against the yoke of autocracy), it is perhaps unsurprising that this quest for martyrdom became, in certain extreme manifestations, suicidal.[32]

A third factor, of decisive importance in Sigida's case (and later in Sozonov's), was that of corporal punishment and the socio-cultural meanings ascribed to it. As Abby Schrader has shown, flogging, from the eighteenth century onwards, was closely linked to imperial Russia's social hierarchies: it was regarded as something reserved for and inflicted upon the peasantry, while exemption from the lash conversely symbolized 'the acquisition of elite status'.[33] Moreover, the use of flogging as a criminal

[30] On the international impact of the 'Kara tragedy' see Phillips, *Siberian Exile*, pp. 81–120.

[31] To quote G. A. Gershuni, *Iz nedavnego proshlogo*, Paris, 1908, p. 123.

[32] The revival of popular interest in the Old Believers from the 1860s onwards was in large part driven by Populist intellectuals who drew parallels (implicitly and explicitly) between the Schism and the political context of their own time. See Alexander Etkind, 'Whirling with the Other: Russian Populism and Religious Sects', *The Russian Review*, 62, 4, 2003, pp. 565–88, and Aleksandr Pyzhikov, *Grani russkogo raskola: tainaia rol' staroobriadchestva ot semnadtsatogo veka do semnadtsatogo goda*, 2nd edn, Moscow, 2018, pp. 67–82. Contemporary scholarly debates over the origins of self-immolation among Old Believer communities were likewise dominated by Populist historians who argued (again, with one eye evidently on the present) that collective suicides were 'an extreme expression of struggle against overwhelming state power'. See Sapozhnikov, *Samosozhzhenie v russkom raskole*, p. 153.

[33] Abby M. Schrader, *Languages of the Lash: Corporal Punishment and Identity in Imperial Russia*, DeKalb, IL, 2002, p. 12.

punishment, once ubiquitous, had been much curtailed during the nineteenth century, such that the jurist N. S. Tagantsev, writing in 1902, could claim that 'in their general direction our laws have been moving towards the abolition of all forms of corporal punishment'.[34] As a result, flogging, when inflicted upon members of the intelligentsia, was not just deeply shocking, but regarded as the gravest imaginable insult. One prisoner who survived the mass suicides at Kara later explained that he had attempted to take his own life because 'neither my education nor my sense of dignity allowed me to live under the constant threat of such shame and degradation'.[35]

In other words, Russian revolutionary terrorism and the prison suicide were linked not just by the simple fact that many who took their own lives in prison had been members of terrorist groups, but on the discursive level too. Both were construed as desperate responses to state violence, a framing that elided the act of revolutionary violence involved (whether directed outwards against state officials or inwards against oneself). Just as Vera Zasulich's attack on Colonel Trepov in 1878, and her subsequent acquittal by a Petersburg jury, set one precedent that government officials who flogged political prisoners would be punished with terrorist reprisals, so the events described above set a second: that imprisoned revolutionaries faced with such intolerable insults to their dignity should respond in the manner of Grachevskii, Sigida and their comrades.

Prison suicides proved an effective tactic: the international outrage prompted by the 'Kara tragedy', in particular, ensured that such episodes remained very rare for some time. After 1907, however, the use of corporal punishment against political prisoners became much more common. Although no statistical data is available, it is clear from the sources that the practice, which seems to have had a degree of official sanction,[36] was very widespread. 'Until recently', one journalist wrote, 'the flogging of political prisoners represented a tragedy that [...] left a lasting mark on the public

---

[34] N. S. Tagantsev, *Russkoe ugolovnoe pravo. Chast' obshchaia*, 2nd edn, 2 vols, vol. 2, St Petersburg, 1902, p. 1112. The upshot of this was that prisons, by the end of the nineteenth century, were in effect the only places where people from the privileged *sosloviia* (who relinquished their rank and status at the point of sentencing) could be flogged. See *Svod zakonov Rossiiskoi imperii*, tom 14: *Ustav o ssyl'nykh*, St Petersburg, 1909, p. 57.

[35] A. Fomin, 'Kariiskaia tragediia po arkhivnym dokumentam', in A. Dikovskaia-Iakimova and V. Pleskov (eds), *Kara i drugie tiur'my Nerchinskoi katorgi*, Moscow, 1927, pp. 120–37 (p. 134).

[36] See I. G. Shcheglovitov's testimony in *Padenie tsarskogo rezhima. Stenograficheskie otchety doprosov i pokazanii, dannykh v 1917 godu v Chrezvychainoi sledstvennoi komissii Vremennogo pravitel'stva*, 7 vols, vol. 2, Leningrad, 1924–27, pp. 422–25.

consciousness. Now such tragedies occur almost constantly: they have become normalized, part of the daily routine of prison life'.[37] For many on the left, the violence of the prison regime, no less than Stolypin's military courts, became a touchstone for the onset of reaction. 'All of Russia is being beaten', one SR deputy declared in the Duma in 1907: '[the government] beats us in prisons, police stations and the Riga fortress; in the towns, the "real Russians" do the job for them'.[38]

The increased use of flogging probably reflected not just a desire on the part of certain officials to revenge themselves on their revolutionary adversaries, but the fact that most political prisoners after 1905 came no longer from the privileged classes, but from the peasantry (i.e. from that part of the population which had never been exempt from corporal punishment in the first place).[39] Whatever the reasons for it, however, the consequences are not in doubt: from 1907 onwards, the suicide rate in Russian prisons more than doubled. In the years 1907–08, no fewer than 221 prisoners took their own lives behind bars.[40]

The 'Zerentui tragedy'

For several years Nerchinsk *katorga* escaped the worst of this backlash. In particular, the Gornyi Zerentui prison – the largest of the seven Nerchinsk prisons, to which Sozonov had been transferred in late 1907 — was distinguished by a relatively liberal regime that still allowed the political prisoners (among other privileges) to live in self-governing communes, and which led the SR leader Viktor Chernov to describe the prison as an 'oasis in the *katorga* desert'.[41] In due course, however, this too began to change, with officials raising concerns not just over what they saw as the excessively indulgent conditions prevailing at Zerentui, but the security risks such indulgence generated. Writing in 1910, one Main Prison Administration (Glavnoe tiuremnoe upravlenie; hereafter,

---

[37] V. Miakotin, 'O sovremennoi tiur'me i ssylke', *Russkoe bogatstvo*, 9, 1910, pp. 124–54 (pp. 134–35).
[38] *Gosudarstvennaia duma vtorogo sozyva: stenograficheskie otchety*, session 2.23, 6 April 1907, p. 1679. 'Real Russians' referred to the 1906 murder of the Kadet M. Ia. Gertsenshtein.
[39] Before 1905 around half of those sentenced for 'state' crimes were from the privileged classes: after 1906, the figure was just 10 per cent. Peasants accounted for some 19 per cent of political offenders before 1905, but 60 per cent afterwards. See E. N. Tarnovskii, 'Statistika svedenii ob osuzhdennykh za gosudarstvennye prestupleniia v 1905–1912 gg', *Zhurnal ministerstva iustitsii*, 9, 1915, pp. 37–69 (pp. 56–57).
[40] 'Iz otcheta po GTU za 1908 god', p. 67. By comparison, some 42 prisoners took their own lives in 1906.
[41] Chernov, 'Pamiati Egora Sozonova', p. 5.

GTU) inspector noted the presence among the prison's political inmates of 'unreconstructed, unbending revolutionaries', who, he argued, had a radicalizing effect on the ordinary criminal convicts.[42] Such concerns were echoed at the highest levels of state: addressing the Council of Ministers in 1909, Minister of Justice I. G. Shcheglovitov complained that Nerchinsk *katorga* no longer resembled 'the image that persists in the popular imagination of our harshest form of criminal punishment, second only to the death penalty'.[43]

From the summer of 1909, conditions for the political prisoners at Zerentui became much harsher. The inmates lost their communal life and many of their privileges: by 1910, their cells were locked night and day, they were obliged to wear both leg and wrist irons and the standard prison garb, and lived in fear of the prison watch, who on more than one occasion used them as target practice.[44] One inmate, the Bolshevik Grigorii Kramarov, wrote that the authorities 'gradually destroyed our free redoubt [*vol'nitsa*]; with fists clenched, they began to enforce a real *katorga* regime'.[45]

This crackdown inevitably created conflict with the political prisoners, who regarded the struggle for their rights not just as a matter of self-preservation, but of wider social and political importance. 'Every one of us knew', Kramarov recalled, that the worsening prison regime was 'the result of the growing reaction at home: as soon as the revolutionary movement began to decline, [the state] began to crush the prisons and insult our dignity'.[46] Initially the inmates registered their protest through insubordination, such as refusing to respond when addressed with the informal pronoun and remaining seated when officers entered their cells. All involved knew, however, that worse was coming, and from 1908 the political prisoners at Nerchinsk carried on an illicit correspondence on tactical questions: in short, how to respond to a vengeful officialdom they regarded as hellbent on their 'physical annihilation'.[47] In these debates, Sozonov emerged as the leader of those who argued for active resistance by all possible means, including suicide: as the terrorist Mariia Spiridonova

[42] Gosudarstvennyi arkhiv Rossiiskoi federatsii (hereafter, GARF), f. 122, op. 1, d. 6157, l. 28, 36. Materialy o komandirovke inspektora GTU Sementovskogo dlia osmotra tiurem, 1910.

[43] 'Po voprosu o preobrazovanii katorgi', 8 December 1909, in B. D. Gal'perina (ed.), *Osobye zhurnaly soveta ministrov Rossiiskoi imperii*, 9 vols, vol. 1, Moscow, 2000–09, pp. 488–92 (p. 488).

[44] GARF, f. 122, op. 1, d. 6157, ll. 30–32; 'U groba Sozonova', *Byloe*, 13, 1910, pp. 157–59; Kramarov, 'Nerchinskaia katorga', p. 69.

[45] Ibid., p. 68.

[46] Ibid.

[47] M. A. Spiridonova, 'Iz zhizni na Nerchinskoi katorge', p. 131.

wrote later, Sozonov saw suicide not just as 'a protest against violence', but as 'liberation from a system that robbed the individual of all humanity'.[48]

For Sozonov, the storm clouds gathering over Nerchinsk in 1909–10 represented the denouement of an eight-year struggle against the prison authorities. From the beginning of his revolutionary career, Sozonov had been deeply affected by the violence and degradation he witnessed in prison, which he saw as representing in microcosm the violence inflicted by the autocracy on Russian society as a whole. In his 1904 court testimony, he noted that his first imprisonment in 1902–03, during which he came face to face with people 'beaten by their guards and the police, people who had spent weeks on hunger strike and contracted tuberculosis due to prison conditions', had contributed to his growing radicalization.[49] As several of his comrades later noted, Sozonov also displayed an almost fanatical devotion to the legacy of the People's Will — a devotion that manifested not just in his initial decision to become a terrorist, but in his evident desire to emulate the stoicism displayed by Vera Figner, Nikolai Morozov and others during their long years in Shlissel'burg.[50] As a result, by the time he arrived in Siberia in 1906, Sozonov saw the 'prison struggle' as nothing less than his 'moral obligation and revolutionary duty'[51] — a duty he was forced to discharge sooner than he might have expected.

Upon arrival in Siberia, Sozonov was assigned to Akatui, which at the time was Nerchinsk's designated 'political' prison and therefore home to some of the most famous revolutionaries in Russia at the time (other celebrity inmates included his fellow SRs Grigorii Gershuni, Petr Karpovich and Mariia Spiridonova). Akatui was distinguished not just by its famous residents, but by a remarkably lax regime that bore less resemblance to a prison than to a socialist commune, with prisoner escapes an everyday occurrence. When Gershuni absconded in a barrel of sauerkraut in October that year, the security risks this situation posed became intolerable in the eyes of the authorities, who, in a sign of things to come, quickly moved to break up the Akatui commune. Early in 1907, Spiridonova and other women were removed to the nearby Mal'tsev

---

[48] Ibid., pp. 131–32; G. Frolov, 'O Egore Sozonove', in *Pis'ma Egora Sozonova k rodnym*, pp. 51–63 (p. 62).

[49] Sozonov, *Ispoved'*, p. 59.

[50] See B. V. Savinkov, *Vospominaniia terrorista*, Moscow, 1990, p. 47, and Ivanovskaia, *V boevoi organizatsii*, pp. 44–45. In 1908, Sozonov claimed that, during his own stint in the fortress, he had 'learned to love life as never before [...] I felt that this was somehow real life, one I wouldn't have swapped for all the temptations Satan offered Christ'. See 'Pis'ma E. S. Sozonova k M. A. Prokof'evoi', *Volia Rossii*, 9, 1930, p. 735.

[51] Frolov, 'O Egore Sozonove', p. 62.

prison, while Sozonov, along with other 'intransigents' (*bespokoinye*), was transferred to a third prison, Algacha, to be broken: upon arrival, his group was subjected to physical abuse and a range of humiliations. In response, Sozonov declared a hunger strike. Two weeks later, faced with negative press coverage and questions in the Duma, the government backed down, relieving the Algacha commandant, Borodulin, of his duties (he was nevertheless assassinated by an SR flying squad several months later).[52]

The immediate upshot of this episode was that Sozonov was transferred to Zerentui and left alone for a few years. Yet it also meant that he was henceforth identified as the de facto leader of the political prisoners at Nerchinsk (or, as one official allegedly put it, 'the king of *katorga*'),[53] a status that may have marked him out as a bigger target in the eyes of officialdom. In the last year of his life, Sozonov was convinced that some in the GTU wanted him dead.[54]

In November 1910, the simmering conflict between the authorities and the Zerentui prisoners came to a head with the appointment of a new commandant, one Lavr Vysotskii. Vysotskii remains a mysterious figure: most sources do not even give his full name, and in the process of preparing this article it has been possible to confirm only scant details. Two such details are relevant here. First, he was an inexperienced prison officer, with just two years' service on his record.[55] Secondly, what he lacked in experience he made up for in personal qualities (or lack thereof), including arrogance and a taste for the arbitrary abuse of power: in a word, the worst attributes of the stereotypical tsarist satrap.[56] His previous appointment had been as warden of a notorious prison near Ekaterinburg known in contemporary parlance as the 'Shlissel´burg of the Urals',[57] and the degree to which his disciplinarian reputation preceded him, given the paucity of concrete information on him in the sources, is striking indeed: news of his impending arrival prompted terror among the political

[52] *Pis´ma Egora Sozonova k rodnym*, pp. 125–30. Borodulin was just one of dozens of prison officers killed in terrorist attacks during this period. See M. Ivich, 'Statistika terroristicheskikh aktov, sovershennykh partiei sotsialistov-revoliutsionerov', in *Partiia sotsialistov-revoliutsionerov: dokumenty i materialy*, 3 vols, vol. 2, Moscow, 1996–2000, pp. 378–89.

[53] Frolov, 'O Egore Sozonove', p. 53; I. N. Bril´on, *Na katorge: vospominaniia revoliutsionera*, Petrograd, 1917, p. 103; G. N. Chemodanov, *Nerchinskaia katorga: vospominaniia byvshego nachal´nika konvoinoi komandy*, 2nd edn, Moscow, 1930, p. 80.

[54] *Pis´ma Egora Sozonova k rodnym*, p. 367; 'U groba Sozonova', p. 159.

[55] *Tiuremnyi vestnik*, 5, 1908, p. 381 gives March 1908 as the date of his first appointment.

[56] See especially the unflattering portrait of him in Chemodanov, *Nerchinskaia katorga*, pp. 86–90.

[57] L. I. Gol´dman, 'Nikolaevskii zastenok', *Katorga i ssylka*, 15, 1925, pp. 224–30.

prisoners at Zerentui. Rumours that he had been appointed with an unspecified 'special mission', and of his alleged connections to the Black Hundreds began to circulate within the prison, leading some inmates to contemplate killing him upon arrival.[58] Sozonov, for his part, interpreted Vysotskii's appointment as confirmation of his worst fears. In an exchange with the outgoing commandant, G. M. Chemodanov, Sozonov alleged that Vysotskii's arrival was connected to his own imminent release and complained that he was 'being handed over to one of the most ferocious prison officers in the whole of Russia [...] Mark my words: I won't leave here alive'.[59]

Were Sozonov's suspicions about Vysotskii correct? In the days and weeks after his death, some on the revolutionary left, including the SR leadership, alleged that Sozonov had been the victim, and Vysotskii the executioner, of what Chernov called a 'premeditated murder': a conspiracy by hardliners in the GTU, linked to the Black Hundreds, to drive him to his death before he could be released from prison.[60] Yet the evidence cited in support of this interpretation, which is also advanced in some Soviet-era sources, is circumstantial at best.[61] There are grounds to conclude that Vysotskii did have connections on the right, and Chemodanov (whose memoirs, written in the 1920s, include the most detailed account of Vysotskii available) was in little doubt that he sought to provoke a confrontation with the political prisoners in order to 'fulfil the wicked task of those who had sent him'.[62] This view was shared by other prison officials, who testified against Vysotskii before an official investigating commission.[63] Yet none of this indicates a specific plot against Sozonov, and the limited evidence available suggests other possible reasons for Vysotskii's appointment. A number of escape plots, intended to free (among others) Sozonov and Spiridonova, had been foiled in 1909–10;

[58] On the prisoners' mood, see V. Pleskov, 'Pamiatnye dni', *Katorga i ssylka*, 3, 1922, pp. 45–50 (p. 45), and I. Minaev, 'Neudavshchaiasia vstrecha', *Katorga i ssylka*, 34, 1927, pp. 123–27.

[59] Chemodanov, *Nerchinskaia katorga*, p. 81.

[60] Ibid., p. 7; 'U groba Sozonova', pp. 157–59; 'Smert' E. S. Sozonova: pis'mo s katorgi', *Znamia truda*, 33, 1911, pp. 24–27.

[61] See N. Rostov, 'Smert' Egora Sozonova', in *Pis'ma Egora Sozonova k rodnym*, pp. 29–46, and idem, *Zerentuiskaia tragediia*, Moscow, 1926. Both works are conspicuously lacking in hard evidence, while some of the evidence Rostov does present (including on Vysotskii's track record) appears on closer inspection to be fabricated.

[62] Chemodanov, *Nerchinskaia katorga*, p. 90.

[63] N. Grave, 'Sekretnoe soobshchenie prokurora Chitinskogo okruzhnogo suda ob otravlenii ssyl'no-katorzhnogo Egora Sozonova', *Istoricheskii arkhiv: sbornik materialov i statei*, 1, 1921, pp. 205–06 (p. 206).

it would also appear that some security officials had concerns about Chemodanov's political reliability.[64] In any event, what happened next was by no means a foregone conclusion.

On 24 November 1910, Vysotskii formally took command of the Zerentui prison: upon doing so, he delivered a provocative speech to the assembled inmates in which he announced that henceforth no distinction between political and ordinary criminals would be recognized and vowed to flog 'for the slightest infraction' (*za maleishie prostupki*) of the rules. The following day, while making his rounds of the political wing, Vysotskii forced the prisoners to stand to attention while addressing them individually with the informal pronoun (*ty*). Finally, on 27 November, he made good on his initial threats by having two political prisoners, Slomianskii and Petrov, flogged for minor disciplinary breaches. In response, the inmates declared a hunger strike and began to prepare for collective suicides. That night, Sozonov — who, isolated from his comrades in a solitary confinement cell, was apparently under the impression that suicides had already begun — took a fatal overdose of morphine in his cell. He was discovered still alive in the early hours of the morning (28 November), but the efforts of the prison medics to save him proved fruitless.[65]

This was not Sozonov's first suicide attempt: he had tried at least once before (in 1907, at the height of his confrontation with his previous nemesis Borodulin),[66] and it is clear, both from general context and from epistolary evidence, that his willingness — perhaps determination — to die in prison was to some degree motivated by the example of the 1889 'Kara tragedy'.[67] Seen from this perspective, it is all the more striking that while Sozonov's death followed the Kara 'script' in most respects (corporal punishment as the trigger, morphine as the method), he departed from that script in one important respect. Unlike Sigida and her comrades, who enacted a suicide pact and died as a collective, Sozonov — as he explained in a note addressed to his fellow prisoners, and later reprinted in an SR newspaper — took his own life precisely so that his comrades would be spared such a fate:

---

[64] 'Ot glavnogo tiuremnogo upravleniia', *Novoe vremia*, 30 November 1910, p. 2; Figner, *PSS*, tom 3: *Posle Shlissel´burga*, pp. 228–81; Chemodanov, *Nerchinskaia katorga*, pp. 78–79; GARF, f. 122, op. 1, d. 6157, ll. 30–34.

[65] This version of events is set out in virtually all memoir sources and in a memorandum received by Shcheglovitov at the time. See Grave, 'Sekretnoe soobshchenie', pp. 205–06.

[66] Chernov, 'Pamiati Egora Sozonova', p. 6.

[67] Sozonov refers to the events of 1889 (both explicitly and implicitly) in several letters to Mariia Prokof´eva. See 'Pis´ma E. S. Sozonova', *Volia Rossii*, 3, 1930, p. 238 and 5–6, 1930, p. 441.

Comrades! Tonight I will try to end my life. If anyone's death can prevent further sacrifices, it is surely mine. And so I must die. I feel this with all my heart: it pains me only that I could not prevent the deaths of those who died today. I ask and beg you, comrades, not to imitate me and not to seek a hasty death! If not for the vanishing hope that my death might lower the price demanded by Moloch, I would stay to fight alongside you [...] but to wait another day will mean more victims. Warmest greetings, my friends, and goodnight. Egor.[68]

The public response

News of what had taken place in Zerentui reached St Petersburg by telegram the following day (29 November), and immediately provoked a scandal. Left-wing deputies in the Duma tabled an urgent question — ultimately defeated by a narrow margin — demanding a public enquiry. The Menshevik N. S. Chkheidze, who spoke for the motion, was heckled during his speech by the parties of the right, who were openly jubilant at news of Sozonov's death. Responding to Chkheidze, the leader of the Union of Russian People (Soiuz russkogo naroda; hereafter, URP), N. E. Markov, suggested that the opposition, if they found corporal punishment so distasteful, should simply vote to ban it. 'I bitterly regret', Markov added, 'that the murderer of Pleve, that most eminent of statesmen, was not hung at the time, and if he is now dead, I am delighted'.[69] The behaviour of the Duma majority prompted revulsion in educated society — even the conservative *Novoe vremia* denounced those 'who rejoiced in the martyrdom of such criminals as if it were a feast day'[70] — and did little to allay the suspicions of those on the left who believed Sozonov had been the victim of an official conspiracy.

The forces of opposition reacted with outrage to the news from Siberia. All the major revolutionary committees and newspapers hailed Sozonov as a hero and martyr to the cause: the SR Central Committee devoted an entire issue of the party newspaper *Znamia truda* to his memory, while the Menshevik Fedor Dan wrote that 'every revolutionary, even those who followed a different political trajectory to Egor Sozonov, will cherish the memory of a man who remained, to his dying breath, a fighter'.[71]

---

[68] Chernov, 'Pamiati Egora Sozonova', p. 6.
[69] *Gosudarstvennaia duma tret'ego sozyva: stenograficheskie otchety* (hereafter, *Gosudarstvennaia duma*), session 4.27, 29 November 1910, St Petersburg, 1910, p. 2223.
[70] Chernov, 'Pamiati Egora Sozonova', p. 7; 'Zametki', *Novoe vremia*, 2 December 1910, p. 4.
[71] F. D. [F. I. Dan], 'Zerentuiskaia tragediia i liberal'noe obshchestvo', *Golos sotsial'demokrata*, 24, 1911, pp. 3–4 (p. 3).

The major liberal dailies (*Russkoe slovo* and the Kadet organ *Rech'*) gave several days' blanket coverage to the story. In an editorial, *Rech'* described Sozonov's suicide as 'an incident that had stirred the public conscience', the inevitable nadir of the government's war on educated society.[72] Inasmuch as it revolved around the arbitrary abuse of state power, Sozonov's case indeed represented in microcosm the liberal critique of autocracy, since it showed Russia to be a lawless state in which the individual was powerless in the face of unaccountable petty tyrants: in other words, it epitomized the frustrated hopes of 1905 for responsible government and an open society. 'After 17 October [1905]', one liberal columnist wrote, 'I have the right to know what happened [in Zerentui], what Sozonov died from, why suicides took place, and whether the prison authorities broke the law [...] I want the truth, the whole truth'.[73] Speaking in the Duma, the Kadet Fedor Rodichev urged the government to investigate properly in order to maintain public confidence in the constitutional system: otherwise, he argued, Russia would be known as 'a country where people are flogged and driven to suicide with the consent of a representative government', and Sozonov remembered 'not as Pleve's murderer, but as a man who took poison because he could not witness people being subjected to the most unbearable tortures'.[74]

As this suggests, much of the public debate focused not on Sozonov himself, but on the role of corporal punishment (and thus, more broadly, the problem of state violence). The opposition motion tabled in the Duma alleged that floggings were used by the government as a way of driving imprisoned revolutionaries, who 'in the majority of cases have a strong sense of their own human dignity [*chelovecheskoe dostoinstvo*]' and 'naturally cannot bear such abuse', to death by suicide.[75] 'Whatever the law says', the left-wing journalist Afanasii Petrishchev wrote in *Russkoe bogatstvo*, 'common sense cannot tolerate the use of such shameful punishments against the offspring of educated Russian society, those who follow, from one generation to the next, in the footsteps of the Decembrists and Petrashevists'.[76] Several newspapers drew parallels between Sozonov's case and that of Sigida — *Rech'*, for instance, described the Zerentui scandal as 'an incident the likes of which we have seen only once in

---

[72] *Rech'*, 1 December 1910, p. 2.
[73] V. Azov, 'Pravdu!', *Rech'*, 1 December 1910, p. 2.
[74] *Gosudarstvennaia duma*, 4.27, 29 November 1910, pp. 2227–28.
[75] Ibid., p. 2217.
[76] A. Petrishchev, 'Khronika vnutrennei zhizni', *Russkoe bogatstvo*, 12, 1910, pp. 70–78 (p. 71).

recent decades, and even then only in the darkest moments of our public life'[77] — while others on the left invoked the image of indiscriminate state violence unleashed on society at large. Chkheidze, for whom floggings were symbolic of 'oriental despotism' (*aziatshchina*), suggested that the Duma majority would soon vote to introduce 'flogging for all', while Chernov wrote that human rights abuses in prisons were 'the reflection of a still more terrible tragedy: that all of Russia is one huge prison in which the Russian people have been left to rot'.[78] Responding to reports of violence against student protestors in St Petersburg, the Menshevik Evgenii Gegechkori argued that floggings of political prisoners and police attacks on students were two sides of the same coin: 'just a man who says A must also say B', he argued, 'so [a government] that tortures prisoners bound hand and foot will go on to punish students, subjecting them to violence and abuse'.[79]

For the revolutionary left, calls for the abolition of corporal punishment or a transparent investigation were insufficient. Instead, they sought to leverage public outrage for a revivified struggle against autocracy. In a statement, the Petersburg SR committee summoned 'all those in whom the desire for freedom still burns to active protest against the actions of the government'.[80] These calls were quickly answered: in the days and weeks that followed, large-scale student demonstrations took place in virtually every university town across the Russian Empire. Protests were largest in Petersburg, where almost all higher education institutions were bought to a standstill for the best part of two weeks: similar manifestations were reported in Moscow, Kyiv, Odesa, Kharkiv and elsewhere.[81] Participants observed minutes of silence in Sozonov's memory, sang revolutionary songs, passed resolutions condemning the use of corporal punishment in prisons, listened to speeches that extolled Sozonov as a revolutionary martyr and called for violent reprisals against the government.[82] These protests represented, in effect, a continuation of a nationwide wave of unrest that had begun weeks earlier in connection with the death on 7 November of the writer Lev Tolstoi, whose funeral gave rise to the largest street demonstrations seen in Russia since 1905: on that day (10 November),

---

[77] Ibid., p. 78; *Rech'*, 1 December 1910, p. 2.
[78] *Gosudarstvennaia duma*, 4.27, 29 November 1910, p. 2217; Chernov, 'Pamiati Egora Sozonova', p. 8.
[79] *Gosudarstvennaia duma*, 4.30, 3 December 1910, pp. 2482, 2486.
[80] *Znamia truda*, 33, 1911, p. 23.
[81] See *Russkoe slovo*, 3 December 1910, p. 5, and *Novoe vremia*, 4 December 1910, p. 17.
[82] 'Korrespondentsiia', *Znamia truda*, 33, 1911, p. 17.

one in every four Moscow workers, according to one estimate, went on strike.[83] The pathos of two such iconic oppositional figures dying in close proximity to one another — a pathos that may, in fact, have been all the greater for the obvious differences between them — was not lost on contemporary observers. Writing in *Znamia truda*, the SR leader Viktor Chernov argued that Sozonov and Tolstoi personified in equal measure 'the highest peaks of the human spirit and moral conscience'. Both, Chernov wrote, had lived harmoniously, in accordance with their ideals, and had 'served in death the causes to which they devoted their lives [*smert′iu sluzhili delu zhizni*]'.[84]

In retrospect, it is clear that the coalition of protest of winter 1910, which united the Duma opposition, the liberal press and student radicals, represented a forerunner to the anti-government 'social consensus' (to borrow Michael Melancon's term) that emerged in the aftermath of the Lena goldfields massacre just two years later.[85] The significance of this was not lost on contemporary observers: in particular, the re-emergence of student radicalism prompted hopes on the left for a new revolutionary 'upsurge' (*pod″em*) in the offing. Party newspapers drew comparisons with the student movement of the 1890s, while Iulii Martov devoted a lengthy article to arguing that students, who 'understood instinctively that what happened in Zerentui was their affair too', were reclaiming their traditional place as the vanguard of revolutionary opposition to the regime.[86] The public response certainly unnerved Stolypin's government. Several student demonstrations were violently suppressed by the police, who were supported, in some cases, by the far-right: in Odesa, one student was killed by counter-protestors linked to the URP.[87] Disturbances continued unabated, and eventually, on 4 January 1911, the Council of Ministers banned all student meetings other than those of a 'strictly academic nature', demanding the expulsion of any students who disobeyed.[88]

---

[83] For a discussion of the events surrounding Tolstoi's funeral, see William Nickell, *The Death of Tolstoy: Russia on the Eve, Astapovo Station, 1910*, Ithaca, NY, 2010, pp. 115–41.

[84] Chernov, 'Pamiati Egora Sozonova', p. 7.

[85] Michael Melancon, *The Lena Goldfields Massacre and the Crisis of the Late Tsarist State*, College Station, TX, 2006, p. 183.

[86] L. M. [Iu. O. Martov], 'Probuzhdenie studenchestva', *Golos sotsial′demokrata*, 24, 1911, pp. 2–3.

[87] 'Korrespondentsiia', p. 17; Bogdanovich, *Tri poslednikh samoderzhtsa*, p. 492; V. S. Diakin, *Samoderzhavie, burzhuaziia i dvorianstvo v 1907–1911 gg*, Leningrad, 1978, p. 180.

[88] 'O merakh k obespecheniiu uchashcheisia molodezhi vozmozhnosti besprepiatstvenno prodolzhit′ uchebnye zaniatiia', 4 January 1911, in *Osobye zhurnaly soveta ministrov*, vol. 3, pp. 19–20.

Sozonov the martyr

In the years after his death, Sozonov was celebrated as a martyr to the revolutionary cause. The martyr-myth that developed around him was highly allegorical: underneath its secular content (tributes to his courage and commitment to the revolutionary cause) lay a religious narrative, according to which Sozonov was a Christ-like figure who had sacrificed his life so that others might live. This framing originated, of course, from Sozonov himself, both in terms of the circumstances of his death (i.e. his decision to die alone rather than alongside his fellow prisoners) and his final letter in which he explained his decision. The point was emphasized in a brief note Sozonov conveyed to the SR leadership on the eve of his death, in which he referenced the torments of Christ in the Garden of Gethsemane:

> A new commandant, Vysotskii — a second Borodulin — has arrived. [The inmates] are awaiting the end. Let this cup pass from me.[89]

All the major themes of Sozonov's martyr-myth — both religious and secular — feature in a lengthy obituary written by Chernov and published in *Znamia truda* in 1911. For Chernov, Sozonov was the SR ideal, 'a product of the humble black earth' guided in all that he did by a 'stern, implacable conscience'. Moved by the sufferings of the workers and peasants, he had come first to identify with the radical intelligentsia, then to take up arms against the regime. His absolute commitment to the revolutionary cause — Sozonov was, Chernov wrote, 'always, and in everything, a man who went all the way [*idushchii do kontsa*]' — was matched by his 'remarkable, bright and crystalline-pure' personality.[90] For Chernov, both Sozonov's original decision to become a terrorist and his willingness to die in defence of his fellow prisoners were acts of moral asceticism. The religious subtext of Chernov's obituary was reinforced by the portrait of Sozonov that accompanied it, reminiscent of Orthodox icon painting. Clad in grey prison robes, Sozonov's facial expression is serious, yet otherworldly — a snapshot of revolutionary transcendence.

Such saintly representations of Sozonov also appear in many memoir accounts written in later years, virtually all of which emphasize both his personal religiosity and moral qualities — his kindness and sweetness of nature — and link them to his final act of self-sacrifice. Several memoirists

---

[89] *E. S. Sozonov: materialy dlia biografii*, p. 99. The reference is to Matthew 26:40.
[90] Chernov, 'Pamiati Egora Sozonova', pp. 3–4.

(including Sozonov's own mother) dwell upon his Old Believer background, a detail that added considerably to the pathos of his biography: Praskov´ia Ivanovskaia (his co-conspirator of 1903–04) wrote that as a young man Sozonov had undergone a period of 'religiosity bordering on fanaticism', something she connected to the 'selflessness and perseverance' he later displayed as a revolutionary.[91] For Spiridonova, Sozonov possessed not just a 'compassionate heart moved [...] by human suffering', but 'spiritual energy of great power and intensity', characteristics that she too attributed to his religious upbringing and which compelled his fellow prisoners to 'humble themselves before his goodness and love'.[92] Perhaps suspecting that readers might draw a different conclusion from the facts of his biography, Spiridonova insisted, in a further allegorical twist, that Sozonov had not wanted to die. '[Sozonov] loved life vividly and joyously', she wrote, 'but when the bell tolled for him, when his brothers were threatened with a mortal insult, his unwavering hand tore through the thousand threads [...] that bound him to life'.[93]

For another fellow inmate, Izrail Bril´on, Sozonov was an 'unforgettable and remarkably noble soul':

Everyone loved Sozonov [...] He often received money and parcels from home, [and] when he was in a position to help someone, he would never refuse them, so he was always poorer than the other prisoners — people took advantage of his good nature. Soon enough, however, the common criminals saw what kind of person he was and, out of shame, stopped cheating him. I once saw a convict asking Sozonov for money when one of the prison elders came up and took him aside, unleashing a tirade: 'Do you know who you're stealing from? Don't you know he won't refuse you, he'll give you his last kopeck and go hungry himself — he's not a man, but a saint.'[94]

The religious elements of Sozonov's mythology — although to some degree typical of Russian revolutionary martyrologies — cannot be fully understood outside the context of the SR Combat Organization, and the culture of revolutionary terrorism as a whole. Although the degree of asceticism and self-abnegation he demonstrated in life and death was highly unusual (even by the standards of the Russian revolutionary

[91] Sozonova, 'Po vospominaniiam', p. 47; Ivanovskaia, *V boevoi organizatsii*, pp. 43–44.
[92] Spiridonova, 'Iz zhizni na Nerchinskoi katorge', pp. 117–18.
[93] Ibid., p. 132.
[94] Bril´on, *Na katorge*, p. 103.

movement), Sozonov was in many ways a typical representative of the Combat Organization, which was conspicuous among revolutionary organizations for the presence in its ranks of many pious Christians who seem to have regarded bombings and assassinations not just as political acts, but as transfigurative in a wider sense, and who believed that one should kill, to quote a character in one of Boris Savinkov's novels, 'so that love transforms the world'.[95] In 1910, moreover, the SRs were deeply divided on a range of moral and ethical questions connected with their use of terrorist tactics: since there was (as we have seen) a strong discursive link between terrorism and political suicides, it is not surprising that Sozonov's death was interpreted and understood in this context.

Here it should be noted that there was a significant discrepancy between what one might term, on the one hand, the official SR narrative of the terror and how the terrorists themselves, on the other, understood the act of killing in the name of an idea. In public, the SRs, as Daniel Beer notes, 'subsumed [assassinations] in a language of political struggle'.[96] In party proclamations and courtroom speeches, terrorist attacks on the state were framed as a purely political tactic — a means of energizing the revolutionary masses and of punishing tyrannical officials for their crimes against the people — in a way that elided the moral side of the question (i.e. whether noble ends truly justified such violent means) altogether.[97] It is nonetheless clear that many of the terrorists, albeit privately, were wracked with doubts about such moral and ethical issues, and Sozonov was no exception. In a letter to his parents from prison in 1906, he acknowledged that he had 'committed the greatest sin possible for a man'.[98] The same theme emerges from the memoir sources. Spiridonova, for instance, writes that Sozonov was traumatized by the memory of Pleve's killing — often asked to tell the story by younger political prisoners who regarded him with awe, he could not oblige without visibly shuddering — while Savinkov reveals that Sozonov, who had previously claimed to feel only 'pride and

---

[95] So says the terrorist Vania in Boris Savinkov, *Pale Horse*, trans. Michael Katz, Pittsburgh, PA, 2019, p. 108. Vania's real-world prototype was Ivan Kaliaev, whose politics were underpinned by a 'deep and powerful religious sensibility' and who saw terror not just as a means of political struggle, but 'as a moral and perhaps even religious sacrifice'. Savinkov, *Vospominaniia terrorista*, p. 37.

[96] Daniel Beer, 'The Morality of Terror: Contemporary Responses to Political Violence in Boris Savinkov's *The Pale Horse* (1909) and *What Never Happened* (1912)', *Slavonic and East European Review*, 85, 1, 2007, pp. 25–46 (p. 25).

[97] For the official line, see V. M. Chernov, 'Terroristicheskii element v nashei programme', in *Partiia sotsialistov-revolutionserov*, vol. 1, pp. 78–88.

[98] *Pis'ma Egora Sozonova k rodnym*, p. 84.

joy' from his participation in the terror, later wrote from Siberia to confess that 'the knowledge of having sinned has never left me'.[99] When Savinkov wrote a short novel, *Kon' blednyi* (*The Pale Horse*, 1909), that made public the moral torments experienced by the terrorists, Sozonov defended its contents in conversations with his fellow prisoners, many of whom thought the book heretical. When he heard that Savinkov had been threatened with expulsion from the party for this alleged breach of discipline, he wrote to the Central Committee stating that, if Savinkov were to be expelled, they should expel him too.[100]

These moral and ethical dilemmas became inescapable during the winter of 1908–09 with the revelation that Evno Azef, the longtime head of the Combat Organization, had been a double agent in the pay of the police for over a decade.[101] Some at the time suspected a connection between the Azef affair and Sozonov's death the following year: in comments quoted in the press, Vladimir Burtsev, the SR-adjacent journalist and historian who had exposed Azef, suggested that the Zerentui affair was suspicious because Sozonov would have been an important witness in an investigation into the scandal.[102] There was, of course, a connection, albeit one that only became evident years later with the publication of the relevant archival materials: Azef's betrayal was a crushing psychological blow to Sozonov (as to many SRs). The emotional distress he experienced at this time is clear from a series of anguished letters he wrote to his girlfriend, Mariia Prokof'eva, and is confirmed by the memoirs of his cellmate, Grigorii Frolov, who wrote that Sozonov was severely depressed in the last year of his sentence: unable to leave his cell for days at a time, he lay on his bed in silence, 'his eyes heavy with sadness'.[103]

Many years after these events, the prominent SR (and himself onetime member of the Combat Organization) Vladimir Zenzinov noted that assassinations, however justifiable they might have been in socio-political terms, were nevertheless regarded by most of the terrorists as a grave sin in moral terms. Consequently, Zenzinov wrote, such sins could only be

---

[99] Spiridonova, 'Iz zhizni na Nerchinskoi katorge', pp. 118–19; Savinkov, *Vospominaniia terrorista*, p. 47.

[100] Bril'on, *Na katorge*, p. 102; V. M. Chernov, *Pered burei: vospominaniia*, New York, 1953, p. 294.

[101] See Anna Geifman, *Entangled in Terror: The Azef Affair and the Russian Revolution*, Wilmington, DE, 2000.

[102] 'Zapros o sobytiakh v katorzhnikh tiur'makh', *Russkoe slovo*, 30 November 1910, p. 4.

[103] Frolov, 'O Egore Sozonove', p. 58. For Sozonov's letters to Prokof'eva on this subject, see *Volia Rossii*, 9–10, 1930, pp. 972–1000.

exculpated by the willing sacrifice of the terrorist's own life.[104] This 'moral economy of terror' — to borrow Susan Morrissey's phrase — added a new layer of interpretation to Sozonov's suicide, which could accordingly be construed not just as a desperate response to the brutal prison regime (as such suicides had been for the revolutionaries of the nineteenth century), but as an act of atonement for past sins. None other than Chernov, in his obituary for Sozonov, came close to exactly this conclusion. 'Even when killing a beast in human form [*v chelovecheskom obraze*]', Chernov wrote, 'Sozonov could not forget that he was taking a human life. He struggled to accept the idea that he had the "right to the blood" of such a beast [as Pleve], and when he did accept it, he accepted it as an obligation of violence against himself.'[105]

Conclusion

Sozonov's martyr-myth was largely created after 1917 and, in particular, during the 1920s, a decade that saw an 'explosion of memoir writing'[106] by former revolutionaries and in which the collective memory of the anti-tsarist struggle was constructed and contested. After the revolution there emerged, in effect, two narratives about Sozonov. One was created by his former SR comrades — Chernov, Ekaterina Breshko-Breshkovskaia, Savinkov, Spiridonova and others — who, now writing from emigration or internal exile in the Soviet Union, remembered him in their memoirs. Yet Sozonov also loomed large in the emergent state-sanctioned narrative of the revolutionary struggle: from 1921 onwards he was the subject of (or featured in) numerous memoirs written by his fellow inmates and published by the Society of Former Political Prisoners (Obshchestvo byvshikh politkatorzhan i ssyl´noposelentsev; hereafter, OPK).[107]

These narratives, as one might expect, served somewhat distinct purposes. The first (i.e. that associated with the exiled SR leadership) tended to collapse Sozonov's deeds as a terrorist, his struggle against the prison authorities and his final act of self-sacrifice into a single, coherent moral narrative that emphasized his altruism and willing acceptance of suffering in the name of higher ideals — characteristics that became, in

[104] V. M. Zenzinov, *Perezhitoe*, New York, 1953, p. 271.
[105] Chernov, 'Pamiati Egora Sozonova', p. 7.
[106] Ben Eklof and Tatiana Saburova, *A Generation of Revolutionaries: Nikolai Charushin and Russian Populism from the Great Reforms to Perestroika*, Bloomington, IN, 2017, pp. 307–08.
[107] On the OPK see Mark Iunge, *Revoliutsionery na pensii: Vsesoiuznoe obshchestvo politkatorzhan i ssyl´noposelentsev, 1921–1935*, Moscow, 2015.

turn, emblematic of the terrorist struggle against autocracy. The second (Soviet) narrative focused less on Sozonov's terrorist career and much more on his time as a political prisoner, a focus that reflected not just the ostensible mission of the OPK to document the barbarities of the tsarist prison system, but political sensitivities around the legacies of terrorism (Lenin, famously, had often criticized 'individual terror' as mere 'adventurism') and the SRs, who by the 1920s were officially regarded as counter-revolutionaries (in 1922, the party's Central Committee was prosecuted in Moscow in the first of the major Soviet show trials). These narratives, however, were not neatly separable: in fact, as we shall now see, they overlapped considerably.

In November 1921, Vera Figner — a veteran of the People's Will, one of the most famous political prisoners in pre-revolutionary Russia and, at the time, among the most visible representatives of the old revolutionary tradition in the new Soviet state[108] — gave a lecture marking the anniversary of Sozonov's death at an OPK meeting in Moscow. In this lecture, Figner sought to combine the two narratives noted above: while on the one hand accounting for Sozonov's 'objective' significance in the history of the anti-tsarist struggle, she also sought to portray him subjectively, as the embodiment of the highest virtues of the Populist-SR political tradition. In so doing, she attempted not just an intervention in the revolutionary 'memory wars' of the 1920s, but a heartfelt tribute to a comrade whom she had never met, yet to whom she felt, nevertheless, a strong personal attachment. For Figner, Sozonov, among all the revolutionaries of the younger generation, most closely resembled the revolutionaries of her own time (i.e. the 1870–80s) in his moral and psychological makeup.[109]

Figner's lecture on Sozonov began by asserting that the SRs — and not, as emergent dogma had it, the Bolsheviks — were the rightful heirs of the People's Will. It was the SRs, she noted, that took up the programme of the People's Will two decades hence and applied it to a mass worker-peasant movement that had not existed in the late nineteenth century, and who carried on the Populist tradition of armed struggle against the regime.[110] Having made this argument, she turned to Sozonov, using the facts of his biography to defend the SR terror campaign against autocracy both in moral

[108] On Figner's place in the revolutionary memory politics of the 1920s, see Lynne Hartnett, *The Defiant Life of Vera Figner: Surviving the Russian Revolution*, Bloomington, IN, 2014, pp. 236–61.
[109] Figner, *Posle Shlissel'burga*, p. 179–80.
[110] Figner, 'Rech' na vechere pamiati E. Sozonova', pp. 450–51. For this assertion Figner earned herself an admonitory footnote from the editors of her collected works.

and political terms. Figner conceded that she and the other *narodovol'tsy* of the 1870s were 'idealists, who knew little of life or the masses'. They had a 'rose-tinted' view of the coming revolution and lacked visceral experience of oppression by the state. Accordingly, when they adopted terrorism as a means of struggle, they did so not out of true moral conviction, but rather for want of an alternative.[111] With the SRs in the early 1900s, Figner argued, the case was quite different. Quoting from Sozonov's letters and his court testimony, she argued that his encounters with state violence in prison and exile were quite different to anything her own generation had experienced. His was 'the psychology of a man who personally experienced violence, who saw before him the degradation of his fellow man and bore witness to bloody acts of vengeance against the defenceless'.[112] When the SRs took up arms against the regime, Figner argued, they did so not pragmatically, but as an act of moral obligation.

For Figner, Sozonov's determination to fight the regime's violence and abuse of power was the defining theme of his life (and death):

> I never met Egor Sozonov, never saw him, and I know of him only from those who worked with him and knew him in prison. I will say only one thing: Sozonov sacrificed his life twice — once on the streets of Petersburg [...] That time fate did not accept the offer of his life. The second time, he took poison to spare his comrades the shame of corporal punishment. This double self-sacrifice [*dvukratnaia otdacha*] gives us the measure of Sozonov as a revolutionary. To sacrifice oneself as he did, one must of course have a very big heart: perhaps unique in all the history of the revolutionary movement.[113]

The pathos of these words comes, first and foremost, from Figner — an iconic terrorist and prison martyr of the previous generation — bestowing her blessing upon the memory of a younger comrade, one to whom she felt connected both by their common ideological convictions and a shared experience of suffering. Yet it also derives from the wider historical context in which they were spoken. The martyr-myths of Sozonov, Figner and many others represented not just the cultural system of the revolutionary underground, but, in a sense, the spiritual values of the old intelligentsia — values for which there was little room in the worker-peasant state. Within a decade, Sozonov and many like him would be all but forgotten, and the

[111]   Ibid., p. 453.
[112]   Ibid., p. 455.
[113]   Ibid., pp. 455–56.

Soviet penal archipelago would produce horrors he and his generation could scarcely have imagined.

A Living Martyrdom?
Representing Life in Emigration in
Katorga i ssylka

LARA GREEN

Introduction

Many political radicals and revolutionaries shared in the experience of life
in emigration in the nineteenth and twentieth centuries. Across the globe,
those who imagined and fought for new political structures and freedoms
travelled in search of liberty and opportunity to continue their political
work as well as intellectual encounters with their counterparts abroad.
Particularly well known among them were those who had left the Russian
Empire. Once abroad, they could continue their political activism beyond
the reach of the tsarist authorities who threatened arrest, imprisonment
and exile to the more remote regions of the empire. Conditions in
Russian prisons were often dire, and life in exile, even if it did not involve
some of the harshest forms of hard labour (*katorga*), were difficult and
exhausting.[1] However, life in emigration came with its own hardships and
compromises. Émigrés often struggled to earn enough money to support
themselves and their families and found themselves in petty squabbles
with their compatriots or frustrated by the impulses of their foreign
sympathizers.[2] Many who left had experienced periods of imprisonment

Lara Green is Lecturer in History at the Erasmus University Rotterdam.
    I would like to thank the editors of this special issue for organizing many panels
and discussions which helped to guide this article in its development. I would also like
to thank the three anonymous reviewers who provided comments on the first version of
the manuscript as well as colleagues at the ASEEES Annual Convention 2022 who gave
invaluable suggestions on an earlier draft.

[1] See Sarah Badcock, *A Prison without Walls? Eastern Siberian Exile in the Last Years
of Tsarism*, Oxford, 2016.
[2] Faith Hillis, *Utopia's Discontents: Russian Émigrés and the Quest for Freedom,
1830s–1930s*, Oxford, 2021, demonstrates the impact of intra-émigré tensions on political
life. For a discussion of the tensions between the goals and ideas of émigrés and those
of their foreign sympathizers, see Ben Phillips, *Siberian Exile and the Invention of*

and exile at home, or at least shared similar stories of political activism in their youth as those who had,[3] while many who had established lives and communities in emigration also regularly traversed borders. As a result, life in emigration was merely one piece of a patchwork of experiences of revolutionary political life in this period.

Scholars of transnational political activism in the late nineteenth and early twentieth centuries have demonstrated that émigrés were vital in sustaining political movements, particularly through their publishing activities.[4] In the case of émigrés from the Russian Empire, there was an extensive history of groups abroad printing and smuggling revolutionary materials. Publishing work was something in which a wide range of individual émigrés were involved in throughout the late nineteenth and early twentieth centuries. In the 1860s and 1870s, the centres of revolutionary émigré print culture were often associated with the established radical and activist communities in Switzerland, where, for example, Aleksandr Gertsen's *Kolokol* was produced. But as time passed, the geographies of émigré print culture grew. In the 1890s, London became an important centre for the production, sale and smuggling of revolutionary literature with the establishment of the Russian Free Press Fund, their associated publications and their postal bookshop. Paris became another centre in the early years of the twentieth century, with the establishment of the Socialist Revolutionary (SR) community there.[5]

Within the print culture of revolutionary political activism of the later imperial period there was a strong tradition of martyrology, associated

Revolutionary Russia, 1835–1917: Exiles, Émigrés and the International Reception of Russian Radicalism, Abingdon, 2022.

[3] Often their experiences in exile became part of their public image abroad, such as the case of Feliks Volkhovskii who frequently lectured on his life. See Donald Senese, 'Felix Volkhovsky in London, 1890–1914', *Immigrants and Minorities*, 2, 3, 1983, pp. 67–78.

[4] See, for example, Sabine Freitag, '"The Begging Bowl of Revolution": The Fund-raising Tours of German and Hungarian Exiles to North America, 1851–1852', in Sabine Freitag (ed.), *Exiles from European Revolutions: Refugees in Mid-Victorian England*, New York and Oxford, 2003, pp. 164–86; Davide Turcato, 'Italian Anarchism as a Transnational Movement, 1885–1915', *International Review of Social History*, 52, 3, 2007, pp. 407–44; Constance Bantman, *The French Anarchists in London, 1880–1914: Exile and Transnationalism in the First Globalisation*, Liverpool, 2013; Pietro di Paola, *The Knights Errant of Anarchy: London and the Italian Anarchist Diaspora (1880–1917)*, Liverpool, 2013, and Constance Bantman and Ana Cláudia Suriani da Silva (eds), *The Foreign Political Press in Nineteenth-Century London: Politics from a Distance*, London, 2018.

[5] For discussion of various émigré publishing activities related to smuggling, see Alfred Erich Senn, 'M. K. Elpidin: Revolutionary Publisher', *The Russian Review*, 41, 1, 1982, pp. 11–23; Martin A. Miller, *The Russian Revolutionary Emigres, 1825–1870*, Baltimore, MD, 1986, pp. 111–34, and Helen Williams, '"Vesti i slukhi": The Russian Émigré Press to 1905', *Revolutionary Russia*, 13, 2, 2000, pp. 45–61.

in particular with execution, imprisonment and hard labour in Siberia. Figures such as the members of the Executive Committee of *Narodnaia volia*, who were executed following their assassination of Alexander II in 1881, and their comrade Vera Figner, who was arrested two years later and spent many years in prison and then exile, were regularly memorialized in both visual and textual forms. Journals, pamphlets and commemorative prints historicized stories of political activism, memorialized lost comrades and recorded their achievements for future generations. Among the most well-known figures in this sphere was Vladimir Burtsev, whose various ventures, but particularly the journal *Byloe* (The Past), reflected the impetus to gather and preserve revolutionary history and memory.[6] Prior to 1917, many of these activities had centred on émigré communities across Europe, as the print culture of revolutionary history and memory would not have been possible inside the Russian Empire. Yet, after the February Revolution of 1917, it once again became possible to conduct such publishing work inside Russia, where former revolutionaries continued these activities under Bolshevik rule. Chief among the architects of revolutionary memory from a more grassroots perspective than other state-led practices in the post-1917 period was the Society of Former Political Prisoners and Exiles (Obshchestvo byvshikh polikatorzhan i ssylnoposelentsev) and its journal, *Katorga i ssylka* (Hard Labour and Exile), which it published between 1921 and 1935. As this article will demonstrate, narrative structures and features of the memoir, as well as (auto)biographical articles in *Katorga i ssylka* representing life in emigration, drew on tropes of emigration as integral to the revolutionary cause, while bodily and emotional suffering and displacement in space/time also characterized the martyrology of pre-1917 revolutionary print culture.

The Society (and its journal) was a non-partisan organization funded by the Bolshevik regime.[7] Although its members represented the political spectrum of the anti-tsarist revolutionary movement, and there were Bolsheviks among their number, many were former Socialist Revolutionaries who were themselves also often former *narodniki* (or Populists). As Ben Eklof and Tatiana Saburova have shown, the *narodnik* generation forged a particularly strong identity through shared experiences

---

[6] See F. M. Lur'e, *Khraniteli proshlogo. zhurnal 'Byloe': Istoriia, redaktory, izdateli*, Leningrad, 1990, and Robert Henderson, *Vladimir Burtsev and the Struggle for a Free Russia: A Revolutionary in the Time of Tsarism and Bolshevism*, London, 2017.

[7] Sandra Pujals, 'When Giants Walked the Earth: The Society of Former Political Prisoners and Exiles of the Soviet Union, 1921–1935', unpublished PhD thesis, Georgetown University, 1999, pp. 24–25.

of activism and imprisonment.[8] Former Socialist Revolutionaries were also close comrades of other émigrés of the pre-1917 period who decided to go back into emigration during the years of Civil War. These included Nikolai Chaikovskii (1850/1–1926), who lent his name to a prominent *narodnik* circle. Though émigrés had dreamed of revolution, and many travelled back to the Russian Empire initially after the outbreak of revolutionary feeling in 1905 and again after February 1917, they were ultimately disappointed with the October Revolution of 1917. Prominent and respected revolutionary figures found themselves fighting the Bolsheviks in the Civil War years, making it impossible for them to remain. Chaikovskii was one such eminent figure in the revolutionary movement who had gone on to participate in anti-Bolshevik militancy and politics during the Civil War before returning to Britain. Alongside this group of disappointed revolutionary elders were those who had not even lived to see the end of the tsarist regime in February 1917, having died in emigration. As a result, members of the Society represented the political plurality of the pre-1917 revolutionary movement and carried with them the friendships and networks formed over long years of life in prison, exile and emigration. This memory and community permeated the pages of *Katorga i ssylka*.

Former émigrés were, therefore, an important group numerically in the Society, connected across borders and with experience of previous publishing activities, but which often felt disconnected from political life. *Katorga i ssylka* became the space in which they attributed revolutionary meaning to their lives and those of their comrades and through which they inscribed their stories into the canon of 1917. As *lieux de mémoire*, revolutionary journals and other publications had regularly printed biographies, memoirs and documents of famous activists. The perpetrators of noted terrorist acts, such as the assassins of the tsar in 1881 and of the tsar's uncle in 1905, were among the most frequent personalities appearing in the publications of the pre-1917 period, including those written by later members of the society and authors in *Katorga i ssylka* such as Vera Figner.[9] In such stories, revolutionaries could locate the meaning

---

[8]   Ben Eklof and Tatiana Saburova, '"Remembrances of a Distant Past": Generational Memory and the Collective Auto/Biography of Russian Populists in the Revolutionary Era', *Slavonic and East European Review*, 96, 1, 2018, pp. 67–93.

[9]   See, for example, V. N. Figner, 'Pamiati narodovol'tsev (o portretakh Perovskoi, Zheliabova, Kibalchicha, Gelfman, Barranikova, Kalodkevicha, Sukhanova i Bogdanovicha)', *Byloe*, no. 7 (1908), pp. 139–47, and 'Pamiati Egora Sazonova', *Za narod!*, no. 35, December 1910, pp. 1–2. *Byloe*'s seventh number (1908) also featured a number of

of their political activism and the sacrifices they and their comrades had made. However, not all those who had lived to see the end of the tsarist regime could count themselves among these illustrious figures. Alongside memorializing those less well-known but associated with infamous acts of revolutionary terrorism, the everyday and the mundane were also important in revolutionary history — and memory-making.[10] The inclusion of stories of life in emigration align with this wider theme in revolutionary (auto)biography and literature, with one piece in *Katorga i ssylka* even giving a detailed account of what one revolutionary usually ate.[11]

One such mundane figure whose memoirs were given extensive space in *Katorga i ssylka* was Lazar Goldenberg (1846–1916), a former *narodnik* and SR who had worked closely with Chaikovskii in emigration as a member of the London-centred Russian Free Press Fund (RFPF). Goldenberg was less famous than the other members of the Fund, and his primary activities had included running its bookselling business. The Fund was also central to several SR publications which included memory-making elements, such as *Za narod!* (For the People!), a publication which ran between 1907 and 1912. Although the Fund lay at the periphery of SR networks both geographically and politically, because of its location in London and promotion of terrorism respectively, this organization was a key node in the transfer of information, printed materials, funds and even weapons. Even when terrorism became viewed with much suspicion after SR terrorist leader Evno Azef was exposed as a police spy, publications led by the members of the RFPF continued to prominently memorialize terrorists as martyrs for the cause. Through this work, they became influential figures in the historical and memory cultures of the revolutionary movement, which later shaped *Katorga i ssylka*.

To serve as a meaningful *lieu de mémoire* for revolutionaries as a wider community, *Katorga i ssylka* embraced a conception of martyrdom which was rooted in these former revolutionaries' own experiences. The journal served readers with representations of familiar characters, lives and experiences, as well as everyday stories of political activism such as

commemorative pieces for the terrorist Ivan Kaliaev, by famous comrades Boris Savinkov and Egor Sazonov.
[10] For example, an early issue of the journal included an extensive memoir/biography of the less well-known (as the author described him) SR terrorist Aleksei Pokotilov. V. O. Levitskii, 'A. D. Pokotilov (Iz lichnykh vospominanii)', *Katorga i ssylka*, no. 3 (1922), pp. 157–72.
[11] M. F. Frolenko, 'A. I. Zundelevich', *Katorga i ssylka*, no. 8 (1924), pp. 219–20 (p. 219).

publishing work. Representations of a diverse range of revolutionary life narratives as a patchwork of interconnected revolutionary experiences illustrate the ways in which members of the Society sought to understand their own experiences and those of close comrades as meaningful political and moral experiences. *Katorga i ssylka* repurposed the tropes and languages of martyrdom associated with execution, imprisonment and Siberian exile to maintain continuity of content, authors and subjects, and in pursuit of an impulse to locate significance in these examples of ordinary or everyday revolutionary activism.

The representation of life in emigration echoed similar tropes across the period up to 1927. In *Katorga i ssylka*, however, the framing of emigration in the journal underwent one important change during this period. Memoir and (auto)biography of emigration had appeared in the journal before 1925, but in the first issue of the journal of that year (no. 14), the topic became a specific part of the title of the section which contained stories of exile, imprisonment and hard labour. The more explicit acknowledgement of emigration as a form of suffering and martyrdom through this framing indicates a greater emphasis on the diversity of revolutionary experiences. At the same time, the emigration narrative seems to have experienced its high point in 1927, a year before the high point of memoir content more broadly, as identified by a quantitative study of the pieces in the journal by L. A. Kolesnikova.[12] Indeed, the theme also seems to have dissipated almost entirely after 1927. Although it seems that the Society and *Katorga i ssylka* sought to avoid conflict with the regime in order to keep favour (and funds), it was perhaps inevitable due to its composition that there was both continual friction and regular upheaval. However, despite the increasing 'Bolshevization' of the organization and its journal with the installation of the 'Old Bolshevik' Feliks Kon as editor in late 1927, it does not appear that it was the changing of personnel *per se* which altered the character of the journal's output from 1928 onwards. After all, as recently as 1926, Kon had authored a biography of Nikolai Chaikovskii published in the journal, albeit one which strategically elided his subject's anti-Bolshevik activities.[13] Rather, it was the changing political environment in which the journal operated, within which the Society's members were required to commit to the official propaganda line and the envisioned role for the Society as the transmitter of the official revolutionary history.[14] Therefore, as well as

[12] L. A. Kolesnikova, *Narodnicheskaia memuaristika (po materialiam istochnikovogo kompleksa zhurnala 'Katorga i ssylka')*, Nizhnii Novgorod, 1999, p. 62.
[13] Feliks Kon, 'N. V. Chaikovskii', *Katorga i ssylka*, no. 5/26 (1926), pp. 211–13.
[14] Pujals, 'When Giants Walked the Earth', pp. 60–64.

examining the various tropes of representation, this article also explores how narratives of life in emigration constituted a part of the negotiated space of history and memory-making during the 1920s.

The émigré and the cause

The construction of the émigré as a revolutionary martyr relied upon a collective understanding of what constituted useful work towards the cause. Committing oneself completely to this work at the expense of individual autonomy or wishes could be constructed as a form of martyrdom. An émigré could participate in a range of activities which might either replicate or directly support those ongoing inside pre-revolutionary Russia, or, alternatively, which might be specific to the émigré context. One way in which revolutionaries in emigration could serve the cause was by writing, printing and distributing (including smuggling across borders) items to contribute to propaganda work inside the Russian Empire. Another task émigrés could perform that directly contributed to concurrent efforts inside the empire was organizing and supplying uprisings or terrorist activities from abroad, including raising money among foreigners to do so. Alongside these widely accepted forms of activism, which supported action inside the empire through transnational networks of émigré activists, sat the more controversial and much debated role of influencing foreign sympathizers to campaign against tsarist despotism. At the same time as activities that were directly aimed at political change inside the Russian Empire, less directly related to the progress of the revolutionary cause were activities which intended to improve the conditions of living for fellow comrades abroad, especially those from less wealthy backgrounds. Such work was necessary, as tasks which specifically aided agitation inside Russia could not provide a living for large numbers of émigrés. The final way in which an émigré could usefully contribute to the cause was doing nothing at all. By taking themselves away from the revolutionary front line, émigrés reduced the risk of arrest, or attracting unwanted attention, potentially leading to more arrests, disruption and more comrades in exile requiring humanitarian assistance and advocacy. Although such activities rarely led to imprisonment (Vladimir Burtsev's time in an English prison being one exception), bodily harm or death, the construction of representations of these activities in *Katorga i ssylka* demonstrates how revolutionaries conceived of such work as fighting for the revolution. Through these representations of life in emigration, the Society reclaimed the lives of

those who had died of old age or non-revolutionary causes abroad, and
the shared and multivariant experiences of revolutionary life experienced
by its members as revolutionary hagiographies. Such representations
also reveal the extent to which emigration, as a substantial part of the
revolutionary experience, framed and structured memories of political
activism before 1917.

At the same time as performing useful work for the cause, in the
tradition of revolutionary martyrology it was important for the individual
to demonstrate the right motivations for the sacrifices that they made and
to behave in ways which were considered morally and ethically correct.
Despite revolutionaries' widespread rejection of religion, the figure of Jesus
played an important role in revolutionary thought as a symbol of self-
sacrifice for the right cause.[15] The idea of behaving with 'innocence' also
permeated representations and debates on terrorism.[16] In the decade before
1917, however, these idealistic images of activism came increasingly under
attack from within the revolutionary movement.[17] What is evident in the
representations of émigré life in *Katorga i ssylka* is the reinscription of this
idealism in stories of revolutionary activism as a means of constructing the
émigré as martyr.

Although émigré life might have appeared to have been an easier option
when compared to the existence of those who remained inside the Russian
Empire, *Katorga i ssylka* emphasized that émigrés continued to work on
behalf of the cause. It was not possible to think of a simple and peaceful
life in emigration since it was necessary to be 'alert and on guard' to defend
the revolutionary movement.[18] Revolutionary émigrés also kept busy and
'did not sit with idle hands'.[19] This same trope can be identified in memoir
literature of comrades who died in emigration published before 1917.[20]

---

[15] Jay Bergman, 'The Image of Jesus in the Russian Revolutionary Movement: The Case
of Russian Marxism', *International Review of Social History*, 35, 1990, pp. 220–48.
[16] Susan K. Morrissey, 'The "Apparel of Innocence": Toward a Moral Economy of
Terrorism in Late Imperial Russia', *Journal of Modern History*, 84, 3, 2012, pp. 607–42.
[17] Sergei Bulgakov, 'Heroism and Asceticism: Reflections of the Religious Nature of
the Russian Intelligentsia', in *Vekhi: Landmarks. A Collection of Articles about the Russian
Intelligentsia*, trans. and ed. Marshall S. Shatz and Judith E. Zimmerman, Armonk, NY
and London, 1994, pp. 26–31.
[18] 'G. V. Plekhanov (iz vospominanii 1902–1904 g.g.)', *Katorga i ssylka*, no. 7 (1923), pp.
21–32 (p. 24).
[19] L. S. Fedorchenko ([N.] Charov), 'V Shveitsarskoi emigratsii (iz vospominanii 1902–
1904 godov)', *Katorga i ssylka*, no. 14 (1925), pp. 225–36 (p. 228).
[20] An obituary of one SR and member of the Russian Free Press Fund Leonid Shishko
described him as 'working tirelessly [*neustanno*]'. 'Leonid Emmanuilovich Shishko',
Narodnoe delo. Sbornik, no. 5 (1910), pp. 9–22 (p. 19).

However, it was also important for the journal to emphasize that some of the revolutionary movement's most respected figures had maintained their hard work in emigration. One short memoir printed in 1924 recounted the author's meeting with Aaron Zundelevich (d.1923), an old *narodnik*. The author, Mikhail Frolenko (1848–1938), another elderly and respected *narodnik*, described meeting 'Zund' in 1908 in London:

> According to everyone who knew the man well, his personality, industriousness [*delovitost'*] and dignity were extraordinary.[21]

Such personal encounters gave an air of authenticity to the works of revolutionary memoir and (auto)biography appearing in the journal. Including such a piece, in place of something which might have been more obviously about self-sacrifice, if it had focused on Zundelevich's more than a quarter of a century spent in some of the most notorious prisons and hard labour camps in the empire, is an example of how emigration was an important element of the extant memory of the living members of the Society. This story demonstrated that life in emigration could be an overwhelming burden, requiring the revolutionary to place the cause above all else, and implicitly equated it to the self-sacrifice of those in prison and exile.

Publishing work was one form of émigré activism which had clear links to agitation at home. *Katorga i ssylka* printed narratives which focused on the minutiae of the operations of revolutionary journals abroad, including who was working on them, where they were based, and the various political positions taken by members of the different groups associated with them, including on the issue of terrorism. For example, the memoir by L. S. Fedorchenko (N. Charov) identifies revolutionaries by listing the publications they worked on and published in, including more established journals such as *Iskra* as well as other, more ephemeral, pamphlets. However, the piece does not particularly offer much by way of personal insights, instead being for the most part a rather dry list.[22] There were also stories of smuggling printed materials into the Russian Empire.[23]

---

[21] Frolenko, 'A. I. Zundelevich', p. 220.

[22] Fedorchenko, 'V Shveitsarskoi emigratsii', pp. 225–36. The journal had also printed another similar memoir by the same author focusing on the life of Georgii Plekhanov. L. S. Fedorchenko (N. Charov), 'G. V. Plekhanov (Iz vospominanii 1902–1904 g.g.)', *Katorga i ssylka*, no. 7 (1923), pp. 21–32.

[23] N. I. Drago, 'Zapiski starogo narodnika', *Katorga i ssylka*, no. 6 (1923), pp. 10–22 (pp. 12–13). Drago was another former member of the Chaikovskii Circle.

This reflected the role of print culture in revolutionary activism in the late imperial period, both in terms of its circulation among established party members and its more hopeful but probably less realistic role as a propaganda tool circulating among a receptive wider public of peasants and workers. It is also suggestive of the role print culture played in structuring memory. Late imperial revolutionary obituaries celebrated the writings of émigré activists (which their fellow émigrés had also published) as being important tools for engaging with the wider population.[24] As in the 'going to the people' movement of the 1870s (Khozhdenie v narod), in which many of the older generation of revolutionaries surviving into the 1920s had participated, propaganda and political educational work remained valued as a form of revolutionary activism. The role of members of this generation in writing about such practices in *Katorga i ssylka* demonstrates how important this older generation of *narodniki* and their revolutionary values remained even after the Bolshevik rise to power.

In addition to supplying their comrades inside the Russian Empire with printed materials, émigrés also found themselves in a position to supply them with weapons.[25] This was especially important during the 1905 revolution, when many émigrés returned to the Russian Empire to take part in revolutionary uprisings.[26] Links with foreign sympathizers could be especially valuable in generating funds, sourcing weapons and arranging transport.[27] In this way, émigré activism could be more concretely linked with revolutionary processes inside the Russian Empire. Even though many of those involved in smuggling weapons might have been too old or infirm to consider taking up arms themselves, their involvement was crucial. Soviet historians considered 1905, which Lenin described as the 'dress rehearsal' for 1917, as a source of legitimacy for Bolshevism.[28] By featuring the contribution of non-Bolshevik émigrés to these events, the members of the Society claimed their role in an important moment for the founding of the new regime.

---

[24] F. Volkhovskii, 'Vechnaia pamiat'!', *Narodnoe delo. Sbornik*, no. 5, (1910), pp. 23–26 (p. 25).

[25] Kon, 'Chaikovskii', *Katorga i ssylka*, pp. 211–13 (p. 212).

[26] See Michael Futrell, *Northern Underground: Episodes of Russian Revolutionary Transport and Communications through Scandinavia and Finland 1863–1917*, London, 1963.

[27] Raymond Challinor, 'Gun-Running from the North-East Coast, 1905–7', *Bulletin of the North-East Group for the Study of Labour History*, 6, 1972, pp. 1–5. This story also appeared in *Katorga i ssylka*: Frolenko, 'Chaikovskii', p. 223.

[28] Abraham Ascher, *The Revolution of 1905*, vol. 1: *Russia in Disarray*, Stanford, CA, 1988, pp. 1–2.

While supplying printed items and weapons was widely thought acceptable as forms of émigré revolutionary activism, the issue of whether propaganda work among foreigners could be useful to the revolutionary cause had been a continual point of debate among revolutionaries prior to 1917. Some revolutionaries felt that foreign interference was either useless, in the form of persuading foreign monarchs and politicians to put pressure on the tsar to enact political reform, or went against the principle that the people of the Russian Empire needed to liberate themselves. The only real support foreigners could offer, therefore, was financial.[29] *Katorga i ssylka* did print some items, however, which suggested that the editors saw the perspectives of foreign sympathizers as important. This included pieces in the thirtieth number of the journal, which appeared in 1927 to mark the tenth anniversary of the fall of tsarism and to mark the liberation of revolutionaries from Siberian exile. The focus on February enabled a broader telling of the story of the revolution perhaps than October, reflected in the content of the issue. The issue printed a speech by the American journalist George Kennan, a sympathizer of the revolutionary movement with personal links to many SRs. Clearly the perspective of foreign observers was important to the editors of *Katorga i ssylka*, as the foreword to the speech noted how writers and artists in the USA were a more ready source of support for the revolution than American workers.[30] Kennan had long been associated with the SRs who were members of the Russian Free Press Fund and had supported their efforts to gain foreign sympathizers.[31] However, Kennan's was a rare foreign and non-socialist voice found in the journal and the stories of life in emigration mostly focused on memoirs and (auto)biography of less contentious work connected to the revolutionary cause.

As well as reporting the everyday lives of more well-known revolutionary émigrés, *Katorga i ssylka* mobilized the representation of the minutiae of émigré life to commemorate those whose lives and work in emigration might otherwise have gone unnoticed in the historical record. In fact, because *Katorga i ssylka* did not feature the quantity and regularity of

---

[29] See, for example, Lara Green, 'Russian Revolutionary Terrorism in Transnational Perspective: Representations and Networks, 1881–1926', unpublished PhD thesis, Northumbria University, 2019, pp. 60–61.

[30] Ia. D. B., 'Pisateli i khudozhniki v russkoi revoliutsii: Predislovie', *Katorga i ssylka*, no. 30 (1927), pp. 99–100 (p. 100)

[31] See, for example, D. M. Nechiporuk, '"Chto amerikantsy mogut sdelat dlya Rossii?": agitatsiia amerikanskogo Obshchestva druzei russkoi svobody i zhurnal "*Free Russia*" (1891–1894 gody)', *Istoricheskii ezhegodnik* (2008), pp. 137–50.

stories of (in)famous individuals to the extent journals such as the pre-1917 *Byloe* had, it framed the story of the 'ordinary' émigré as more important in revolutionary history. In one article in 1923, *Katorga i ssylka* memorialized a comrade named Zolotarev whom, they noted, 'no-one would remember at all', but who had established a school to train émigrés in electrical work.[32] Political and activist writing, printing and publishing, which was often ephemeral and transient in nature, could not have provided a living for all émigrés. Those who managed to focus on this work abroad seem often to have been those who had already established their reputation as propagandists at home and who continued this work in emigration. They included the London Fund member Feliks Volkhovskii who was known for his work on a Siberian exile newspaper.[33] Those who established strong links with foreign sympathizers were also best prepared for this lifestyle, or those whose political writings had wider philosophical appeal, such as Peter Kropotkin.[34] The ordinary émigré political activist could not tap into these alternative and more lucrative income streams of publishing and lecturing for foreign audiences and may have been forced by circumstances to turn to an alternative occupation. Such a decision could also be considered a form of self-sacrifice, as it entailed an individual giving up on their own revolutionary dreams having been forced to leave Russia in order to avoid becoming a threat or burden to their comrades. The Society also democratized the memory of political activism to some extent by including such ordinary stories. By establishing the importance of the everyday in the lives of revolutionary émigrés, *Katorga i ssylka* thereby reinscribed their individual experiences in the story of the revolution.

Although decisive action was naturally a key element in revolutionary history — and memory-making — inaction was also an important contribution the émigré revolutionary could make to the cause. The literary writings of revolutionaries prior to 1917 featured examples in which misdirected and inappropriate enthusiasm to participate in revolutionary terrorist acts was considered a threat.[35] As an activist, subordinating your

---

[32] Ia., 'Tovarishch Zolotarev', *Katorga i ssylka*, no. 7 (1923), p. 253 (p. 253).

[33] Donald Senese, 'S. M. Kravchinskii and the National Front Against Autocracy', *Slavic Review*, 34, 3, 1975, pp. 506–22 (p. 507).

[34] See Haia Shpayer-Makov, 'The Reception of Peter Kropotkin in Britain, 1886–1917', *Albion*, 19, 3, 1987, pp. 373–90.

[35] For example, the characters Zina in Sergei Stepniak's 1889 novel, *Career of a Nihilist* (later published in Russian translation under the name of its protagonist Andrei Kozhukov), and Erna in Boris Savinkov's *Pale Horse*, which first appeared in serialized form in the journal *Russkaia mysl'* (Russian Thought) in 1909. Erna is a fictionalized version of Savinkov's comrade Dora Brilliant who was a participant in the real events

own interests and desires to the collective was valuable, even when it might tell you to stay away.[36] By commemorating the commitment of those who had sacrificed their personal activism in favour of the revolution, *Katorga i ssylka* reinserted the stories of those who had not been able to do anything, thus recognizing them in the martyrology of 1917.

By claiming the importance of émigré political activism, the members of the Society of Former Political Prisoners and Exiles established a historical narrative which placed their work in the canon of 1917. By asserting their status among those who had caused the downfall of tsarist despotism, they laid claim to a place at the heart of political life in the early Soviet period, even though the regime denied them that role. As long as they made contributions which were considered valuable, the personal, social and political sacrifices that revolutionaries made could be considered a form of martyrdom.

Physical and emotional suffering
Although the pinnacle of self-sacrifice remained dying in the pursuit of the revolutionary cause, physical suffering in other forms took a central position in revolutionary history and memory-making activities. In part, this was due to the ways in which bodily suffering had become a central experience of imprisonment and exile for revolutionaries in the late imperial period.[37] This meant that many revolutionaries suffered ill-health to varying degrees for the rest of their lives, even long after a period of only comparatively few years in the tsarist carceral system.[38] Reflecting this, the harsh treatment of exiles and prisoners was a common theme in the journal, which printed stories of the brutal (and sometimes deadly) forms of *katorga* in mines and factories in the section of the journal dedicated to this theme. At the same time, suffering sacralized the body in the rebirth of the revolutionary cause. In revolutionary culture, this spirit of renewal was particularly associated with Siberia, which embodied this alongside the suffering of prisoners and exiles.[39] As a result, time spent in

Savinkov depicts in the novel.

[36] For example, Andrei Kozhukov in Stepniak's *Career of a Nihilist* faced 'disappointment' when fellow activists refused his request to return. Stepniak, *The Career of a Nihilist*, 2nd edn, London, 1890, p. 14. The waiting echoed Stepniak's own experiences of life in emigration.

[37] See Badcock, *A Prison Without Walls?*, pp. 139–68.

[38] Among them was Feliks Volkhovskii, whose 'hair had gone white, he was almost deaf, spoke in a cracked voice and suffered from splitting headaches' at the age of only twenty-five. Senese, 'Volkhovsky', p. 68.

[39] Phillips, *Siberian Exile and the Invention of Revolutionary Russia*, pp. 24–25.

prison and exile literally inscribed the history of the revolutionary cause upon the bodies of prisoners and exiles and through their experiences of suffering.[40] Alongside this, their time in exile was also time spent in a space imagined to be both 'empty' and a place of new beginnings, from which revolutionaries would emerge reborn.

Many émigrés had experienced prison and/or exile prior to, or interspersed with, the time they spent living abroad. However, by echoing the same tropes and emphasizing the particularity of the suffering experienced in emigration, *Katorga i ssylka* incorporated émigré experiences into the canon of revolutionary self-sacrifice. They reclaimed the revolution for those whose varied experiences made up the patchwork of revolutionary history, both for themselves as members of the Society of Former Political Prisoners and Exiles and for those who had died or whose anti-Bolshevik activism had forced them once again into emigration. Such efforts challenged the Bolshevik authorities' efforts to restrict the definition of who counted as a member of the Society over the course of the 1920s and, thereby, to whom the revolution belonged.[41]

The trope of bodily suffering in emigration appeared in stories of life in emigration in *Katorga i ssylka*, although the parameters can seem somewhat contrived. For example, one memoir depicted hard labour in a factory in France while wearing uncomfortable clogs.[42] According to the author, it was important to become accustomed to the discomfort. In late nineteenth-century Russia, coats, more so than shoes, had been the main emblems of socio-economic status. The insufficient coat, old, worn or thin, was the noticeable uniform of someone suffering from economic hardship, with the archetypal Akakii Akakievich in Gogol''s *The Overcoat* inspiring the representation of subsequent figures such as Prince Myshkin in Dostoevskii's *The Idiot*.[43] Throughout Dostoevskii's *Poor Folk*, however, it is boots (or indeed the lack of footwear) which mark out a character's poverty and are a source of humiliation.[44] Revolutionaries also embraced

---

[40] See also, Lynn Ann Hartnett, *The Defiant Life of Vera Figner: Surviving the Russian Revolution*, Bloomington, IN, 2014, and Lara Green, 'The Transnational Life and Death of Peter Kropotkin, 1881–1921: Terrorism, the Anarchist Body, and the Russian Revolution', *Anarchist Studies*, 30, 1, 2022, pp. 83–119.

[41] Pujals, 'When Giants Walked the Earth', pp. 34–35

[42] L. Goldenberg, 'Vospominaniia', *Katorga i ssylka*, no. 5/12 (1924), pp. 106–20 (p. 114). Goldenberg's lengthy memoirs were serialized across multiple issues of the journal.

[43] David Herman, *Poverty of the Imagination: Nineteenth-Century Russian Literature about the Poor*, Evanston, IL, 2001, p. 179.

[44] V. V. Vinogradov, 'Shkola sentimentalnogo naturalizma: Poman "Bednye liudi" na fone literaturnoi evoliutsii 40-kh godov', in *Poetika russkoi literatury: Izbrannye Trudy*,

dress as a means to demonstrate their political sympathies. Particular clothing could also help to conceal themselves in a crowd. The would-be terrorist Dmitrii Karakozov, for example, wore a peasant *armiak* (overcoat) during his attempt to assassinate the tsar in 1866.[45] Inhabiting the shoes of a French factory worker was thus evidence of this émigré's sacrifice for their politics, while being symbolic of their sharing in the suffering of those living under oppression and in poverty.

Although the labour of the émigré in a factory abroad was not precisely the same as in the tsarist carceral system and did not present the same level of danger as some forms of *katorga*, such as in mines, given the revolutionary socialist politics of those involved it could nevertheless be comparable. Rather than the oppressive tsarist regime being the exploiter of labour, it was the capitalist system which oppressed the émigré abroad. One of the freedoms sought by late imperial revolutionaries was economic liberation, therefore they were the victims of violence in similar ways. At the same time, labour in a foreign factory echoed the work undertaken by the activists who took part in the 'going to the people' of the 1870s, who were sometimes those very same émigrés. Through performing manual labour alongside workers and peasants they sought to enamour themselves and their politics to them as well as to gain the credentials of being a true revolutionary. The trope of salvation through labour permeated revolutionary literary culture of the late nineteenth and early twentieth centuries, including the classic text *What is to be Done?* by Nikolai Chernyshevskii.[46] By laying claim to the suffering of hard labour and bodily harm, émigrés could tap into the connotations of rebirth and revolutionary salvation which accompanied them. The bodily suffering of émigrés had also been a feature of pre-1917 émigré obituaries, such as that of Volkhovskii who died in 1914, and who had persisted in travelling

Moscow 1976, pp. 141–87 (p. 174); Makar Devushkin is embarrassed by his boots, which are among the aspects of his appearance that fellow employees criticize. He ponders whether if he were able to publish a book he would not be able to be seen in public or that he would be mocked by satirical writers because of the condition of his boots. He also feels sympathy for a child without shoes. Fyodor Dostoevsky, *Poor Folk*, trans. Robert Dessaix, Ann Arbor, MI, 1982, pp. 61, 69, 81, 90, 113–14.

[45] Claudia Verhoeven, *The Odd Man Karakozov: Imperial Russia, Modernity, and the Birth of Terrorism*, Ithaca, NY, 2009, pp. 107–08.

[46] Chernyshevskii's radical heroes provided the models for revolutionary self-improvement and inspired many activists. This took a variety of forms, including imitating the extreme asceticism of Rakhmetov or the work of Vera Pavlovna, who in the novel sets up a cooperative sewing shop. See Michael R. Katz and William G. Wagner, 'Introduction', in Nikolai Chernyshevsky, *What Is to Be Done?*, translated by Michael R. Katz and annotated by William G Wagner, Ithaca, NY, 1989, pp. 28–32.

between London and Paris despite his illnesses requiring bed rest.[47] Continuing to perform revolutionary work despite such bodily hardships showed the resolve of the individual revolutionary to serve the cause. The Society recognized and, at least at first, also paid pensions to its members, recognizing the suffering caused by imprisonment and exile. However, by the end of 1924 this particular form of veneration of the revolutionary body diminished in favour of promoting the contribution that the Society's members could make in the present, thereby side-lining many old *narodniki*.[48] In the same way that bodily suffering was not the same as giving one's life for the cause but was still a focus of commemoration, émigré suffering through labour could also be incorporated into the revolutionary canon.

For many, emigration meant economic hardship and privation, and often involved a struggle for food and accommodation. According to one memoirist writing about the time of the February Revolution in Switzerland, '[l]ife in emigration, especially during times of war, differs little from life in exile'.[49] The difficulty of travelling to the scene of the action was the same for both the émigré and the exile, and the high cost of living, unemployment and absence of support from comrades at home made life very difficult. One author even described emigration as being 'worse than exile' for the large mass of political émigrés that left Russia after the 1905 revolution.[50] The early years of the twentieth century saw an increase in the number of political exiles from less wealthy backgrounds who were particularly vulnerable.[51] Being without work could also lead to having to move again, even to another country.[52] There was also concern that when the time came, there would be no money with which to return to Russia.[53] Despite its various difficulties, the émigré community always found money for publishing work and for donations to funds to assist political prisoners. *Katorga i ssylka* thus recognized the material sacrifices made by émigré revolutionaries to support the cause.

[47] In. Ritina [I. I. Rakitnikova], 'Feliks Vadimovich Volkhovskii', *Mysl'*, no. 40, 1 January 1915, pp. 2–3.

[48] Pujals, 'When Giants Walked the Earth', pp. 36–37.

[49] Olga Ravich, 'Fevral´skie dni 1917 goda v Shveitsarii', *Katorga i ssylka*, no. 30 (1927), pp. 180–86 (p. 180).

[50] I. Sheinis, 'Amnistiia v emigratsii', *Katorga i ssylka*, 4/33 (1927), pp. 145–50 (p. 145).

[51] Iadov, 'Parizhskaia emigratsiia v gody voniny', *Katorga i ssylka*, no. 10 (1924), pp. 196–204 (p. 197).

[52] Goldenberg, 'Vospominaniia', p. 114.

[53] E. Stepanov, 'Iz zagranichnii vospominanii starogo narodovolstvo', *Katorga i ssylka*, no. 24 (1926), pp. 123–44 (p. 124).

In addition to bodily suffering and physical hardship, *Katorga i ssylka* also included emotional suffering among the experiences of the revolutionary émigré. As going abroad to avoid hindering the revolutionary cause was considered a legitimate contribution, the emotional suffering that resulted from being unable to play an active role in some revolutionary activities could be commemorated as a form of self-sacrifice. The sense of being unable to do anything, particularly during wartime, had a significant emotional impact on émigrés. The war was a more pressing matter for their foreign contacts, whether activists or workers, even if there was some sympathy for their cause.[54] Contact with comrades still inside the Russian Empire was weakened by war, with travel becoming impossible,[55] leaving émigrés little sense of connection to their comrades at home. This physical separation and lack of opportunities to carry on propaganda work among foreigners meant that the ways in which émigrés could commonly be commemorated as contributing to the revolutionary cause could not be applied. Therefore, although the Society's role as arbiter of who was a deserving member, and distributing pensions and paying for medical care was not officially constrained until the end of 1927, it cannot have escaped them that they needed to continually reassert the contributions of their members in the shifting political climate. While October remained the central moment of Bolshevik commemoration, non-Bolsheviks could therefore insert themselves into the story of February as part of their efforts to lay claim to the canon of revolutionary history.

Despite living outside the empire, Russian exiles and émigrés never really felt themselves out of reach of the tsarist secret police, who made it their business to destroy the means by which they could find a peaceful and secure (*vernoe*) life abroad.[56] Several memoirists writing in *Katorga i ssylka* reported being harassed while abroad.[57] They also came under regular threat from spies and *agents provocateurs*.[58] While the risks of life in emigration were hardly the same as in the Russian Empire, perhaps excepting individuals such as Vladimir Burtsev, who spent time in a British prison in terrible conditions, depictions of the threat from the police were drawn out in *Katorga i ssylka*. In addition, the journal recounted how

---

[54] Ravich, 'Fevral´skie dni 1917 goda', pp. 181–83.

[55] Ibid., p. 181.

[56] R. M. Kantor, 'Frantsuzskaia okhranka o russkikh emigrantakh (neizdannye materialy)', *Katorga i ssylka*, no. 2/31 (1927), pp. 81–88 (p. 82)

[57] See, for example, Stepanov, 'Iz zagranichnii vospominanii', and Goldenberg, 'Vospominaniia', *Katorga i ssylka*, no. 5/12.

[58] Fedorchenko, 'V Shveitsarskoi emigratsii', p. 236.

émigrés were targeted by foreign police forces, often acting cooperatively with the tsarist police force.[59]

Although the experience of life in emigration was unlikely to have involved the same degree of physical suffering as time spent in prison or exile inside the Russian Empire, the same tropes of bodily suffering and poverty infused accounts of émigré life in *Katorga i ssylka*. Furthermore, the émigré body was often one which had suffered abuse and lasting damage in the prison and exile system, so physical suffering continued in emigration. Emotional suffering as an expression of self-sacrifice was also something unique to the émigré experience. While such representations may not have been as powerful or significant as stories of execution, imprisonment and exile in revolutionary culture, their inclusion in the journal demonstrates a continuity in the tropes used in memory practices across the revolutionary divide and the importance of the commemoration of self-sacrifice to the members of the Society of Former Political Prisoners and Exiles.

Time and the émigré revolutionary

One form of martyrdom unique to representations of the émigré revolutionary was the suffering they experienced due to their relationship with time. The specific experience of the passing of time reflected in memoir literature derived from the temporal construction of revolution, modernity and history in revolutionary culture of the late imperial period. It is also useful to think of conceptions of temporality as spatial, as in Mikhail Bakhtin's concept of the chronotope which proposes that time and space are integrative and constitutive elements of the writing and reading of literature.[60] The specific combination communicates meaning to readers, who also bring their own perceptions. According to James Lawson, narratives and their chronotopes are also useful tools which permit diverse ways of knowing and of truth-telling about complex, polyvocal and contested pasts. Such narratives allow for contestations of identity, memory and history in the present because of how they interact with present experiences of time, or other chronotopes.[61] *Katorga i ssylka*

---

[59] L. Goldenberg, 'Vospominaniia', *Katorga i ssylka*, no. 5/12, pp. 106–20. The tsarist regime requested that Goldenberg's permit to live in Geneva be refused in the 1870s (p. 110).

[60] Mikhail Bakhtin, 'Forms of Time and of the Chronotope in the Novel: Notes Towards a Historical Poetics', in Michael Holquist (ed.), *The Dialogic Imagination: Four Essays by M. M. Bakhtin*, trans Caryl Emerson and Michael Holquist, Austin, TX, 1981, pp. 84–258 (p. 84).

[61] James Lawson, 'Chronotope, Story, and Historical Geography: Mikhail Bakhtin and the Space-Time of Narratives', *Antipode*, 43, 2, 2011, pp. 384–412.

employed chronotopes which reflected conceptions of revolution and temporality which the Bolsheviks also embraced, but which mainly echoed pre-existing and broader cultural connections between temporality and modernity. Using such chronotopes, authors in the journal asserted that émigré life had been a valuable form of martyrdom before 1917.

Revolutionaries fighting tsarist oppression inherited the legacy of ideas which presented revolution as both disrupting the experience of temporality and heralding the arrival of 'new time'. These temporal conceptions, which infused the memoir and (auto)biographical writings of members of the Society of Former Political Prisoners and Exiles, as well as other texts printed in *Katorga i ssylka*, had their roots in the French Revolution. Prior to 1917, many looked back to the French Revolution and saw themselves as its intellectual heirs and as inheritors of the legacy of what could be constructed either as a popular revolution usurped, a cautionary tale, or a lesson on historical materialism and the inevitability of revolution.[62] One memoirist writing in *Katorga i ssylka* recorded how, at the end of the 1880s, a group of exiles decided to write an address to the French Republic on the one-hundredth anniversary of the French Revolution.[63] Lynn Hunt has argued that the revolutionaries of 1789 saw a new conceptualization of time which gave them the agency to 'shape the future and thereby accelerate the effects of time'.[64] New time would therefore have different characteristics than old time, namely that of progress. In addition, there was the idea of the 'mythic present' of the time of revolutionary days, which seemed to stretch even for centuries in length.[65] While revolution brought about new time, participants also experienced the duration of the revolution in a different way to the periods before and after it. Just like their revolutionary predecessors over a century before, the Bolsheviks had also sought to inscribe modernity on time itself, in their case by abandoning the Julian calendar system in favour of the Gregorian, skipping over almost two weeks in the process. Members of the Society found themselves living in the new time, which also shaped their memory of their activism before 1917.

Prior to 1917, however, new time was elsewhere. If the French Revolution had brought new time to Western Europe with the destruction of the *ancien régime*, the space of new time did not cross Russian borders.

[62] Jay Bergman, *The French Revolutionary Tradition in Russian and Soviet Politics, Political Thought, and Culture*, Oxford, 2019, pp. 31–50.

[63] M. V. Bramson, 'Ot russkikh ssylnykh Frantsuzskoi Respublike (Istoriia odnogo dokumenta)', *Katorga i ssylka*, no. 4/11 (1924), pp. 238–41.

[64] Lynn Hunt, *Measuring Time, Making History*, Budapest, 2008, p. 70.

[65] Ibid., p. 69.

revolutionaries saw the promise of new time but lived within the bounds of the old, stagnant time of the Russian Empire. The experience of the passing of time thus became increasingly painful set against the lack of meaningful political change. This led to the emergence of the chronotope of 'elsewhere' in revolutionary memoir literature of the late imperial period, which was subsequently sustained in *Katorga i ssylka*. The representation of ageing in *Katorga i ssylka* was also shaped by the chronotope of elsewhere: as a contrast between the process of ageing inside and outside the Russian Empire. This is visible when comparing the two old *narodniki* Chaikovskii and Ekaterina Breshko-Breshkovskaia, the former having spent most of the four decades prior to 1917 outside of the Russian Empire and the latter having spent over two decades in prison and exile. While age conferred respect, one author described Breshkovskaia as retaining youthfulness in her old age, attributing this to her having been in exile in Siberia, rather than abroad.[66] Spending time in emigration, as opposed to exile or prison, therefore came with its own unique challenges.

Being elsewhere also meant that the revolutionary experienced a kind of enforced timelessness while existing in a space where time was still passing. For example, while some émigrés contributed to terrorist plots and the transport of weapons, they remained separate from the sphere of action. Whether or not the émigré had participated in revolutionary acts from abroad, they were condemned to wait for news of success or failure, escape or arrest, about which they could do nothing. One memoir depicting Vera Zasulich, the infamous revolutionary who had shot the Governor of St Petersburg in 1878, described her as being 'anxious and worried' when speaking with those she did not know well and noted that she almost never left her apartment.[67] She was clearly uncomfortable with émigré life in the early years of the twentieth century, shunning party politics and preferring instead the company either of old comrades or newcomers who brought news of ongoing political protests inside the Russian Empire, 'literally throwing them questions' to find out more.[68] While Zasulich was hardly representative of émigré activists, largely avoiding large social gatherings, it seems that the waiting affected her too.[69] She had little interest in the

---

[66] S. Livshits, 'Chaikovskii (Po povodu ego smerti)', *Katorga i ssylka*, no. 5/26 (1926), pp. 223–32 (226).

[67] L. S. Fedorchenko (N. Charov), 'Vera Zasulich', *Katorga i ssylka*, no. 23 (1926), pp. 197–205 (p. 200).

[68] Ibid., pp. 200–01.

[69] For such a well-known figure of the revolutionary movement, there were few articles in the journal which focused specifically on her. She featured regularly in various pieces

émigré existence, choosing to live disconnected from her own space and time in Geneva and instead anchoring herself to the revolutionary past and present inside the Russian Empire. While *Katorga i ssylka* acknowledged the varieties of émigré labour, such as the writing Zasulich did in emigration, including that published in non-Russian periodicals, it also showed a sense of exclusion from the passage of revolutionary time inside the Russian Empire as a space where ordinary life no longer mattered.[70]

In addition to the chronotope of elsewhere, émigrés also experienced a sense of dislocation abroad. One article in *Katorga i ssylka* described life in Paris during the First World War: 'To be an emigrant is to live on an island with the constant awareness of the temporary nature of your stay.'[71] The uncertainty of life in emigration, which might involve moving regularly, and even to different countries for reasons linked to revolutionary work, persecution or expulsion, or just for practical reasons, was different to life in exile. Furthermore, with the envisaged revolution, it did not seem to make much sense to build a permanent life abroad. If émigrés settled in Britain, they often also struggled to participate in social life because knowledge of English was not prevalent.[72] As a result, their experiences could be constructed as a kind of martyrdom in the form of sacrificing meaningful human interaction.

From this perspective, it might be tempting to see late-imperial revolutionaries as so impatient, so desperate and so obsessed about sacrificing themselves for the cause that they decided to carry out acts of terrorism in order to fulfil their selfish goals and create the break in time that would come with revolution. However, more recent studies of late-imperial revolutionary terrorism have thoroughly interrogated this stereotype, which also permeated scholarship of the late twentieth century.[73] As a result, we can reject the most simplistic of assumptions which underpin this model. As Claudia Verhoeven has shown, revolutionaries experienced the passing of time in a different way, feeling a sense of urgency for political change and seeing terrorism as one method for speeding up the achievement of their revolutionary goals.[74] The spatial-temporal narratives

but was rarely the focus.

[70] A selection of her writings was published in the journal no. 58 (1929).

[71] Iadov, 'Parizhskaia emigratsiia', p. 197.

[72] Goldenberg, 'Vospominaniia', *Katorga i ssylka*, no. 5/12, p. 112.

[73] An important example of this interpretation of the 'turn to terror' is Deborah Hardy, *Land and Freedom: The Origins of Russian Terrorism, 1876–1879*, Westport, CT, 1987.

[74] Claudia Verhoeven, 'Oh Times, There Is No Time (But the Time that Remains): The Terrorist in Russian Literature (1863–1913)', in Thomas Austenfeld, Dimiter Daphinoff, and Jens Herlth (eds), *Terrorism and Narrative Practice*, Berlin, 2011, pp. 117–36 (pp. 123–25).

of emigration in *Katorga i ssylka* reflect how experiencing time was painful because of this sense of being unable to act, therefore this became commemorated as a meaningful form of self-sacrifice in itself.

Members of the Society of Former Political Prisoners and Exiles also found themselves in a kind of temporal dislocation after the Bolshevik rise to power. Many former SRs felt dissatisfied with the outcome of the revolution, in which the Constituent Assembly, dominated by Socialist Revolutionaries and tasked with constructing the new politics, was just one example of the victims of the Bolsheviks' 'dictatorship of the proletariat'. It was a result which perhaps tainted the memory of their own suffering and that of their deceased comrades. The space of the former Russian Empire had now entered the space of new time and the language of speed, progress and modernity infused Bolshevik discourse. However, to some this felt like a temporal experience of which they were not a part. Embracing the memory of the anti-Bolshevik émigré activist might also represent a way to tell alternative narratives about their present, as demonstrated perhaps by the inclusion of many narratives that either focused on or included prominent anti-Bolshevik figures. Many revolutionaries had chosen to leave during and after the Civil War years, returning to lives already well-established in emigration or else to found new communities and lives in new places. Although these old revolutionaries writing for *Katorga i ssylka* were not living abroad, they might draw on the experience of pre-revolutionary times as a means of reassurance. In addition to this, in a world that grew more alien to them, the émigré space-time was a place where comrades, predecessors, often as well as their past selves, lived. It was a place they could recreate through memory practices as a way of finding meaning in their present.

The chronotope of elsewhere provided a means by which former émigrés could claim a unique form of martyrdom. Although emigration was not a form of death, it was constructed as a loss of time in living through the acceleration of ageing, as a dislocation in the revolutionary's experience of lived time and in isolation from meaningful social and political activities. As emigration had been established as a meaningful and helpful contribution to the revolutionary cause, the physical and emotional loss experienced by those living in emigration became a legitimate form of martyrdom.

Conclusion
Katorga i ssylka provided the members of the Society of Former Political Prisoners and Exiles with a space in which they could explore the meanings of their revolutionary activism in the years before 1917. Among the many narratives, biographies and memoirs of revolutionary life that the editors might have chosen, the decision to include pieces about revolutionary émigrés seems somewhat remarkable. However, in the context of the post-1917 period, the political exclusion and dislocation experienced by many members of the Society may explain their desire to resurrect the minutiae of revolutionary activism in order to claim its contribution to the cause, give meaning to the suffering of those for whom October did not represent *their* revolution, and to make sense of their current situation.

Looking for articles depicting the lives of revolutionary émigrés in *Katorga i ssylka* it becomes clear that 1927 was a high point in the publication of narratives, biographies and memoirs on the subject. In particular, the issue commemorating the tenth anniversary of the February Revolution printed several pieces. While the focus of the pieces was naturally on the receipt of the long-awaited news from home of the end of the tsarist regime, they established the significance of the émigré as part of these world-changing events. February 1917 was also the moment which invited more diverse commemorations. While largely absent from Bolshevik histories of 1917 prior to 1922, after 1922 February was presented in a way which contrasted its character to the October Revolution.[75] The February Revolution as a marker of the end of tsarism was also largely overshadowed by the celebration of Red Army Day and International Women's Day (whether by accident or design is unclear) until it was lost from the list of official calendar of holidays in 1930.[76] The absence of a dominant narrative for the memory of February 1917 may have created the space for polyvocal narratives. However, while this phenomenon in the pages of *Katorga i ssylka* could be interpreted as a triumph for the Society's members, it also marked the beginning of the end for the journal. Explicit emigration narratives disappeared somewhat abruptly and the wider theme of memoir and (auto)biography soon followed, although emigration remained a part of the title of the section of the journal. Some émigré content remained, such as the reprinting of letters, but became more sporadic. With the shift in the state's reimagining of the role of the Society and its journal in the

[75] James D. White, 'Early Soviet Historical Interpretations of the Russian Revolution 1918–24', *Soviet Studies*, 37, 3, 1985, pp. 330–52 (pp. 346–48).
[76] Elizabeth A. Wood, 'February 23 and March 8: Two Holidays that Upstaged the February Revolution', *Slavic Review*, 76, 3, 2017, pp. 732–40 (pp. 739–40).

present, and the more extensive codification of revolutionary history, the more expansive memory culture of *Katorga i ssylka* no longer seemed to fit.

Examination of the representation of emigration in *Katorga i ssylka* reveals the extent to which the journal challenged the cult of celebrity in revolutionary history and memory. While pre-1917 publications regularly dedicated significant space to memorializing the well-known figures of revolutionary terrorism, among them the assassins of Alexander II, Grand Duke Sergei and Ministers of the Interior Viacheslav von Pleve and Petr Stolypin, *Katorga i ssylka* fundamentally reoriented the focus of revolutionary history and memory. Instead, the protagonist of their version of the revolutionary movement was the ordinary activist whose work often took place behind the scenes of the great revolutionary dramas of the later imperial period.

Although *Katorga i ssylka* told the stories of very different revolutionary heroes, it mobilized the same tropes of representation as the earlier publications had ascribed to the celebrities of the revolutionary movement. Its emphasis on the usefulness of emigration to the cause echoes the same emphasis on the selflessness of terrorism in pre-1917 émigré literature which contested accusations that they were revolutionaries whose only motivation was self-interest. The representation of physical and emotional suffering in emigration ensured the continued centrality of the body in revolutionary history and memory. Alongside these familiar tropes, the memoir and (auto)biography printed in the journal also established emigration as a specific form of revolutionary suffering due to its specific spatial-temporal character. The émigré narrative was a *lieu de mémoire* for the non-Bolshevik majority of members of the Society of Former Political Prisoners and Exiles whose own situation echoed that of life in emigration. Increasingly alone as their numbers dwindled, excluded from public life and identified only by reference to their pasts, they found themselves again on islands where time stood still while Bolshevik modernity surged around them.

Publications Received

Abely, Christine. *The Russia Sanctions: The Economic Response to Russia's Invasion of Ukraine*. Cambridge University Press, Cambridge and New York, 2023. £90.00; £29.99: $39.99 (e-book).

Aliyev, Nurlan. *Reassessing Russia's Security Policy*. Contemporary Russia and East Europe Series. Routledge, Abingdon and New York, 2023. £135.00; £39.99 (e-book).

Azarieva, Janetta; Brudny, Yitzhak M. and Finkel, Eugene. *Bread and Autocracy: Food, Politics, and Security in Putin's Russia*. Oxford University Press, Oxford and New York, 2023. £64.00; £19.99.

Baer, Brian James and Fiks, Yevgeniy (eds). *Queer(ing) Russian Art: Realism, Revolution, Performance*. Myths and Taboos in Russian Culture. Academic Studies Press, Boston, MA, 2023. $139.00.

Birgy, Philippe (ed.). *Understanding Bakhtin, Understanding Modernism*. Understanding Philosophy, Understanding Modernism. Bloomsbury Academic, London, New York and Dublin, 2023. £95.00; £85.90 (e-book).

Baumann, Fabian. *Dynasty Divided: A Family History of Russian and Ukrainian Nationalism*. NIU Series in Slavic, East European, and Eurasian Studies. Northern Illinois University Press, Ithaca, NY and London, 2023. $125.00; $29.95.

Bill, Stanley and Lewis, Simon (eds). *Multicultural Commonwealth: Poland-Lithuania and Its Afterlives*. Pitt Series in Russian and East European Studies. Pittsburgh University Press, Pittsburgh, PA, 2023. $55.00.

Boyd-Barrett, Oliver and Marmura, Stephen (eds). *Russiagate Revisited: The Aftermath of a Hoax*. Palgrave Macmillan, Cham, 2023. £74.99; £59.99 (e-book).

Bozovic, Marijeta. *Radical Poetics after the Soviet Union*. Harvard University Press, Cambridge, MA and London, 2023. $39.95: £34.95: €36.95.

Brintlinger, Angela. *Why We (Still) Need Russian Literature: Tolstoy, Dostoevsky, Chekhov and Others*. Russian Shorts. Bloomsbury Academic, London, New York and Dublin, 2024. £45.00; £12.99; £11.69 (e-book).

Caron, Jean-François. *Putin's War and the Re-Opening of History*. Palgrave Macmillan, Singapore, 2023. £34.99; £27.99 (e-book).

Cassiday, Julie A. *Russian Style: Performing Gender, Power, and Putinism*. The University of Wisconsin Press, Madison, WI, 2023. $79.95.

David-Fox, Michael (ed.). *The Secret Police and the Soviet System: New Archival Investigations*. Pitt Series in Russian and East European Studies. Pittsburgh University Press, Pittsburgh, PA, 2023. $50.00.

Donaldson, Robert H. and Nadkarni, Vidya. *The Foreign Policy of Russia: Changing Systems, Enduring Interests*. Seventh edition. Routledge, Abingdon and New York, 2024. £165.00; £45.99 (paperback & e-book).

Eriksroed-Burger, Magdalena; Hein-Kircher, Heidi and Malitska, Julia (eds). *Consumption and Advertising in Eastern Europe and Russia in the Twentieth Century*. Palgrave Macmillan, Cham, 2023. £119.99; £95.50 (e-book).

Evdokimova, Svetlana. *Staging Existence: Chekhov's Tetralogy*. The University of Wisconsin Press, Madison, WI, 2023. $79.95.

Galeotti, Mark. *Russia's Wars in Chechnya, 1994–2009*. Essential Histories. Osprey Publishing, an imprint of Bloomsbury Publishing, London, New York and Dublin, 2024. £12.99 (paperback); £10.39 (e-book).

Glaser, Marina; Krivushin, Ivan and Morini, Mara (eds). *The Presidentialization of Political Parties in Russia, Kazakhstan and Belarus*. Palgrave Studies in Presidential Politics. Palgrave Macmillan, Cham, 2023. £109.99; £87.50 (e-book).

Hale, Henry E., Johnson, Juliet and Lankina, Tomila V. (eds). *Developments in Russian Politics, 10*. Bloomsbury Academic, London, New York and Dublin, 2024. £110.00; £34.99; £31.49 (e-book).

Hasanli, Jamil. *Stalin's Early Cold War Foreign Policy: Southern Neighbours in the Shadow of Moscow, 1945–1947*. Routledge Contemporary Russia and East Europe Series. Routledge, Abingdon and New York, 2024. £39.99 (paperback).

Hauter, Jakob. *Russia's Overlooked Invasion: The Causes of the 2014 Outbreak of War in Ukraine's Donbas*. Soviet and Post-Soviet Politics and Society, 270. *ibidem*-Verlag, Stuttgart, 2023. €29.90: $34.00 (paperback).

Hellebust, Rolf. *How Russian Literature Became Great*. NIU Series in Slavic, East European, and Eurasian Studies. Northern Illinois University Press, Ithaca, NY and London, 2024. $49.95; $32.99 (e-book).

Hendley, Kathryn and Solomon, Peter H., Jr. *The Judicial System of Russia*. Judicial Systems of the World. Oxford University Press, Oxford and New York, 2023. £90.00; £24.99.

Ishov, Zakhar. *Brodsky in English*. Studies in Russian Literature and Theory. Northwestern University Press, Evanston, IL, 2023. $120.00; $38.00 (paperback & e-book).

Jenkins, J. R. *Picturing Socialism: Public Art and Design in East Germany*. Bloomsbury Visual Arts. Bloomsbury, London, New York and Dublin, 2023. £27.99 (paperback).

Kaganovitch, Albert. *Exodus and Its Aftermath: Jewish Refugees in the Wartime Soviet Interior*. The University of Wisconsin Press, Madison, WI, 2023. $79.95; $32.95.

Kelly, Catriona. *Russian Food since 1800: Empire at Table*. Russian Shorts. Bloomsbury Academic, London, New York and Dublin, 2024. £45.00; £12.99; £11.69 (e-book).

Kenez, Peter. *Before the Uprising: Hungary under Communism, 1949–1956*. Cambridge University Press, Cambridge and New York, 2024. £22.99 (paperback).

Khapaeva, Dina. *Putin's Dark Ages: Political Neomedievalism and Re-Stalinization in Russia*. Routledge Histories of Central and Eastern Europe. Routledge, Abingdon and New York, 2024. £135.00; £36.99.

Khazanov, Pavel. *The Russia That We Have Lost: Pre-Soviet Past as Anti-Soviet Discourse*. The University of Wisconsin Press, Madison, WI, 2023. $89.95.

Klimentov, Vassily. *A Slow Reckoning: The USSR, the Afghan Communists, and Islam*. NIU Series in Slavic, East European, and Eurasian Studies. Northern Illinois University Press, Ithaca, NY and London, 2024. $54.95; $39.99 (e-book).

Kohn, Marek. *The Stories Old Towns Tell: A Journey Through Cities at the Heart of Europe*. Yale University Press, New Haven, CT and London, 2023. $30.00 (hardback & e-book).

Korneeva, Marina and Gillespie, David (eds). *The History of Russian Literature on Film*. The History of World Literatures on Film. Bloomsbury Academic, London, New York and Dublin, 2024. £130.00; £117.00 (e-book).

Kovács, József Ö., Horváth, Gergely Krisztián and Csikós, Gábor (eds). *The Sovietization of Rural Hungary, 1945–1980: Subjugation in the Name of Equality*. Routledge Histories of Central and Eastern Europe, Routledge, Abingdon and New York, 2023. £130.00; £35.09 (e-book).

Kudors, Andis. *Russia and Latvia: A Case of Sharp Power*. Routledge Contemporary Russia and East Europe Series. Routledge, Abingdon and New York, 2024. £135.00; £31.99 (e-book).

Kuzio, Taras (ed.). *Russian Disinformation and Western Scholarship: Bias and Prejudice in Journalistic, Expert, and Academic Analyses of East European, Russian and Eurasian Affairs*. Soviet and Post-Soviet Politics and Society, 262. *ibidem*-Verlag, Stuttgart, 2023. €34.90: $40.00 (paperback).

Legucka, Agnieszka and Kupiecki, Robert. *Disinformation, Narratives and Memory Politics in Russia and Belarus*. Routledge Contemporary Russia and East Europe Series. Routledge, Abingdon and New York, 2024. £39.99 (paperback).

Loftus, Suzanne. *Russia, China and the West in the Post-Cold War Era: The Limits of Liberal Universalism*. New Security Challenges. Palgrave Macmillan, Cham, 2023. £99.99; £79.50 (e-book).

Mahoney, William. *The History of the Czech Republic and Slovakia*. The Greenwood Histories of the Modern Nations. Bloomsbury Academic, London, New York and Dublin, 2023. £21.99: $29.95 (paperback).

McCannon, John. *Nicholas Roerich: The Artist Who Would Be King*. Pitt Series in Russian and East European Studies. Pittsburgh University Press, Pittsburgh, PA, 2022. $50.00.

Miazhevich, Galina (ed.). *Queering Russian Media and Culture*. Contemporary Russia and East Europe Series. Routledge, Abingdon and New York, 2023. £39.99 (e-book).

Mogilner, Marina B., Gerasimov, Ilya V., Glebov, Sergey and Semyonov, Alexander. *A New Imperial History of Northern Eurasia, 600–1700: From Russian to Global History*. Volume 1. Bloomsbury Academic, London, New York and Dublin, 2023. £85.00; £76.50 (e-book).

Nadel, Ira B. *Love and Russian Literature: From Benjamin to Woolf*. Bloomsbury Academic, London, New York and Dublin, 2023. £85.00; £76.50 (e-book).

O'Connor, Kevin. *The House of Hemp and Butter: A History of Old Riga*. NIU Series in Slavic, East European, and Eurasian Studies. Northern Illinois University Press, Ithaca, NY and London, 2023. $125.00; $29.95; $18.99 (e-book).

Popescu, Bogdan G. *Imperial Borderlands: Institutions and Legacies of the Habsburg Military Frontier*. Cambridge Studies in Economic History – Second Series. Cambridge University Press, Cambridge and New York, 2024. £85.00.

Prokofiev, Sergey. *Diaries 1924–1933: Prodigal Son*. Translated and annotated by Anthony Phillips. Faber & Faber, London, 2023. £40.00 (paperback).

Read, Christopher. *Lenin Lives?* Oxford University Press, Oxford and New York, 2024. £30.00.

Rentola, Kimmo. *How Finland Survived Stalin: From Winter War to Cold War, 1939–1950*. Translated by Richard Robinson. Yale University Press, New Haven, CT and London, 2024. $35.00.

Rosenberg, William G. *States of Anxiety: Scarcity and Loss in Revolutionary Russia*. Oxford University Press, Oxford and New York, 2024. £29.99.

Sakwa, Richard. *The Lost Peace: How the West Failed to Prevent a Second Cold War*. Yale University Press, New Haven, CT, 2023. $38.00; $32.50 (e-book).

Sakwa, Richard. *The Russia Scare: Fake News and Genuine Threat*. Innovations in International Affairs. Routledge, Abingdon and New York, 2023. £31.99 (paperback & e-book).

Sätre, Ann-Mari; Gradskova, Yulia and Vladimirova, Vladislava (eds). *Post-Soviet Women: New Challenges and Ways to Empowerment*. Sustainable Development Goals Series. Palgrave Macmillan, Cham, 2023. £109.99; £87.50 (e-book).

Scarborough, Daniel. *Russia's Social Gospel: The Orthodox Pastoral Movement in Famine, War, and Revolution*. The University of Wisconsin Press, Madison, WI, 2023. $79.95.

Service, Robert. *Blood on the Snow: The Russian Revolution 1914–1924*. Picador, London and New York, 2023. £30.00; £12.99.

Shearer, David R. *Stalin and War, 1918–1953: Patterns of Repression, Mobilization, and External Threat*. Routledge Histories of Central and Eastern Europe. Routledge, Abingdon and New York, 2024. £130.00; £35.99; £32.39 (e-book).

Składanowski, Marcin. *Russia's National Security in Aleksandr Dugin's Neo-Eurasianism: A Sacred Fortress*. Lexington Books, Lanham, MD, Boulder, CO, New York and London, 2023. $110.00: £85.00; $45.00: £35.00 (e-book).

Steinberg, John W. *The Military History of the Russian Empire from Peter the Great until Nicholas II*. The Bloomsbury History of Modern Russian Series. Bloomsbury Academic, London, New York and Dublin, 2024. £85.00; £76.50 (e-book).

Sweet, Julia. *Russian Hackers and the War in Ukraine: Digital Threats and Real-World Consequences*. Lexington Books, Lanham, MD, Boulder, CO, New York and London, 2023. $105.00: £81.00; $45.00: £35.00 (e-book).

Tabachnikova, Olga (ed.). *A Culture of Discontinuity? Russian Cultural Debates in Historical Perspective*. Cultural History and Literary Imagination, 34. Peter Lang, Oxford, Bern, Berlin, Brussels, New York and Vienna, 2023. £52.00.

Taras, Raymond (ed.). *Exploring Russia's Exceptionalism in International Politics*. Routledge Contemporary Russia and East Europe Series. Routledge, Abingdon and New York, 2023. £135.00; £39.99 (e-book).

Tazmini, Ghoncheh. *Power Couple: Russian-Iranian Alignment in the Middle East*. I. B. Tauris, an imprint of Bloomsbury Publishing, London, New York and Dublin, 2024. £65.00; £19.99; £17.99 (e-book).

Tihanov, Galin; Lounsbery, Anne and Djagalov, Rossen (eds). *World Literature in the Soviet Union*. Studies in Comparative Literature and Intellectual History. Academic Studies Press, Boston, MA, 2023. $119.00.

Vinokour, Maya. *Work Flows: Stalinist Liquids in Russian Labor Culture*. NIU Series in Slavic, East European, and Eurasian Studies. Northern Illinois University Press, Ithaca, NY and London, 2024. $56.95: $37.99 (e-book).

Voronina, Ol'ga. *Tainopis´: Nabokov, Arkhiv, Podtekst*. Izdatel´stvo Ivana Limbakha, St Petersburg, 2023. ₽990.00.

Wade, Imogen Sophie Kristin. *Innovation and Modernisation in Contemporary Russia: Science Towns, Technology Parks and Very Limited Success*. Routledge Contemporary Russia and East Europe Series. Routledge, Abingdon and New York, 2024. £39.99 (paperback).

Wang, Emily. *Pushkin, the Decembrists, and Civic Sentimentalism*. Publications of the Wisconsin Center for Pushkin Studies. The University of Wisconsin Press, Madison, WI, 2023. $99.95.

Weinberg, Robert. *Jews under Tsars and Communists: The Four Questions*. Russian Shorts. Bloomsbury Academic, London, New York and Dublin, 2024. £45.00; £12.99; £11.69 (e-book).

Yavuz, M. Hakan and Gunter, Michael. *The Nagorno-Karabakh Conflict: Historical and Political Perspectives*. Routledge Contemporary Russia and East Europe Series. Routledge, Abingdon and New York, 2024. £39.99 (paperback).

Yoder, Jennifer A. *World War II Memory and Contested Commemorations in Europe and Russia*. Oxford University Press, Oxford and New York, 2023. £76.00.

Zięba, Ryszard. *Politics and Security of Central and Eastern Europe: Contemporary Challenges*. Contributions to Political Science. Springer, Cham, 2023. £119.99; £95.50 (e-book).

Zusi, Peter. *The Integrity of the Avant-Garde: Karel Teige and the Biography of an Ambition*. Visual Culture, 2. Legenda, Oxford, 2024. £85.00: $115.00: €99.00.

Abstracts

Liberal Funerals, Political Resistance and Sites of Martyrdom in the Late Russian Empire by George Gilbert

This article explores a series of political funerals held for major liberal figures during the early years of the twentieth century within the Russian Empire. Using three major figures — the philosopher and university rector Sergei Trubetskoi, lawyer Lev Kupernik and politician Sergei Muromtsev — as its primary examples, it considers the importance of both space and place, focusing on demonstrations held in support of these individuals in Moscow and Kyiv. Drawing on a range of sources including the periodical press and hitherto untapped police records, it explores the circumstances behind the appearance of liberal political funerals, and the novelty of such events in relation to well-established traditions surrounding the political funeral in the late Russian Empire. It looks at who attended, the size and intensity of the disturbances that followed, and how onlookers and supporters interacted with these events. Conceptually, it assesses whether the causes that the subjects of these political funerals stood for, such as selfhood, subjectivity and citizenship, spoke to a particularly liberal tradition of protest which intersected with the wider currents of dissent by then endemic in different parts of the empire. Finally, it considers whether there was a liberal tradition in terms of political martyrdom in the late Russian Empire and to what extent this was used to advance the political causes espoused by supporters of these liberal figureheads.

An Ephemeral Look at Russian Anarchist Life in the United States by Alison Rowley

In September 1915, San Francisco resident Ernest Kundy received a picture postcard from an unnamed correspondent. Produced by the Anarchist Red Cross of Detroit, the postcard featured a depiction of the Bloody Sunday massacre which sparked Russia's 1905 revolution and served as one of the most important episodes in the history of revolutionary martyrdom. By examining every aspect of the postcard this article reveals, layer by layer, its connections to Russian anarchist life in the United States. The article begins by analysing the image on the front, explaining how illustrations like the one in question by Fortunino Matania were turned into widely disseminated postcards that spread revolutionary messages well beyond Russian borders. Turning to the information on the back, the article next explores the history of the Anarchist Red Cross in the US and the role that it played in keeping anarchism alive for recent immigrants from Russia. Then the links between the sender's handwritten message and an area of Chicago that features prominently in histories of immigrant life, the settlement movement and the US labour movement — Halsted Street — are considered. Finally, the connections between the recipient's family and a 1915 bank robbery in California serve as a window into the history of Russian anarchist circles on the American West Coast.

Nihilists, Fenians and Revolutionary Martyrdom in Transnational Context by Abby Holekamp

Although their goals and the cultural contexts in which they were operating differed, both the so-called nihilists and the so-called Fenians described themselves and were described by others — in the press, in fiction — as martyrs willing to die for their cause. Whether employed with approval or opprobrium, Victorian print culture in particular drew these two sets of radicals together: fear of an impending 'union of Nihilists and Fenians', as one Lancaster newspaper put it in 1882, was a recurring theme in the late Victorian press. However, so too was the idea, expressed in 1896 by an English journalist who had worked in Russia, that it was unbelievable that nihilists would have 'any connection whatsoever' with the Fenians, because the high-minded nihilists supposedly perceived Irish radicals as prosaic dilettantes. By examining such contradictory representations of revolutionary sacrifice and martyrdom in comparative and transnational context (with particular attention paid to gendered representations), we can begin to trace the contours of a shared language of sacrifice both among and outside of these respective movements. In doing so, this article begins to define the role of Russia (and its 'martyrs') as both a focus and a foil in the *fin de siècle* European imagination.

The Martyrdom of Illness: Mariia Spiridonova in Siberian Imprisonment, 1906–17 by Sally A. Boniece

In the summer of 1906 at the age of twenty-one, Mariia Spiridonova, a Russian Socialist Revolutionary (SR) assassin was transported with five other convicted female SR terrorists by railway from Moscow to the Nerchinsk prison complex in eastern Siberia. Only Spiridonova was known as a martyr-heroine to opponents of tsarism across the empire, however, because national newspapers had published her story of physical abuse by police and Cossacks at the time of her arrest. Patterning themselves after an earlier generation of populist terrorists in the 1870s and 1880s, male and female SR terrorists in the revolution of 1905–07 attempted to kill government officials whom the SR party accused of oppressive actions against helpless civilians. Although SR terrorists expected to sacrifice their own lives as compensation for committing political murder, the tsarist government commuted the women's death sentences to penal servitude for life. In Siberian imprisonment, Spiridonova and her five terrorist comrades followed the tradition of preceding generations of revolutionaries by joining a 'socialist collective' or 'commune' of political prisoners with a code of conduct and a shared economy. Male and female socialist prisoners lived by such compacts to prepare themselves for the future revolution and to deepen the political consciousness of their fellow inmates by personal example. Only Spiridonova among the women 'politicals' took no visible role in upholding the prison commune but rather lived in semi-isolation as an invalid throughout her eleven years in the Nerchinsk complex. Suffering from tuberculosis, Spiridonova, who had anticipated a martyr's death on the scaffold, seemingly succumbed to the martyrdom of chronic illness. Yet the fall of the tsarist autocracy in February 1917 did not just liberate Spiridonova from penal servitude but simultaneously restored her health, her energy and her drive to engage in radical politics. Her pattern of revolutionary behaviour thus alternated between active and passive self-sacrifice, the tuberculosis that enhanced her legend of martyrdom apparently waxing and waning according to the degree of her personal freedom.

The Sozonov Case, 1910: The Making of a Russian Revolutionary Martyrology by Ben Phillips

On the night of 27 November (10 December) 1910, the Socialist-Revolutionary terrorist Egor Sozonov, renowned as the assassin of Minister of the Interior Viacheslav von Pleve in July 1904, committed suicide in his Siberian prison cell in protest at the use of corporal punishment against his fellow political prisoners. News of Sozonov's death provoked an outcry across Russia: it was accompanied by questions in the Duma, widespread and hagiographical coverage in the liberal and revolutionary press, and student protests in the major university towns (and, conversely, by barely concealed joy from the Black-Hundredist right). This article serves two purposes. First, it reconstructs, in as much detail as the evidence allows, the events surrounding Sozonov's death, which (despite their infamy at the time) have up to now received little scholarly attention and remain, to some extent, shrouded in mystery. Secondly, it explores how these events came to serve as the basis of a revolutionary martyrology — originally promoted by the SRs, and later appropriated by the Bolsheviks after 1917 — that glorified Sozonov as a 'just assassin', persecuted by a despotic government, who had ultimately sacrificed his own life in order that others might live. The article situates Sozonov's death in the wider political, social and cultural context of the time, considering it in relation to contemporary discourses on suicide (as a transcendentalist political act), corporal punishment (long regarded as the gravest imaginable insult to the dignity of educated Russians), the 'moral economy' of revolutionary terrorism and the quasi-religious mythologies of the revolutionary underground.

A Living Martyrdom? Representing Life in Emigration in *Katorga i ssylka*   by Lara Green
Katorga i ssylka (Hard Labour and Exile, 1921–35) provides important insights into the personal details of revolutionaries' lives as well as the (auto)biographical representation of members and deceased colleagues of the Society of Former Political Prisoners and Exiles. The journal facilitated identity formation at a time when many former revolutionaries found themselves politically marginalized by the Bolshevik rise to power, being a *lieu de mémoire* for revolutionary martyrs of all types. This article suggests that death or bodily harm as forms of martyrdom were only elements of a wider set of revolutionary practices of self-sacrifice. By drawing comparisons with similar practices in late-imperial revolutionary print culture, it suggests a continuity of practices in emigration across 1917. Such practices drew not only on the individuals and communities involved in publishing work but also the tropes and narratives in these representations. As membership of the Society was dominated by former Socialist Revolutionaries, studying the representation of life in emigration provides insights into the contestations of revolutionary memory during the 1920s and the ways in which members of the Society sought to find meaning in their personal experiences of political activism and that of their deceased comrades. The article explores the ways in which memoir and (auto)biography constructed emigration as a space of useful political activism, and provided the basis for the representation of emigration as meaningful self-sacrifice. This involved invoking tropes of suffering common in the memory of imprisonment and exile, while emigration brought with it new challenges linked to the experience of time passing.

THE SLAVONIC & EAST EUROPEAN REVIEW

General Editor	SIMON DIXON
Joint Editors	N. BERMEL, P. R. BULLOCK, R. BUTTERWICK-PAWLIKOWSKI, P. J. CAVENDISH, R. A. CHITNIS, M. CORNWALL, D. DJOKIĆ, P. J. S. DUNCAN, G. GILBERT, T. J. HAUGHTON, C. H. M. KELLY, D. P. KOENKER, J. KUBIK, A. B. McMILLIN, Z. MILUTINOVIĆ, R. MOLE, U. PHILLIPS, M. RADY, K. ROTH-EY, M. RUBINS, C. SHAW, P. WALDRON, K. WILLIAMS, S. YOUNG
Managing Editor	BARBARA WYLLIE

The *Slavonic and East European Review*, the journal of the UCL School of Slavonic and East European Studies, is published quarterly by the Modern Humanities Research Association (MHRA). Issues are numbered serially, the four annual issues constituting a volume. Up to and including 1965 an even-numbered issue (published in December) together with the following and odd-numbered issue (published in June) constituted a volume.

Scholarly contributions are invited on all subjects related to the field of Slavonic and East European Studies. Articles should be between 8,000 and 12,000 words, although contributions falling outside this range may also be considered. Book reviews should be no longer than requested. Other contributions (review articles/essays, marginalia, obituaries, summary notes) should aim at a corresponding and proportionate brevity. Original documents are specially welcome. No correspondence is published in the *Review*.

Contributions should be submitted in English in a form ready for publication and in the final state intended. Contributors should study the leaflet, 'Guide for Contributors', obtainable on request from the Managing Editor, SEER Office, UCL SSEES, Gower Street, London WC1E 6BT (seer@ucl.ac.uk), or online at www.ucl.ac.uk/ssees/publishing/slavonic-and-east-european-review. All contributions must adhere to the *Review*'s house style.

Contributions and other editorial communications should be sent to the Managing Editor. While the editors take every possible care with regard to typescripts, they advise authors to retain duplicate copies. The editors do not consider themselves responsible in the event of the loss of a contribution.

Disclaimer: Views expressed in the content of the *Slavonic and East European Review* are those of the respective authors and contributors and not of the journal editors or of the MHRA. The MHRA makes no representation, express or implied, in respect of the accuracy of the material in this journal and cannot accept any legal responsibility or liability for views expressed or for any errors or omissions that may be made.

Copyright in the individual articles and reviews published in the *Slavonic and East European Review* is vested in the authors. For permission to reproduce material from the *Slavonic and East European Review*, please apply to the Managing Editor.

Further information about the activities of the Modern Humanities Research Association and individual membership may be obtained from the Membership Secretary, email: membership@mhra.org.uk, or from the website at: www.mhra.org.uk. For institutional subscription rates and information, contact subscriptions@mhra.org.uk.

ISSN 0037-6795 (print); ISSN 2222-4327 (online)